Microsoft®
Access 2000
Complete Tutorial™

Sandra Cable

William R. Pasewark, Sr., Ph.D.
Professor Emeritus, Texas Tech University
Office Management Consultant

VISIT US ON THE INTERNET
www.swep.com

South-Western Educational Publishing
an International Thomson Publishing company I(T)P®
www.thomson.com

Cincinnati • Albany, NY • Belmont, CA • Bonn • Boston • Detroit • Johannesburg • London • Madrid
Melbourne • Mexico City • New York • Paris • Singapore • Tokyo • Toronto • Washington

Library of Congress Cataloging-in-Publication Data

Cable, Sandra.
  Microsoft Access 2000 complete tutorial / Sandra Cable, William R.
Pasewark, Sr.
    p.   cm.
  ISBN 0-538-68841-6 (spiral bound)
  ISBN 0-538-68845-9 (soft cover)
  ISBN 0-538-68842-4 (perfect bound)
  1. Database management.   2. Microsoft Access.   I. Pasewark,
William Robert.   II. Title.
  QA76.9.D3C317 1999
  005.75'65—dc21

99-23423
CIP

Team Leader: Karen Schmohe
Managing Editor: Carol Volz
Project Manager: Dave Lafferty
Production Coordinator: Angela McDonald

Art Coordinator: Mike Broussard
Consulting Editor: Custom Editorial Productions, Inc.
Marketing Manager: Larry Qualls
Production: Custom Editorial Productions, Inc.

Copyright © 2000

By SOUTH-WESTERN EDUCATIONAL PUBLISHING/ITP
Cincinnati, Ohio

1 2 3 4 5 6 DR 03 02 01 00 99

Printed in the United States of America

IP®

International Thomson Publishing

South-Western Educational Publishing is a division of International Thomson Publishing, Inc. The ITP® registered trademark is used under license.

PREFACE

You will find much helpful material in this introductory section. The *How to Use This Book* pages give you a visual summary of the kinds of information you will find in the text. The *What's New* section summarizes features new in this version of Microsoft Access. Be sure to review *Guide for Using This Book* to learn about the terminology and conventions used in preparing the pages and to find out what supporting materials are available for use with this book. If you are interested in pursuing certification as a Microsoft Office User Specialist (MOUS), read the information on *The Microsoft Office User Specialist Program.*

An Ideal Book for Anyone

Because computers are such an important subject for all learners, instructors need the support of a well-designed, educationally sound textbook that is supported by strong ancillary instructional materials. *Microsoft Access 2000: Complete Tutorial* is just such a book.

The textbook includes features that *make learning easy and enjoyable*—yet challenging—for learners. It is also designed with many features that *make teaching easy and enjoyable* for you. Comprehensive, yet flexible, *Microsoft Access 2000: Complete Tutorial* is adaptable for a wide variety of class-time schedules.

The text includes a wide range of learning experiences from activities with one or two commands to simulations and case studies that challenge and sharpen learners' problem-solving skills. This book is ideal for computer courses with learners who have varying abilities and previous computer experiences.

The lessons in this course contain the following features designed to promote learning:

- Objectives that specify goals students should achieve by the end of each lesson.

- Concept text that explores in detail each new feature.

- Screen captures that help to illustrate the concept text.

- Step-by-Step exercises that allow students to practice the features just introduced.

- Summaries that review the concepts in the lesson.

- Review Questions that test students on the concepts covered in the lesson.

- Projects that provide an opportunity for students to apply concepts they have learned in the lesson.

- Critical Thinking Activities that encourage students to use knowledge gained in the lesson or from Access's Help system to solve specific problems.

Each unit also contains a unit review with the following features:

- A Command Summary that reviews menu commands and toolbar shortcuts introduced in the unit.

- Review Questions covering material from all lessons in the unit.

- Applications that give students a chance to apply many of the skills learned in the unit.

- An On-the-Job Simulation that proposes real-world jobs a student can complete using the skills learned in the unit.

Acknowledgments

The authors of this book would like to make the following acknowledgments and dedications:

William Pasewark, Sr.: For committing themselves to produce a quality book that will help learners understand computers and for working effectively with each other, I gratefully thank the following colleagues for their fine work:

Laura Melton for her significant experience as a writer and editor.

Rhonda Davis for applying her recent computer business experiences to producing this book.

Scott Pasewark for his computer technology abilities.

Carolyn Denny, Jan Stogner, and Beth Wadsworth for completing a variety of tasks.

Billie Conley, computer instructor at Lubbock High School, for updating the Computer Concepts appendix.

Many professional South-Western sales representatives make educationally sound presentations to instructors about our books. I appreciate their valuable work as "bridges" between the authors and instructors.

Sandy Cable: This book is the result of efforts of many people and I thank each and every one of you. To all the students I have taught and for all that they have taught me, I thank you. This book is dedicated to my brother, Keith Albright. Thank you for always being there for me.

About the Authors

William R. Pasewark, Sr., Ph. D., has authored more than 90 books, including Canadian adaptations and Spanish and Danish translations. He is a management consultant and was the 1972 Texas Business Teacher of the Year.

He won the Textbook and Academic Authors Association *Texty Award* for the best computer book in 1994.

Sandy Cable owns her own computer consulting company and works with companies such as Southwest Airlines, IAMS, and Memorex Telex, just to name a few. She has many years of writing experience with South-Western Educational Publishing, which has resulted in 11 books. Sandy travels nationwide to speak at seminars and in classrooms promoting simple approaches to teaching computer applications.

How to Use This Book

What makes a good computer instructional text? Sound pedagogy and the most current, complete materials. That is what you will find in *Microsoft Access 2000: Complete Tutorial*. Not only will you find an inviting layout, but also many features to enhance learning.

Objectives—Objectives are listed at the beginning of each lesson, along with a suggested time for completion of the lesson. This allows you to look ahead to what you will be learning and to pace your work.

SCANS (Secretary's Commission on Achieving Necessary Skills)—The U.S. Department of Labor has identified the school-to-careers competencies. The eight workplace competencies and foundation skills are identified in exercises where they apply. More information on SCANS can be found on the Electronic Instructor.

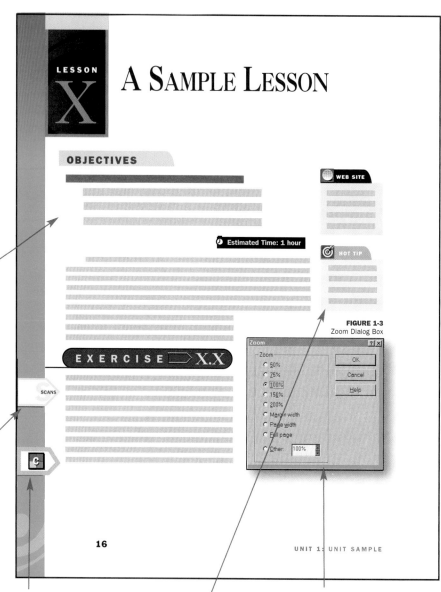

Certification Icon—This icon is shown wherever a criteria for Microsoft Office User Specialist (MOUS) certification is covered in the lesson. A correlation table with page numbers is provided elsewhere in this book and on the Electronic Instructor.

Marginal Boxes—These boxes provide additional information for Hot Tips, fun facts (Did You Know?), Concept Builders, Internet Web Sites, Extra Challenges activities, and Teamwork ideas.

Enhanced Screen Shots—Screen shots now come to life on each page with color and depth.

How to Use This Book

Summary—At the end of each lesson, you will find a summary to prepare you to complete the end-of-lesson activities.

Review Questions—Review material at the end of each lesson and each unit enables you to prepare for assessment of the content presented.

Lesson Projects—End-of-lesson hands-on application of what has been learned in the lesson allows you to actually apply the techniques covered.

Critical Thinking Activities—Each lesson gives you an opportunity to apply creative analysis and use the Help system to solve problems.

Command Summary—At the end of each unit, a command summary is provided for quick reference.

End-of-Unit Applications—End-of-unit hands-on application of concepts learned in the unit provides opportunity for a comprehensive review.

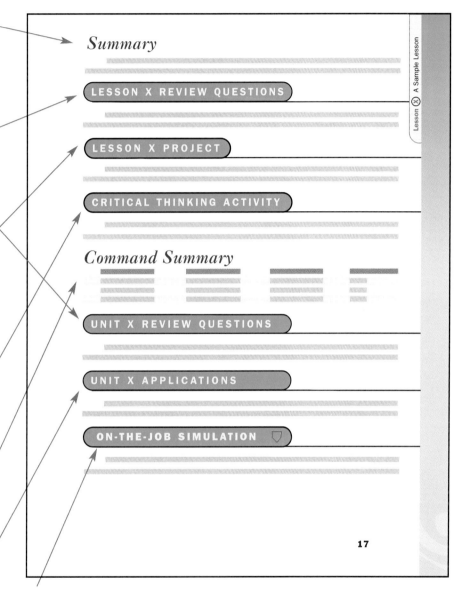

Summary

LESSON X REVIEW QUESTIONS

LESSON X PROJECT

CRITICAL THINKING ACTIVITY

Command Summary

UNIT X REVIEW QUESTIONS

UNIT X APPLICATIONS

ON-THE-JOB SIMULATION

Lesson ⊗ A Sample Lesson

17

On-the-Job Simulation—A realistic simulation runs throughout the text at the end of each unit, reinforcing the material covered in the unit.

Appendices—Appendices include Microsoft Office User Specialist Program, Windows 98, and Computer Concepts.

WHAT'S NEW

Microsoft Access 2000 has many features that help you to be more productive and to enjoy using your computer. Some of the new features covered in this course are listed below.

■ Software is easier to install, use, and manage. Access 2000 installs a set of frequently used features that you can easily supplement if and when you need additional features.

■ New basic features include improved subform and subreport capabilities, plus subdatasheets which let you view and edit data in related or joined tables, queries, and forms. The Objects bar in the Database window has a vertical orientation, making it easier to use and access database objects.

■ Publishing to the Web is easier than ever. All Office documents can be saved in HTML format so that anyone with a Web browser can view the documents just as they were created. You can "round trip" documents to HTML and back without losing Office file formats. Web themes can be used to design sophisticated Web pages.

■ New tools make it possible to collaborate online with other members of a workgroup across intranets and the Web.

■ Access's data access pages let you view, edit, and contribute information to a database object within a browser window.

■ You can easily convert an Access 2000 database to an Access 97 format.

START-UP CHECKLIST

HARDWARE

Minimum Configuration

- ✓ PC with Pentium processor
- ✓ 32 Mb RAM
- ✓ Hard disk with 200 Mb free for typical installation
- ✓ CD-ROM drive
- ✓ VGA monitor with video adapter
- ✓ Microsoft Mouse, IntelliMouse, or compatible pointing device
- ✓ 9600 or higher baud modem
- ✓ Printer

Recommended Configuration

- ✓ Pentium PC with greater than 32 Mb RAM
- ✓ Super VGA 256-color monitor
- ✓ 28,800 baud modem
- ✓ Multimedia capability
- ✓ For e-mail, Microsoft Mail, Internet SMTP/POP3, or other MAPI-compliant messaging software

SOFTWARE

- ✓ Windows 95, 98, or NT Workstation 4.0 with Service Pack 3.0 installed
- ✓ For Web collaboration and Help files, Internet Explorer 5 browser or Windows 98

JOIN US ON THE INTERNET

WWW: **http://www.thomson.com**

E-MAIL: **findit@kiosk.thomson.com**

South-Western Educational Publishing is a partner in *thomson.com,* an on-line portal for the products, services, and resources available from International Thomson Publishing (ITP). Through our site, users can search catalogs, examine subject-specific resource centers, and subscribe to electronic discussion lists.

South-Western Educational Publishing is also a reseller of commercial software products. See our printed catalog or view this page at:

http://www.swep.com/swep/comp_ed/com_sft.html

For information on our products visit our World Wide Web site at:

http://www.swep.com

To join the South-Western Computer Education discussion list, send an e-mail message to: **majordomo@list.thomson.com.** Leave the subject field blank, and in the body of your message key: SUBSCRIBE SOUTH-WESTERN-COMPUTER-EDUCATION <your e-mail address>.

A service of I(T)P®

GUIDE FOR USING THIS BOOK

Please read this Guide before starting work. The time you spend now will save you much more time later and will make your learning faster, easier, and more pleasant.

Terminology

This text uses the term *keying* to mean entering text into a computer using the keyboard. *Keying* is the same as "keyboarding" or "typing."

Text means words, numbers, and symbols that are printed.

Conventions

The different type styles used in this book have special meanings. They will save you time because you will soon automatically recognize from the type style the nature of the text you are reading and what you will do.

WHAT YOU WILL DO	TYPE STYLE	EXAMPLE
Text you will key	**Bold**	Key **Don't litter** rapidly.
Individual keys you will press	**Bold**	Press **Enter** to insert a blank line.

WHAT YOU WILL SEE	TYPE STYLE	EXAMPLE
Filenames in book	**Bold upper and lowercase**	Open **IA Step2-1** from the student data files.
Glossary terms in book	***Bold and italics***	The ***menu bar*** contains menu titles.
Words on screen	*Italics*	Highlight the word *pencil* on the screen.
Menus and commands	**Bold**	Choose **Open** from the **File** menu.
Options and areas in dialog boxes	*Italics*	Key a new name in the *File name* box.

Data CD-ROM

All data files necessary for the Step-by-Step exercises, end-of-lesson Projects, and end-of-unit Applications and Jobs for this book are located on the Data CD-ROM supplied with this text. Data files for the *Activities Workbook* are also stored on the Data CD-ROM.

Data files are named according to the first exercise in which they are used and the unit of this textbook in which they are used. A data file for a Step-by-Step exercise in the Introduction to Microsoft Access unit would have a filename such as **IA Step1-1**. This particular filename identifies a data file used in the first Step-by-Step exercise in Lesson 1. Other data files have the following formats:

- End-of-lesson projects: **IA Project1-1**
- End-of-unit applications: **IA App2**
- On-the-Job Simulation jobs: **IA Job3**

Electronic Instructor® CD-ROM

The *Electronic Instructor* contains a wealth of instructional material you can use to prepare for teaching Access 2000. The CD-ROM stores the following information:

- Both the data and solution files for this course.

- Quizzes for each lesson and unit, and answers to the quizzes, lesson and unit review questions, and *Activities Workbook* exercises.

- Copies of the lesson plans that appear in the instructor's manual, as well as student lesson plans that can help to guide students through the lesson text and exercises.

- Copies of the figures that appear in the student text, which can be used to prepare transparencies.

- Grids that show skills required for Microsoft Office User Specialist (MOUS) certification and the SCANS workplace competencies and skills.

- Suggested schedules for teaching the lessons in this course.

- Additional instructional information about individual learning strategies, portfolios, and career planning, and a sample Internet contract.

Additional Activities and Questions

An *Activities Workbook* is available to supply additional paper-and-pencil exercises and hands-on computer applications for each unit of this book. In addition, testing software is available separately with a customizable test bank specific for this text.

SCANS

The Secretary's Commission on Achieving Necessary Skills (SCANS) from the U.S. Department of Labor was asked to examine the demands of the workplace and whether new learners are capable of meeting those demands. Specifically, the Commission was directed to advise the Secretary on the level of skills required to enter employment.

SCANS workplace competencies and foundation skills have been integrated into *Microsoft Access 2000: Complete Tutorial*. The workplace competencies are identified as 1) ability to use *resources*, 2) *interpersonal* skills, 3) ability to work with *information*, 4) understanding of *systems*, and 5) knowledge and understanding of *technology*. The foundation skills are identified as 1) basic communication skills, 2) thinking skills, and 3) personal qualities.

Exercises in which learners must use a number of these SCANS competencies and foundation skills are marked in the text with the SCANS icon.

THE MICROSOFT OFFICE USER SPECIALIST PROGRAM

APPROVED COURSEWARE

What Is Certification?

The logo on the cover of this book indicates that the book is officially certified by Microsoft Corporation at the **Core** and **Expert** user skill level for Access 2000. This certification is part of the **Microsoft Office User Specialist (MOUS)** program that validates your skills as knowledgeable of Microsoft Office.

Why Is Getting Certified Important?

Upon completing the lessons in this book, you will be prepared to take a test that could qualify you as a **Core** and **Expert** user of Microsoft Access. This can benefit you in many ways. For example, you can show an employer that you have received certified training in Microsoft Access 2000, or you can advance further in education or in your organization. Earning this certification makes you more competitive with the knowledge and skills that you possess. It is also personally satisfying to know that you have reached a skill level that is validated by Microsoft Corporation.

The difference between Expert and Core users is the level of competency. Core users can perform a wide range of basic tasks. Expert users can do all those same tasks, plus more advanced tasks, such as special formatting.

Where Does Testing Take Place?

To be certified, you will need to take an exam from a third-party testing company called an **Authorization Certification Testing Center**. Call **800-933-4493** to find the location of the testing center nearest you. Learn more about the criteria for testing and what is involved. Tests are conducted on different dates throughout the calendar year.

South-Western Educational Publishing has developed an entire line of training materials suitable for Microsoft Office certification. To learn more, call **800-824-5179**. Also, visit our Web site at **www.swep.com**.

TABLE OF CONTENTS

iv   Preface
vi   How to Use This Book
viii   What's New
ix   Start-Up Checklist
x   Guide for Using This Book
xii   The Microsoft Office User Specialist Program

UNIT · INTRODUCTION

IN-2 Lesson 1: Office 2000 Basics and the Internet

IN-2   Introduction to Office 2000
IN-8   Office 2000 Help

IN-11   Accessing the Internet
IN-13   Summary

UNIT · INTRODUCTION TO MICROSOFT ACCESS

IA-2 Lesson 1: Access Basics

IA-2   Database Basics
IA-3   Starting Access
IA-3   Opening a Database
IA-7   Creating a Database
IA-18   Summary

IA-25 Lesson 2: Manipulating Data

IA-25   Editing Records
IA-30   Changing Datasheet Layout
IA-36   Summary

IA-42 Lesson 3: Creating and Modifying Forms

IA-42   Creating Forms
IA-49   Modifying Forms
IA-55   Compacting and Repairing a Database
IA-56   Summary

IA-60 Lesson 4: Finding and Ordering Data

IA-60   Using Find
IA-62   Using Queries
IA-64   Sorting
IA-71   Indexing
IA-72   Setting a Primary Key
IA-72   Relationships
IA-77   Creating a Multitable Query
IA-79   Summary

IA-84 Lesson 5: Reports and Macros

IA-84   Reports
IA-97   Macros
IA-101   Summary

IA-105 Lesson 6: Integrating Access

IA-105   Sharing Data
IA-108   Form Letters
IA-114   Summary
IA-119   Unit Review

UNIT ADVANCED MICROSOFT ACCESS

AA-2 Lesson 1: Modifying Table Design

AA-2 Introduction
AA-2 Choosing an Input Mask
AA-8 Setting Validation Rules
AA-9 Setting Required Properties
AA-10 Creating Lookup Fields
AA-12 Summary

AA-16 Lesson 2: Relationships in Tables and Queries

AA-16 Introduction
AA-16 Understanding Table Relationships
AA-18 Defining Relationships Between Tables
AA-23 Setting and Removing Joins in a Query
AA-27 Summary

AA-30 Lesson 3: Advanced Form Features

AA-30 Creating a Subform
AA-35 Adding a Record in the Subform
AA-36 Modifying a Subform
AA-37 Creating and Modifying a Form in Design View
AA-38 Summary

AA-42 Lesson 4: Analyzing Data

AA-42 Introduction
AA-42 Using Queries to Calculate Data
AA-46 Building Summary Queries
AA-48 Using Concatenation
AA-49 Creating an AND Query
AA-50 Creating an OR Query
AA-51 Applying Filters to a Query
AA-52 Summary

AA-55 Lesson 5: Advanced Queries

AA-55 Modifying a Query's Design
AA-57 Creating a Parameter Query
AA-59 Understanding Action Queries
AA-65 Summary

AA-69 Lesson 6: Advanced Report Features

AA-69 Understanding Bound, Unbound, and Calculated Controls
AA-72 Creating a Title Page
AA-73 Customizing Report Footers
AA-74 Adding a Chart to a Report
AA-79 Creating and Modifying a Report in Design View
AA-81 Summary

AA-85 Lessson 7: Importing and Exporting Data

AA-85 Importing Data
AA-91 Exporting Data to Other Programs
AA-92 Using Drag-and-Drop to Integrate Data
AA-93 Summary

AA-96 Lesson 8: Creating Macros and Switchboards

AA-96 Creating a Basic Macro
AA-101 Creating a Switchboard
AA-104 Creating Conditional Macros
AA-109 Using the Macro Builder
AA-110 Summary

AA-115 Lesson 9: Working with Web Features

AA-115 Creating a Hyperlink
AA-118 Understanding Data Access Pages
AA-125 Summary

AA-130 Lesson 10: Using Advanced Access Tools

AA-130 Compacting a Database
AA-131 Encrypting and Decrypting a Database
AA-131 Securing a Database
AA-133 Setting Startup Options
AA-134 Using Add-Ins
AA-137 Summary
AA-140 Unit Review

A-1 **Appendix A**

B-1 **Appendix B**

C-1 **Appendix C**

G-1 **Glossary**

IX-1 **Index**

UNIT

INTRODUCTION

lesson 1   1.5 hrs.

**Office 2000 Basics
and the Internet**

⏱ Estimated Time for Unit: 1.5 hours

LESSON 1

OFFICE 2000 BASICS AND THE INTERNET

OBJECTIVES

Upon completion of this lesson, you should be able to:

- Explain the concept of an integrated software package.

- Start an Office application from Windows 98.

- Open an existing document.

- Save and close an Office document.

- Know the shortcuts for opening recently used documents.

- Use the Help system.

- Use the Office Assistant.

- Quit an Office application.

- Access the Internet and use a Web browser.

⏱ Estimated Time: 1.5 hours

Introduction to Office 2000

O ffice 2000 is an integrated software package. An ***integrated software package*** is a program that combines several computer applications into one program. Office 2000 consists of a word processor application, a spreadsheet application, a database application, a presentation application, a schedule/organization application, a desktop publishing application and a Web page application.

The word processor application (Word) enables you to create documents such as letters and reports. The spreadsheet application (Excel) lets you work with numbers to prepare items such as budgets or to determine loan payments. The database application (Access) organizes information such as addresses or inventory items. The presentation application (PowerPoint) can be used to create slides, out-

Web Site

For more information on Microsoft Word and other Microsoft products, visit Microsoft's Web site at *http://www.microsoft.com*.

lines, speaker's notes, and audience handouts. The schedule/organization application (Outlook) increases your efficiency by keeping track of e-mail, appointments, tasks, contacts, events, and to-do lists. The desktop publishing application helps you design professional-looking documents. The Web page application (FrontPage) enables you to create and maintain your own Web site.

Because Office 2000 is an integrated program, the applications can be used together. For example, numbers from a spreadsheet can be included in a letter created in the word processor or in a presentation.

Starting an Office 2000 Application

An Office 2000 application can be started from the Programs menu on the Start menu or directly from the Start menu.

OPENING AN OFFICE APPLICATION FROM THE PROGRAMS MENU

To open an Office application from the Programs menu, click the Start button, select Programs, and then click the name of the application you want to open.

OPENING AN OFFICE APPLICATION FROM THE START MENU

To open an Office application and create a new blank document within the application at the same time, click the Start button. Then, click New Office Document on the Start menu. On the General tab of the New Office Document dialog box that appears (see Figure 1-1), double-click the icon for the type of blank document you want to create. The application for that type of document opens and a new blank document is created. For example, if you double-click the Blank Presentation icon, PowerPoint will open and a blank presentation will be displayed on the screen.

Hot Tip

If the Microsoft Office Shortcut Bar is installed, you can use it to open an Office application and create a blank document at the same time.

Concept Builder

You can also open a new file from within an application by choosing **New** on the **File** menu. The New dialog box appears, which is very similar to the New Office Document dialog box.

FIGURE 1-1

General tab in the New Office Document dialog box

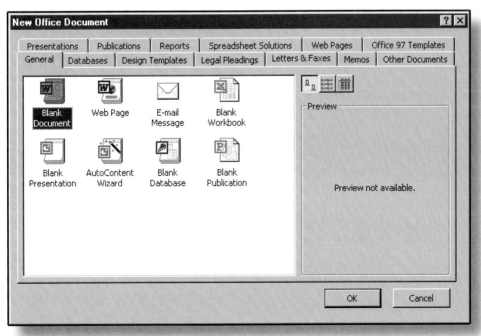

1. Click the **Start** button to open the **Start** menu.

2. Click **Programs**, and then **Microsoft Power-Point**. PowerPoint opens.

3. Click **Cancel** to close the PowerPoint dialog box.

4. Click the **Start** button; then, click **New Office Document**.

5. The New Office Document dialog box appears, as shown in Figure 1-1.

6. Click the **General** tab, if it is not already selected.

7. Double-click the **Blank Document** icon. Word starts and a blank document appears. Leave Word and PowerPoint open for use in the next Step-by-Step.

Opening, Saving, and Closing Office Documents

In Office applications, you *open*, *save*, and *close* files in the same way. Opening a file means loading a file from a disk onto your screen. Saving a file stores it on disk. Closing a file removes it from the screen.

OPENING AN EXISTING DOCUMENT

To open an existing document, you can choose Open on an application's File menu, which displays the Open dialog box (see Figure 1-2). Or, choose Open Office Document on the Start menu, which displays the Open Office Document dialog box.

FIGURE 1-2
Open dialog box

The Open (or Open Office Document) dialog box enables you to open a file from any available disk and folder. The Look in box, near the top of the dialog box, is where you locate the disk drive that contains the file you want to open. Below that is a list that shows you the folders or resources that are on the disk. Double-click a folder to see what files and folders are contained within. To see all the files or office documents in the folder instead of just those created with a particular application, choose All Files or Office Files from the *Files of type* drop-down list box located near the bottom of the dialog box. The bar on the left side of the dialog box provides a shortcut for accessing some of the common places to store documents.

When you have located and selected the file you want to open, click the Open button. If you click the down arrow next to the Open button, a menu is displayed. You can choose to open the document as a ***read-only file*** that can be viewed but not changed, open a copy of the document, or open the document in your browser if it is saved in Web page format.

STEP-BY-STEP ▷ 1.2

1. With Word on the screen, choose **Open** on the **File** menu. The Open dialog box appears, as shown in Figure 1-2.

2. Click the down arrow to the right of the *Look in* box to display the available disk drives.

3. Click the drive that contains your student data files and locate the **Employees** folder, as shown in Figure 1-3.

4. Double-click the **Employees** folder. The folders within the Employees folder appear (see Figure 1-4).

5. Double-click the **Rita** folder. The names of the Word files in the Rita folder are displayed.

6. Click the down arrow at the right of the *Files of type* box and select **All Files**. The names of all files in the Rita folder are displayed.

7. Click **Schedule Memo** to select it and then click **Open** to open the file.

8. Leave the file open for the next Step-by-Step.

FIGURE 1-3
Look in box

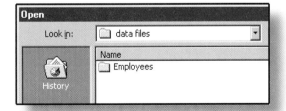

FIGURE 1-4
Employees folder

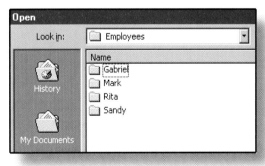

You can see how folders can help organize and identify documents. The Rita folder also contains a spreadsheet with the work schedule for the first two weeks in September. In the next Step-by-Step, you will start Excel, the spreadsheet application of Office 2000, and open the spreadsheet that goes with the memo.

STEP-BY-STEP ▷ 1.3

1. Click the **Start** button.

2. Click **Open Office Document**.

3. Click the down arrow at the right of the *Look in* box and click the drive that contains the student data files.

4. Double-click the **Employees** folder; then, double-click the **Rita** folder.

5. Double-click **September Schedule** to open the file. The Office 2000 spreadsheet application, Excel, opens and *September Schedule* appears on the screen.

6. Leave the file open for the next Step-by-Step.

Saving a File

Saving is done two ways. The Save command saves a file on a disk using the current name. The Save As command saves a file on a disk using a new name. The Save As command can also be used to save a file to a new location.

FILENAMES

Unlike programs designed for the early versions of Windows and DOS, filenames are not limited to eight characters. With Windows 98, a filename may contain up to 255 characters and may include spaces. However, you will rarely need this many characters to name a file. Name a file with a descriptive name that will remind you of what the file contains. The authors of this book have chosen names that are descriptive and easy to use. The filename can include most characters found on the keyboard with the exception of those shown in Table 1-1.

TABLE 1-1
Characters that cannot be used in filenames

CHARACTER	NAME	CHARACTER	NAME
*	asterisk	<	less than sign
\	backslash	.	period
[]	brackets	;	semicolon
:	colon	/	slash
,	comma	"	quotation mark
=	equal sign	?	question mark
>	greater than sign	|	vertical bar

STEP-BY-STEP ▷ 1.4

1. *September Schedule* should be on the screen from the last Step-by-Step.

2. Choose **Save As** on the **File** menu. The Save As dialog box appears, as shown in Figure 1-5.

3. In the *File name* box, key **Sept Work Sched**, followed by your initials.

4. Click the down arrow to the right of the *Save in* box and choose where you want to save the file.

5. Choose **Save** to save the file with the new name.

6. Leave the document open for the next Step-by-Step.

FIGURE 1-5
Save As dialog box

Closing an Office Document

You can close an Office document either by choosing Close on the File menu or by clicking the Close button on the right side of the menu bar. If you close a file, the application will still be open and ready for you to open or create another file.

 **STEP-BY-STEP** ▷ **1.5**

1. Choose **Close** on the **File** menu. *Sept Work Sched* closes.

2. Click the **Microsoft Word** button on the taskbar to make it active. *Schedule Memo* should be displayed.

3. Click the **Close** button (X) in the right corner of the menu bar to close *Schedule Memo*.

4. Leave Word open for the next Step-by-Step.

Hot Tip

When you first use an Office 2000 application, the menus only display the basic commands. To see an expanded menu with all the commands, click the arrows at the bottom of the menu. As you work, the menus are adjusted to display the commands used most frequently, adding a command when you choose it and dropping a command when it hasn't been used recently.

Shortcuts for Loading Recently Used Files

Office offers you two shortcuts for opening recently used files. The first shortcut is to click Documents on the Start menu. A menu will open listing the 15 most recently used documents. To open one of the recently used files, double-click on the file you wish to open.

The second shortcut can be found on each Office application's File menu. The bottom part of the File menu shows the filenames of the four most recently opened documents. The filename with the number 1 beside it is the most recently opened document. When a new file is opened, each filename moves down to make room for the new number 1 file. To open one of the files, you simply choose it as if it were a menu selection. If the document you are looking for is not on the File menu, use Open to load it from the disk.

Hot Tip

If the file is on a floppy disk, you must be sure that the correct disk is in the drive.

Office 2000 Help

This lesson has covered only a few of the many features of Office 2000 applications. For additional information, use the Office 2000 Help system as a quick reference when you are unsure about a function. To get specific help about topics relating to the application you are using, access help from the Help menu on the menu bar. Then, from the Help dialog box, shown in Figure 1-6, you can choose to see a table of contents displaying general topics and subtopics, key a question in the Answer Wizard, or search the Help system using the Index.

Many topics in the Help program are linked. A *link* is represented by colored, underlined text. By clicking a link, the user "jumps" to a linked document that contains additional information.

FIGURE 1-6
Help feature

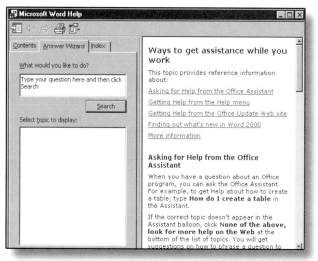

Using the buttons on the toolbar controls the display of information. The Hide button removes the left frame of the help window from view. The Show button will restore it. Back and Forward buttons allow you to move back and forth between previously displayed help entries. Use the Print button to print the help information displayed. The Options button offers navigational choices, as well as options to customize, refresh, and print help topics.

The Contents tab is useful if you want to browse through the topics by category. Click a book icon to see additional help topics. Click a question mark to display detailed help information in the right frame of the help window.

STEP-BY-STEP 1.6

1. Open the Word Help program by choosing **Microsoft Word Help** on the **Help** menu.

2. Click the **Hide** button on the toolbar to remove the left frame.

3. Click the **Show** button to display it again.

4. The Answer Wizard tab is displayed and the right frame displays *Ways to get assistance*

while you work. Your screen should appear similar to Figure 1-6.

5. Click the **Getting Help from the Help menu** link in the right frame.

6. Read the help window and leave it open for the next Step-by-Step.

 **Hot Tip**

If the Office Assistant appears, turn it off by clicking **Options** in the balloon, clearing the *Use Office Assistant* check box, and clicking **OK**.

Using the Answer Wizard tab, you can key in a question about what you would like to do. Then click one of the topics that appears in the box below to display the information in the right frame.

When you want to search for help on a particular topic, use the Index tab and key in a word. Windows will search alphabetically through the list of help topics to try to find an appropriate match, as shown in Figure 1-7. Double-click a topic to see it explained in the right frame of the help window.

FIGURE 1-7
Index tab of the Help system

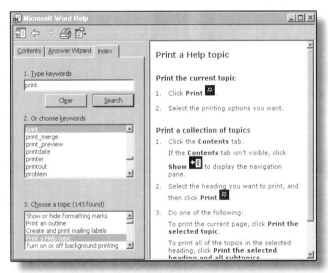

S TEP-BY-STEP ▷ 1.7

1. Click the **Index** tab.

2. Key **print** in the *Type keywords* box and click **Search**.

3. In the *Choose a topic* box, scroll down until you find **Print a Help topic** and click it to display information in the right frame as shown in Figure 1-7.

4. Read the help window; then, print the information by following the instructions you read.

5. Click the **Back** button to return to the previous help entry.

6. Click the **Forward** button to advance to the next help entry.

7. Close the Help program by clicking the **Close** button.

Office Assistant

The Office Assistant is a feature found in all the Office 2000 programs that offers a variety of ways to get help. The Assistant, shown in Figure 1-8, is an animated character that offers tips, solutions, instructions, and examples to help you work more efficiently. The default Office Assistant character is a paperclip. A *default* setting is the one used unless another option is chosen.

The Office Assistant monitors the work you are doing and anticipates when you might need help. It appears on the screen with tips on how to save time or use the program's features more effectively. For example, if you start writing a letter in Word, the Assistant pops up to ask if you want help, as shown in Figure 1-9.

If you have a specific question, you can use the Office Assistant to search for help. To display the Office Assistant if it is not on the screen, choose Show the Office Assistant from the Help menu. Key your question and click Search. The Assistant suggests a list of help topics in response.

FIGURE 1-8
Office Assistant

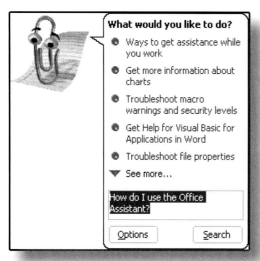

FIGURE 1-9
Office Assistant

S TEP-BY-STEP ▷ 1.8

1. Choose **Show the Office Assistant** on the **Help** menu. The Office Assistant appears.

2. Key **How do I use the Office Assistant?** in the text box.

3. Click **Search**. A list of help topics is displayed, as shown in Figure 1-8.

4. Click **Ways to get assistance while you work**. The Microsoft Word Help box appears.

5. Click the **Asking for Help from the Office Assistant** link.

6. Read about the Office Assistant and print the information.

7. Click the **Close** box to remove the Help window from the screen.

8. Open a new Word document.

9. Key **Dear Zebedee,** and press **Enter**.

10. A message from the Office Assistant appears, asking if you want help writing your letter, as shown in Figure 1-9.

11. Click **Cancel**.

12. Close the Word document without saving.

13. Leave Word on the screen for the next Step-by-Step.

Quitting an Office Application

The Exit command on the File menu provides the option to quit Word or any other Office application. You can also click the Close button (X) on the right side of the title bar. Exiting an Office application takes you to another open application or back to the Windows 98 desktop.

S TEP-BY-STEP ▷ 1.9

1. Open the **File** menu. Notice the files listed toward the bottom of the menu. These are the four most recently used files mentioned in the previous section.

2. Choose **Exit**. Word closes and Excel is displayed on the screen.

3. Click the **Close** button in the right corner of the title bar. Excel closes and the desktop appears

on the screen. The taskbar shows an application is still open.

4. Click the **PowerPoint** button on the taskbar to display it on the screen. Exit PowerPoint. The desktop appears on the screen again.

Accessing the Internet

The **Internet** is a vast network of computers linked to one another. The Internet allows people around the world to share information and ideas through Web pages, newsgroups, mailing lists, chats, e-mail, and electronic files.

Connecting to the Internet requires special hardware and software and an Internet Service Provider. Before you can use the Internet, your computer needs to be connected and you should know how to access the Internet.

The **World Wide Web** is a system of computers that share information by means of hypertext links on "pages." The Internet is its carrier. To identify hypertext documents, the Web uses addresses called **Uniform Resource Locators (URLs)**. Here are some examples of URLs:

http://www.whitehouse.gov
http://www.microsoft.com
http://www.thomson.com/swpco

The Web toolbar, shown in Figure 1-10, is available in all Office 2000 programs. It contains buttons for opening and searching documents. You can use the Web toolbar to access documents on the Internet, on an **Intranet** (a company's private Web), or on your computer. To display the Web toolbar in an application, choose View, Toolbars, Web.

FIGURE 1-10
Web toolbar

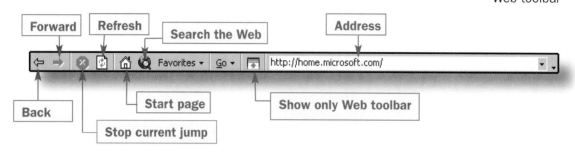

The Back button takes you to the previous page and the Forward button takes you to the next page. Click the Stop Current Jump button to stop loading the current page. The Refresh Current Page button reloads the current page. Click the Start Page button to load your *home page*, the first page that appears when you start your browser. The Search the Web button opens a page in which you can type keywords and search the Web. The Favorites button is a list to which you can add your favorite sites so that you can return to them easily. From the Go button's menu, you can choose to go to different sites or key in an address using the Open command. Click Show Only Web Toolbar when you want to hide all the toolbars except the Web toolbar. When you know the specific address you want to jump to, key it in the *Address* box.

To view hypertext documents on the Web, you need special software. A ***Web browser*** is software used to display Web pages on your computer monitor. Microsoft's ***Internet Explorer*** is a browser for navigating the Web that is packaged with the Office 2000 software. When you click the Start Page button, Search the Web button, or key an URL in the *Address* box of the Web toolbar, Office automatically launches your Web browser. Depending on your type of Internet connection, you may have to connect to your Internet Service Provider first. Figure 1-11 shows a Web page using Word as a browser.

Concept Builder

There are two basic types of Internet connections. *Dial-up access* uses a modem and a telephone line to communicate between your computer and the Internet. Most individual users and small businesses have dial-up access. *Direct access* uses a special high-speed connection between a computer network and the Internet. This access is faster but more expensive than dial-up access. Many businesses and institutions have direct access.

FIGURE 1-11
Web browser

Hot Tip

Since this page is updated every day, your page may not look exactly like the one shown.

STEP-BY-STEP 1.10

1. Connect to your Internet Service Provider if you're not connected already.

2. Open Word. Choose **Toolbars** on the **View** menu, and **Web** from the submenu if the Web toolbar isn't displayed already.

3. Click the **Start Page** button on the Web toolbar. The Start Page begins loading, as shown in Figure 1-11. Wait a few moments for the page to load. (Your start page may be different from the one shown, since this page can be changed easily by choosing Set Start Page on the *Go* button menu.)

4. Click the **Show Only Web Toolbar** button on the toolbar.

5. Click the **Search the Web** button. A new page loads where you can search for a topic on the Web.

6. Click the **Back** button to return to the Start Page.

7. Close all the Word windows that are open. (If a message appears asking you if you want to save changes, click **No**.)

8. Disconnect from your Internet Service Provider.

 Hot Tip

Toolbars display buttons for basic commands only. To see additional buttons, click **More Buttons** on the toolbar and choose from the list that appears. When you use a button from the list, it is added to the toolbar. If you haven't used a button recently, it is added to the More Buttons list.

 Hot Tip

You can display the Web toolbar in any Office application and use it to access the World Wide Web.

Concept Builder

To search for topics on the Web using Microsoft's Search page, key your topic in the *Search* box, choose a search engine, and click **Search**.

Summary

In this lesson, you learned:

■ Microsoft Office 2000 is an integrated software package. The professional version consists of a word processor application, a spreadsheet application, a database application, a presentation application, a schedule/organizer application, and a Web page application. The documents of an integrated software package can be used together.

■ Office applications can be started from the Programs menu and from the Start menu.

■ You can open an existing document from the File menu or from the Start menu. The Open dialog box will be displayed enabling you to open a file from any available disk or directory.

■ No matter which Office application you are using, files are opened, saved, and closed the same way. Filenames may contain up to 255 characters and may include spaces.

■ Recently used files can be opened quickly by choosing the filename from the bottom of the File menu. Or, click the Start button, and select Documents to list the 15 most recently used files. To exit an Office application, choose Exit from the File menu or click the Close button (X) on the title bar.

- The Office 2000 Help program provides additional information about the many features of Office 2000 applications. You can access the Help program from the menu bar and use the Contents, Answer Wizard, and Index tabs to get information.

- The Office Assistant is a help feature found in all Office applications. It offers tips, advice, and hints on how to work more effectively. You can also use it to search for help on any given topic.

LESSON 1 REVIEW QUESTIONS

WRITTEN QUESTIONS

Write a brief answer to the following questions.

1. List four of the applications that are included in Office 2000.

2. What is one way to start an Office application?

3. What is the difference between the Save and Save As commands?

4. If the Web toolbar is not on the screen, how do you display it?

5. What are two of the options you can choose in the Help dialog box?

TRUE/FALSE

Circle T if the statement is true or F if the statement is false.

T   F   1.   In all Office applications, you open, save, and close files in the same way.

T   F   2.   A read-only file is a printed copy of a document.

T   F   3.   The Office Assistant is available in all Office 2000 programs.

T   F   4.   The Web uses addresses called URLs to identify hypertext links.

T   F   5.   A default setting is one that cannot be changed.

LESSON 1 PROJECTS

PROJECT 1-1

You need to save a copy of September's work schedule in Gabriel, Mark, and Sandy's folders as well as in Rita's.

1.   Use the **New Office Document** command to open a new Word document.

2.   Use the **Open Office Document** command to open the **September Schedule** file in Excel.

3.   Use the **Save As** command to save the file as **Sept Work Sched**, followed by your initials, in Gabriel's folder.

4.   Repeat the process to save the file in Mark and Sandy's folders as well.

5.   Close **Sept Work Sched** and exit Excel.

6.   Close the Word document without saving and exit Word.

PROJECT 1-2

1.   Open Word and access the Help system.

2.   Click the **Index** tab.

3.   Key **tip** in the *Type keywords* box to find out how to show the Tip of the Day when Word starts.

4. Print the information displayed in the right frame.

5. Click the **Answer Wizard** tab.

6. In the *What would you like to do?* box, key **What do I do if the Office Assistant is distracting?**

7. Click **Search**.

8. In the *Select topic to display* box, select **Troubleshoot the Office Assistant**.

9. In the right frame, click on the link **The Office Assistant is distracting**.

10. Print the information about what to do if the Office Assistant is distracting.

11. Close the Help system and exit Word.

PROJECT 1-3

1. Connect to your Internet Service Provider.

2. Open your Web browser.

3. Search for information on the Internet about Microsoft products.

4. Search for information about another topic in which you are interested.

5. Return to your home page.

6. Close your Web browser and disconnect from the Internet.

Extra Challenge

If you are using Microsoft Internet Explorer as your Web browser, choose **Web Tutorial** on the **Help** menu and use the tutorial to learn more about the Internet.

CRITICAL THINKING

SCANS

ACTIVITY 1-1

Describe how you would use each of the Office 2000 applications in your personal life. Imagine that you are a business owner and describe how each of the Office 2000 applications would help you increase productivity.

SCANS

ACTIVITY 1-2

Use the Office 2000 Help system to find out how to change the Office Assistant from a paper clip to another animated character. Then find out how you can download additional Assistants.

SCANS

ACTIVITY 1-3

Open your Web browser. Compare the toolbar of your browser with the Web toolbar shown in Figure 1-10. Use the Help system if necessary and describe the function of any buttons that are different. Then describe the steps you would take to print a Web page.

UNIT

INTRODUCTION TO MICROSOFT® ACCESS

lesson 1 — 1.5 hrs.
Access Basics

lesson 2 — 1.5 hrs.
Manipulating Data

lesson 3 — 1.5 hrs.
Creating and Modifying Forms

lesson 4 — 1.5 hrs.
Finding and Ordering Data

lesson 5 — 1.5 hrs.
Reports and Macros

lesson 6 — 1.5 hrs.
Integrating Access

Estimated Time for Unit: 9 hours

LESSON

1

ACCESS BASICS

OBJECTIVES

Upon completion of this lesson, you should be able to:

- Understand databases.

- Start Access and open a database.

- Identify parts of the Access screen.

- Identify the database objects.

- Understand database terminology.

- Create a new database and a new table.

- Design, modify, name, and save a table.

- Navigate a database and enter records.

- Print a table and exit Access.

⏱ **Estimated Time: 1.5 hours**

Database Basics

Access is a program known as a *database management system*. A computerized database management system allows you to store, retrieve, analyze, and print information. You do not, however, need a computer to have a database management system. A set of file folders can be a database management system. Any system for managing data is a database management system. There are distinct advantages, however, to using a computerized database management system.

A computerized database management system (often abbreviated DBMS) is much faster, more flexible, and more accurate than using file folders. A computerized DBMS is also more efficient and cost-effective. A program such as Access can store thousands of pieces of data in a computer or on a disk. The data can be quickly searched and sorted to save time normally spent digging through file folders. For example, a computerized DBMS could find all the people with a certain ZIP code faster and more accurately than you could by searching through a large list or through folders.

Starting Access

To start Access, click the Start button on the taskbar. Select Programs, and then click the Microsoft Access icon to load Access. After a few moments, the Access startup dialog box appears, as shown in Figure 1-1. The dialog box gives you the option of creating a new database or opening an existing one. You can also choose to use a Database Wizard to guide you through the process of creating a database.

FIGURE 1-1
Access startup dialog box

STEP-BY-STEP ▷ 1.1

1. With Windows 98 running, click **Start** on the taskbar.

2. Point to **Programs** on the **Start** menu, and click **Microsoft Access**.

3. Access opens and the Access startup dialog box appears as shown in Figure 1-1. Leave the dialog box on the screen for the next Step-by-Step.

Opening a Database

You can open an existing database from the startup dialog box or from the File menu. To open a database from the startup dialog box, click the *Open an existing file* option and choose a database from the file list. To create a new database, click the *Blank Access database* or *Access database wizards, pages, and projects* option. If you choose *Blank Access database*, you must manually create the database. If you choose *Access database wizards, pages, and projects*, you will be guided through the creation of the database. You will learn more about creating databases later in this lesson.

When you open an existing database, the Database window appears, like that shown in Figure 1-2. The Objects bar on the left side of the window lists the types of database objects. The database objects window lists the various functions for creating the selected object and any objects that already exist. In Figure 1-2, for example, three functions for creating a table and one table named *service club members* are listed. You will learn about database objects later in this lesson.

FIGURE 1-2
Database window

STEP-BY-STEP ▷ 1.2

1. Click the **Open an existing file** option, if it is not already selected.

2. Make sure the **More Files** option is highlighted in the list box, and click **OK**.

3. Open the file **IA Step1-2** from the student data files. The Database window appears, as shown in Figure 1-2. Leave the database open for the next Step-by-Step.

The Access Screen

Like other Office 2000 applications, the Access screen has a title bar, menu bar, and toolbar. At the bottom of the screen is the status bar. Click the down arrow in the Objects bar to view the other objects. Figure 1-3 shows the Access screen with the *IA Step1-2* database open.

As you use Access, various windows and dialog boxes will appear on the screen. Unlike Word and Excel, Access does not have a standard document view. Instead, the screen changes based on how you are interacting with the database.

 Did You Know?

As in other Office programs, you can access the Office Assistant for help. To display the Office Assistant, choose **Show the Office Assistant** on the **Help** menu. Key in a question and click **Search**.

Database Objects

When a database is saved, the file that is saved contains a collection of objects. These objects work together to store data, retrieve data, display data, print reports, and automate operations. The Objects bar

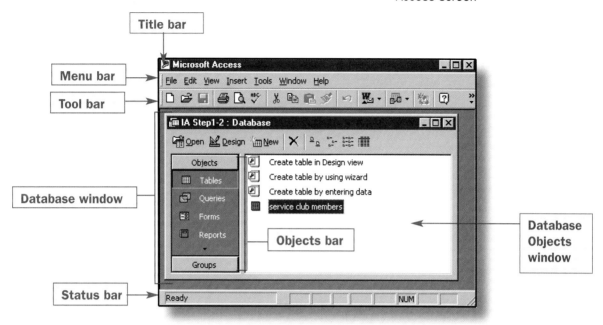

FIGURE 1-3
Access screen

in the Database window displays a button for each type of object. Click the down arrow on the bar to view the additional objects.

Table 1-1 briefly explains the purpose of each type of object.

TABLE 1-1
Database objects

OBJECT	DESCRIPTION
Table	Tables store data in a format similar to that of a worksheet. All database information is stored in tables.
Query	Queries search for and retrieve data from tables based on given criteria. A query is a question you ask the database.
Form	Forms allow you to display data in a custom format. You might, for example, create a form that matches a paper form.
Report	Reports also display data in a custom format. Reports, however, are especially suited for printing and summarizing data. You can even perform calculations in a report.
Page	Data access pages are a new object in Access 2000. They let you design other database objects so that they can be published to the Web.
Macro	Macros automate database operations by allowing you to issue a single command that performs a series of operations.
Module	Modules are like macros but allow much more complex programming of database operations. Creating a module requires the use of a programming language.

1. Make sure **Tables** is selected on the Objects bar. Highlight the **service club members** table in the database objects window, and click the **Open** button. The table appears, as shown in Figure 1-4.

2. Choose **Close** on the **File** menu to close the table. The database objects window is visible again.

3. Click **Queries** on the Objects bar. There is one query object named *Lubbock*. This query locates members who live in Lubbock.

4. Click **Forms** on the Objects bar. There is one form object named *service members form*.

5. Choose **Close** on the **File** menu to close the database. Leave Access open for the next Step-by-Step.

FIGURE 1-4
Database table

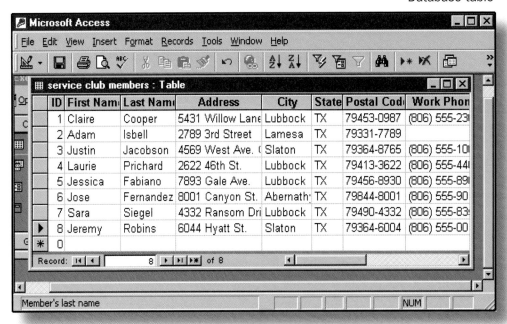

Database Terminology

Four terms are essential to know when working with databases. These terms relate to the way data is organized in a table. A *record* is a complete set of data. In the service club members table, each member is stored as a record. In a table, a record appears as a row, as shown in Figure 1-5.

Each record is made up of *fields*. For example, the first name of each member is placed in a special field that is created to accept first names. In a table, fields appear as columns. In order to identify the fields, each field has a *field name*. The data entered into a field is called an *entry*. In the service club members database, for example, the first record has the name *Claire* as an entry in the First Name field.

FIGURE 1-5
Records and fields

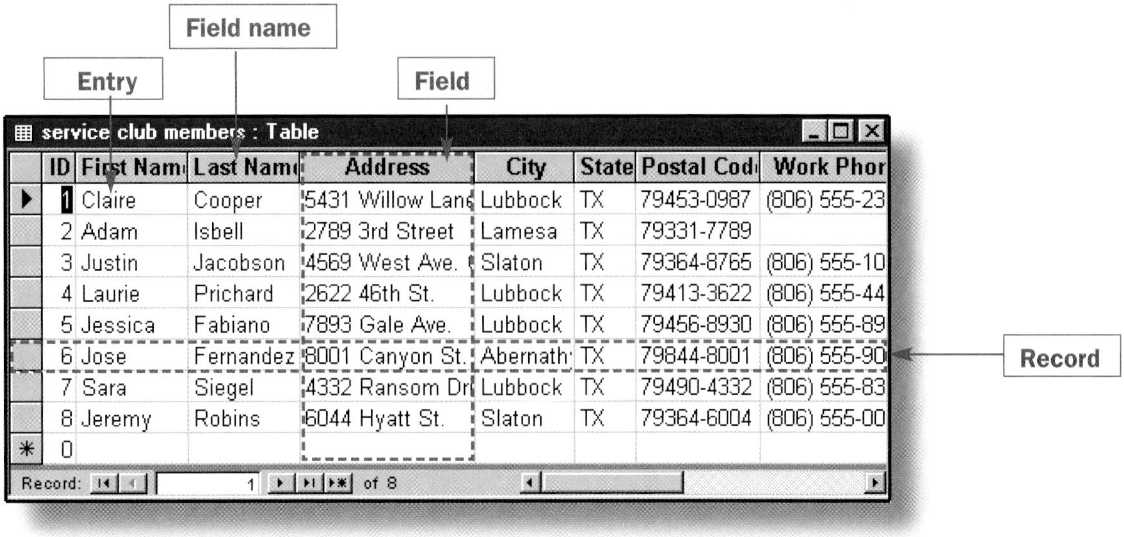
Field name
Entry
Field
Record
service club members : Table
ID
First Nam
Last Nam
Address
City
State
Postal Cod
Work Phor
1 Claire Cooper 5431 Willow Lan Lubbock TX 79453-0987 (806) 555-23
2 Adam Isbell 2789 3rd Street Lamesa TX 79331-7789
3 Justin Jacobson 4569 West Ave. Slaton TX 79364-8765 (806) 555-10
4 Laurie Prichard 2622 46th St. Lubbock TX 79413-3622 (806) 555-44
5 Jessica Fabiano 7893 Gale Ave. Lubbock TX 79456-8930 (806) 555-89
6 Jose Fernandez 8001 Canyon St. Abernath TX 79844-8001 (806) 555-90
7 Sara Siegel 4332 Ransom Dr Lubbock TX 79490-4332 (806) 555-83
8 Jeremy Robins 6044 Hyatt St. Slaton TX 79364-6004 (806) 555-00
0
Record: 1 of 8

Creating a Database

The first step in creating a database is to create the file that will hold the database objects. To do this, you choose New on the File menu. The New dialog box appears, as shown in Figure 1-6. With the General tab already selected, choose Database and the File New Database dialog box appears. This is where you will name the file and store it with your other data files. Choose Create and the Database window appears, as shown in Figure 1-7. It will not contain any objects yet, because none have been created.

FIGURE 1-6
New dialog box

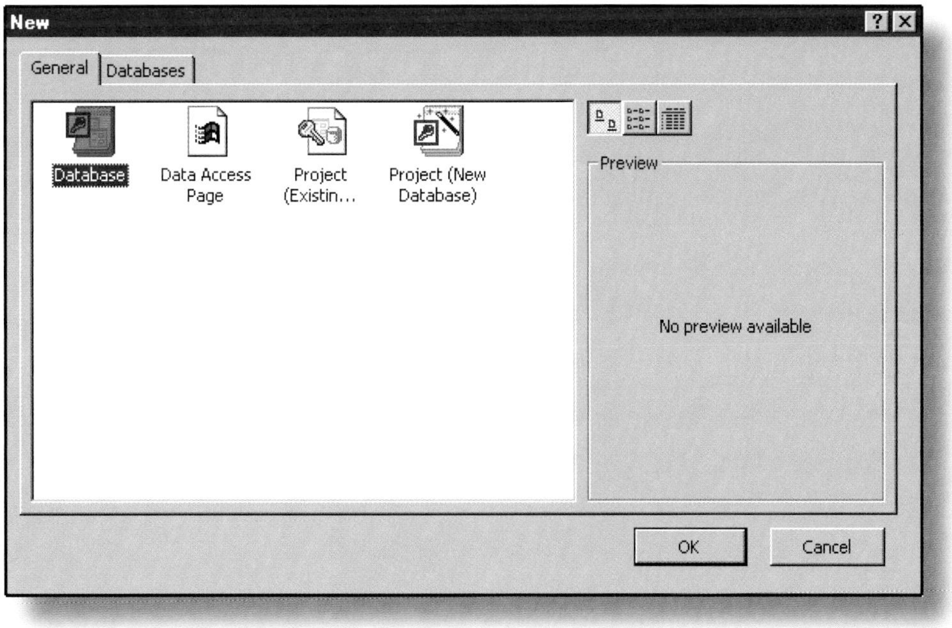
New
General
Databases
Database
Data Access Page
Project (Existin...
Project (New Database)
Preview
No preview available
OK
Cancel

FIGURE 1-7
Database window

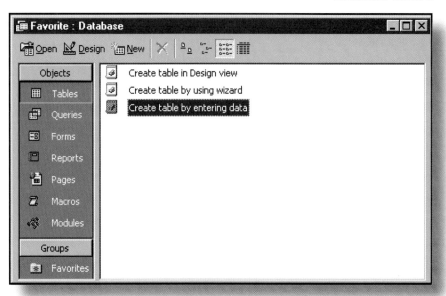

STEP-BY-STEP ▷ 1.4

1. Choose **New** on the **File** menu. The New dialog box appears, as shown in Figure 1-6.

2. With the **General** tab selected, choose **Database**, and then click **OK**. The File New Database dialog box appears.

3. Save the database as **Favorite**, followed by your initials, and then click **Create**. Your Database window should look like that shown in Figure 1-7.

4. Double-click **Create table by entering data**. A new table appears in Datasheet view, as shown in Figure 1-8.

5. Choose **Close** on the **File** menu to go back to the Database window. Leave the window open for the next Step-by-Step.

 Extra Challenge

Create a new database. In the New dialog box, choose the **Databases** tab. Select one of the database formats already designed for you and add your own information.

FIGURE 1-8
New table in Datasheet view

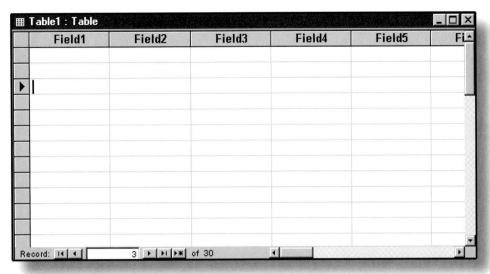

Creating Tables

Because all other database objects rely on the existence of a database table, creating a table is the next step after creating a database. In many database management systems, data is stored using more than one table. To create a table, click Tables on the Objects bar. Click the New button and the New Table dialog box appears, as shown in Figure 1-9.

Hot Tip

You can create a table manually in Design view. Or, you can select the *Table Wizard* option in the New Table dialog box. A series of wizards guides you step-by-step through the process of creating a table.

The New Table dialog box lists several ways to create a table. The most common way is to create the table in ***Design view***. This is the view where you will design new tables and modify the design of existing tables. You can also create a table in Design view by double-clicking *Create table in Design view* in the Database window.

FIGURE 1-9
New Table dialog box

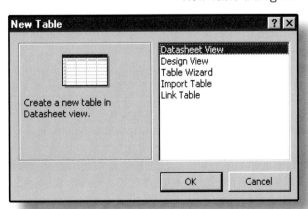

STEP-BY-STEP ▷ 1.5

1. Click **Tables** on the Objects bar, if necessary, and then click **New**. The New Table dialog box appears, as shown in Figure 1-9.

2. Choose the **Design View** option and click **OK**. The Design view window opens. Leave the window on the screen for the next Step-by-Step.

Designing a Table

Now you are ready to design your table. You create the table's fields in the Design view window. As you can see in the window on your screen, each field in a table is divided into three sections: Field Name, Data Type, and Description. You will insert data in each of these three sections to create a table.

FIELD NAMES

First you have to decide what data you need to store. You should divide the data into categories to create fields. For example, suppose you want to create a database of your family members' birthdays. Some fields to include would be the person's name, address, and birth date. An example of a record would be: Halie Jones (name), 3410 Vicksburg Ave., Dallas, TX 75224 (address), and 10/28/89 (birth date).

You key the names of these fields in the Field Name column of the Table design window. It is helpful if you create meaningful field names that identify the types of data stored.

DATA TYPE

After keying the field name, press the Tab key to move to the Data Type column. Then, determine the type of data to be stored in each field and choose an appropriate data type. The *data type* tells Access what kind of information can be stored in the field. Table 1-2 briefly describes the basic data types.

Choosing the correct data type is important. For example, you might think a telephone number or ZIP code should be stored in a field with a Number data type. However, you should only use Number data types when you intend to do calculations with the data. You won't be adding or subtracting ZIP codes. Numbers that will not be used in calculations are best stored as Text.

For a table of favorite restaurants, the name of the restaurant and address would be stored in fields of Text type, which is the default data type. The typical meal cost is ideal for the Currency type. The date you last ate at the restaurant would be Date type, and a Yes/No data type could specify whether reservations are required.

To choose a data type, click the arrow that appears in the Data Type column when the insertion point is in that column or when you key the first letter of the word. This button is called a drop-down arrow. A menu appears allowing you to choose a data type.

> **Did You Know?**
>
> You can set a default value for a field that usually contains the same value. For example, if most of the people in a database of names and addresses live in Texas, you can enter TX as the default value of the State field. The State field will automatically contain TX, unless you change it.

DESCRIPTION

The last step in designing a table is to key a description for each field. The description explains the data in the field. For example, a field for the *Restaurants* database named Last Visit could have a description such as Date I Last Ate at the Restaurant. The description clarifies the field name. It does not appear in a table, but does display in the status bar when you select the field.

TABLE 1-2
Data types

DATA TYPE	DESCRIPTION
Text	The Text data type allows letters and numbers (alphanumeric data). A text field can hold up to 255 characters. Data such as names and addresses is stored in fields of this type.
Memo	The Memo data type also allows alphanumeric data. A memo field, however, can hold thousands of characters. Memo fields are used for data that does not follow a particular format. For example, you might use a Memo field to store notes about a record.
Number	The Number data type holds numeric data. There are variations of the Number type, each capable of storing a different range of values.
Date/Time	The Date/Time data type holds dates and times.
Currency	The Currency data type is specially formatted for dealing with currency.
AutoNumber	The AutoNumber data type is automatically incremented by Access for each new record added. Counters are used to give each record in a database a unique identification.
Yes/No	The Yes/No data type holds logical values. A Yes/No field can hold the values Yes/No, True/False, or On/Off.
OLE Object	The OLE Object data type is used for some of the more advanced features. It allows you to store graphics, sound, and even objects such as spreadsheets in a field.
Hyperlink	The Hyperlink data type is used to store a hyperlink as a UNC path or URL.
Lookup Wizard	The Lookup Wizard creates a field that allows you to choose a value from another table or from a list of values.

STEP-BY-STEP ▷ 1.6

1. Key **Name** in the first row of the Field Name column.

2. Press **Tab** (or **Enter**). The data type will default to Text, which is appropriate for the name of the restaurant.

3. Press **Tab** to move to the Description column.

4. Key **Name of restaurant** and press **Enter** to move to the next row.

5. Key the other fields and descriptions shown in Figure 1-10. All of the fields are the Text data type.

(continued on next page)

FIGURE 1-10
Defining fields in a table

Field Name	Data Type	Description
Name	Text	Name of restaurant
Address	Text	Address of restaurant
Phone	Text	Phone number of restaurant
▶ Specialty	Text	Restaurant's specialty foods

6. Key **Last Visit** in the Field Name column and press **Tab**.

7. Click the arrow in the Data Type field and choose **Date/Time** from the drop-down menu that appears, as shown in Figure 1-11.

8. Press **Tab**.

9. Key **Date I last ate at the restaurant** in the Description column. Press **Tab**.

10. Key **Reservations** in the Field Name column, choose **Yes/No** as the data type, and key **Are reservations required?** in the Description column.

11. Leave the Design view window on the screen for the next Step-by-Step.

FIGURE 1-11
Data types

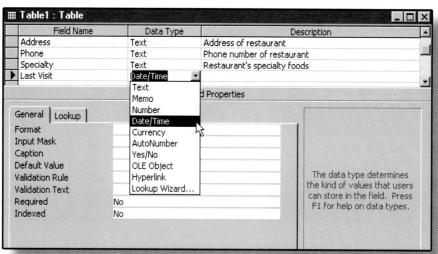

Naming and Saving a Table

After designing a table, you must give it a name and save the design. To save a table, choose Save on the File menu. The Save As dialog box appears, as shown in Figure 1-12. Key a name for the table and click OK. A message appears asking you if you want to create a ***primary key***, which is a special field that assigns a unique identifier to each record. You can have Access create the primary key for you, in which case each record is automatically assigned a unique number. Or you can designate an existing field to be a primary key. For example, in a table containing the names and addresses of customers, you might create a field that contains a customer identification number. You could set this as the primary key, since it will be a unique number for each customer.

FIGURE 1-12
Save As dialog box

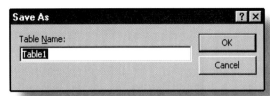

S TEP-BY-STEP ▷ 1.7

1. Choose **Save** on the **File** menu. The Save As dialog box appears, as shown in Figure 1-12.

2. Key **Restaurants** in the *Table Name* box and click **OK**.

3. You will be asked if you want to create a primary key. Click **No**.

4. Choose **Close** on the **File** menu to close the Design view window and return to the Database window. Note that your *Restaurants* table now appears as an object, as shown in Figure 1-13.

5. Leave the Database window open for the next Step-by-Step.

FIGURE 1-13
Database window showing *Restaurants* table as an object

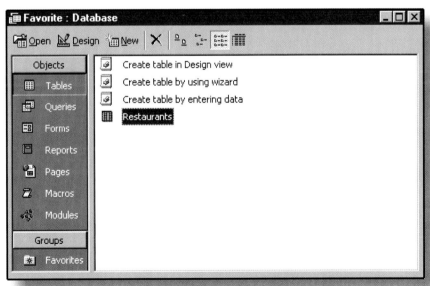

Modifying Tables

To modify the design of a table, you must be in Design view. Go to Design view by highlighting the name of the table in the Database window and clicking the Design button. In Design view, you can make changes to the names of fields, data formats, and descriptions.

You can add fields to the end of the list, or you can insert a new row for a field between existing fields. To insert a new row, place the insertion point in the row *below* where you want the new row to appear. Then, choose Rows on the Insert menu. You can delete a field by placing the insertion point in the row you want to delete and choosing Delete Rows on the Edit menu. You can also insert and delete rows by clicking the Insert Rows or Delete Rows button on the standard toolbar.

It is important to make sure you don't delete the wrong data in Design view; but if you do, you can click the Undo Delete button on the toolbar. The Undo Delete button reverses your last command.

You can delete an entire table by highlighting the table in the Database window and choosing Delete on the Edit menu.

When you finish changing fields, choose Save on the File menu or click the Save button on the toolbar.

 Did You Know?

A primary key field is a unique identifier for a record. To set a field as a primary key, open the table in Design view and click the row selector for the desired field. Click the Primary Key button on the toolbar.

 TEP-BY-STEP 1.8

1. Highlight the **Restaurants** table in the Database window if it's not selected already.

2. Click the **Design** button. The table appears in Design view.

3. Click in the first blank row's Field Name column to place the insertion point there. You may need to scroll down.

4. Key **Meal Cost** in the Field Name column. Press **Tab**.

5. Choose **Currency** as the data type. Press **Tab**.

6. Key **Typical meal cost** as the description.

7. Place the insertion point in the **Last Visit** field name.

8. Click the **Insert Rows** button on the toolbar. A blank row is inserted above the *Last Visit* field.

9. In the blank row, key **Favorite Dish** as the field name, choose **Text** as the data type, and key **My favorite meal** as the description.

10. Place the insertion point in the **Reservations** field name.

11. Click the **Delete Rows** button on the toolbar. The Reservations field is deleted.

12. Click the **Undo Delete** button on the toolbar. The Reservations field reappears.

13. Click the **Save** button on the toolbar to save the design changes. Remain in this screen for the next Step-by-Step.

Navigating and Entering Records in Datasheet View

Once a table is created and designed, you can enter records directly into the table using *Datasheet view*. In Datasheet view, the table appears in a form similar to a spreadsheet, as you saw earlier in the lesson. As with a spreadsheet, the intersection of a row and a column is called a cell. To get to Datasheet view, select the table in the Database window and click the Open button, or click the View button on the toolbar while in Design view. You can switch back to Design view by clicking the View button again.

View, Datasheet

View, Design

The techniques used to enter records in the table are familiar to you. Press Enter or Tab to move to the next field as you enter the data. Access will consider the data types as you enter data. For example, you must enter a valid date in a Date/Time field and you must enter a number in a Number field. If you don't, an error message appears.

After entering records in a table in Datasheet view, you do not need to save the changes. Access saves them for you automatically. Remember to always save changes to the table design in Design view.

You can use the mouse to move the insertion point to a particular cell in the table. You can also use the keys in Table 1-3 to navigate through a table.

 Did You Know?

You can switch to the Datasheet or Design view using options on the View menu.

TABLE 1-3
Navigating in Datasheet View

KEY	DESCRIPTION
Enter, Tab, or right arrow	Moves to the following field
Left arrow or Shift+Tab	Moves to the previous field
End	Moves to the last field in the current record
Home	Moves to the first field in the current record
Up arrow	Moves up one record and stays in the same field
Down arrow	Moves down one record and stays in the same field
Page Up	Moves up one screen
Page Down	Moves down one screen

1. Click the **View** button in the Design view window to switch to Datasheet view. The *Restaurant* table looks like that shown in Figure 1-14. Notice how the View button now displays a different icon to indicate that clicking it will switch you back to Design view.

2. Key **Rosa's** in the Name field. Press **Tab**.

3. Key **8722 University Ave.** in the Address field. Press **Tab**.

4. Key **555-6798** in the Phone field. Press **Tab**.

5. Key **Mexican** in the Specialty field. Press **Tab**.

6. Key **Chicken Fajitas** in the Favorite Dish field. Press **Tab**.

7. Key today's date in the Last Visit field. Press **Tab**. (If you do not key the year, it will be added automatically.)

8. The Reservations field has a check box in it. Click the check box or press the spacebar to place a check in the box. Press **Tab**.

9. Key **5.95** as the typical meal cost. Press **Tab**. Leave the database table open for the next Step-by-Step.

Extra Challenge

Create a database of your own favorite local restaurants. Use the fields from this *Restaurants* exercise, and any others that may apply.

FIGURE 1-14
Datasheet view

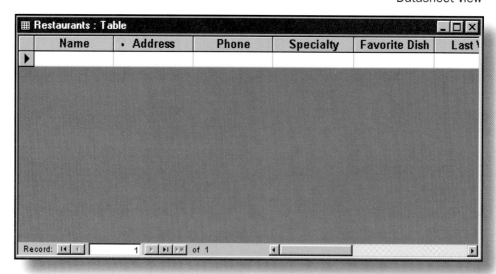

Printing a Table

You can print a database table in Datasheet view. Choose the Print command on the File menu to display the Print dialog box. As shown in Figure 1-15, you can choose to print all the records, only those selected, or for long tables you can specify the pages to print. Click the Setup button and the Page Setup dialog box appears, as shown in Figure 1-16. Here you can change the margins. To change the orientation, click the Properties button in the Print dialog box.

You can also click the Print button on the toolbar to print the database table. However, the Print dialog box will not appear for updates to the page setup.

FIGURE 1-15
Print dialog box

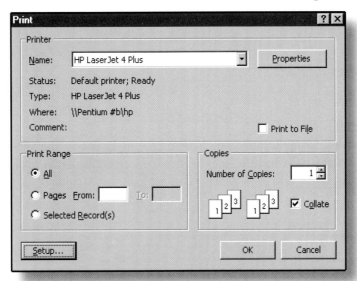

FIGURE 1-16
Page Setup dialog box

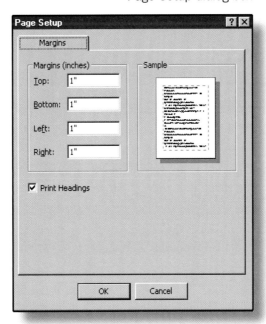

STEP-BY-STEP ▷ 1.10

1. Choose **Print** on the **File** menu. The Print dialog box appears, as shown in Figure 1-15.

2. Click **Setup**. The Page Setup dialog box appears, as shown in Figure 1-16.

3. For the margins, key **.5** in the Left box and **.5** in the Right box.

4. Click **OK**.

5. In the Print dialog box, click **Properties**. The Properties dialog box appears.

6. From the *Orientation* options, click **Landscape**.

7. Click **OK**.

8. In the Print dialog box, click **All** from the *Print Range* options, if it isn't already selected. Click **OK**.

9. Close the table. The record has been saved in the table automatically.

Exiting Access

As in other Office 2000 programs, you exit Access by choosing the Exit command on the File menu. Exiting Access takes you back to the Windows 98 desktop. Remember to remove any floppy disks, and properly shut down Windows 98 before turning off the computer.

STEP-BY-STEP ▷ 1.11

1. Choose **Close** on the **File** menu. The database closes.

2. Choose **Exit** on the **File** menu. The Windows 98 desktop appears.

Summary

In this lesson, you learned:

■ Access is a program known as a database management system. A computerized database management system allows you to store, retrieve, analyze, and print information. Start Access from the Programs menu.

■ You can open an existing database from the File menu or by clicking the toolbar button. The Access screen has a title bar, menu bar, and toolbar. Access, however, does not have a standard document view.

■ A database is a collection of objects. The objects work together to store data, retrieve data, display data, print reports, and automate operations. The object types are tables, queries, forms, reports, macros, and modules.

■ A record is a complete set of data. Each record is made up of fields. Each field is identified by a field name. The actual data entered into a field is called an entry.

■ Creating a database creates a file that will hold database objects. To store data, a table must first be created. In Design view, you can create fields and assign data types and descriptions to the fields. Once a table has been created and designed, you can enter records in Datasheet view.

■ As in other Office 2000 applications, you exit Access by choosing the Exit command from the File menu.

LESSON 1 REVIEW QUESTIONS

TRUE/FALSE

Circle T if the statement is true or F if the statement is false.

T   F   1.   A computerized DBMS is more efficient than paper filing.

T   F   2.   Opening a database automatically displays the data in the table.

T   F   3.   Access has a standard document view that remains on the screen as long as a database is open.

T   F   4.   A database file is a collection of database objects.

T   F   5.   Fields are identified by field names.

WRITTEN QUESTIONS

Write a brief answer to the following questions.

1.   Which window appears after you open a database?

2.   List three types of database objects.

3. Which database object allows you to search for and retrieve data?

4. What is the term for the data entered in a field?

5. Which view is used to design tables?

LESSON 1 PROJECTS

PROJECT 1-1

1. Start Access.

2. Open the **Favorite** database.

3. Open the **Restaurants** table in Datasheet view.

4. Insert the records shown in Figure 1-17.

5. Print the table in landscape orientation.

6. Close the table.

FIGURE 1-17

Lesson ① Access Basics

Name	Address	Phone	Specialty	Favorite Dish	Last Visit	Reservations	Meal Cost
Health Hut	3440 Slide Rd.	555-6096	Healthy foods	Fruit Delight	6/30/98	☐	$5.50
Stella's	7822 Broadway	555-8922	Italian	Lasagna	7/6/98	☑	$9.95
Tony's BBQ	2310 82nd St.	555-3143	BBQ	Baby Back Ribs	5/1/98	☑	$10.95
Morning Glory	5660 Salem	555-6621	Breakfast	Daybreak Muffins	7/12/98	☐	$2.95
Salads and Stuff	8910 Main St.	555-3440	Salads	Chicken Caesar Salad	4/29/98	☐	$5.95
Saltlick Steakhouse	2100 Highway 281	555-6700	Steaks	Rib Eye	3/10/98	☑	$13.50
Alamo Diner	451 San Jacinto	555-9833	American	Cheeseburger	8/4/98	☐	$5.50

PROJECT 1-2

SCANS

1. With the *Favorite* database open, create a new table named **Stores** using the field names, data types, and descriptions shown in Figure 1-18.

FIGURE 1-18

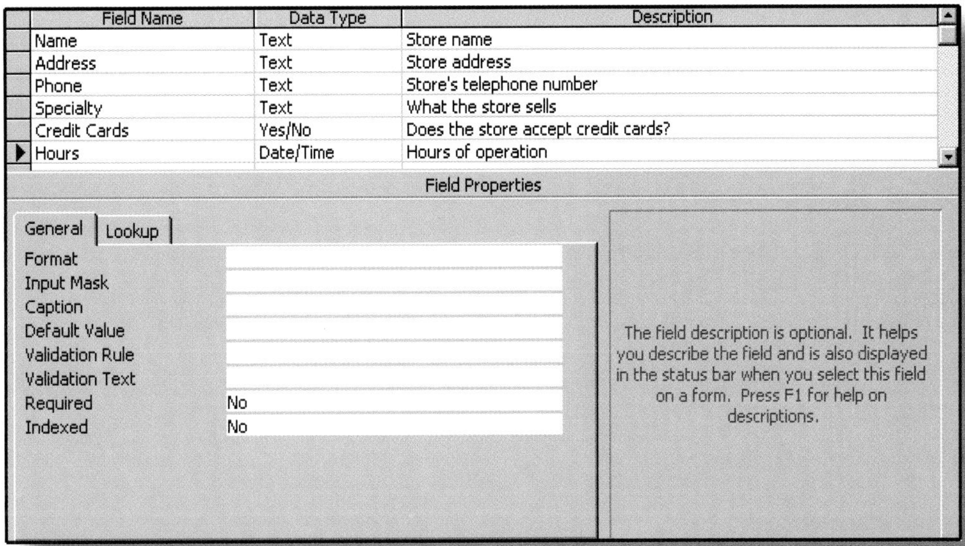

Field Name	Data Type	Description
Name	Text	Store name
Address	Text	Store address
Phone	Text	Store's telephone number
Specialty	Text	What the store sells
Credit Cards	Yes/No	Does the store accept credit cards?
▶ Hours	Date/Time	Hours of operation

Field Properties

General | Lookup

Format	
Input Mask	
Caption	
Default Value	
Validation Rule	
Validation Text	
Required	No
Indexed	No

The field description is optional. It helps you describe the field and is also displayed in the status bar when you select this field on a form. Press F1 for help on descriptions.

2. Save the table as **Stores** and close it. No primary key is necessary.

3. Open the table in Datasheet view and enter the record shown in Figure 1-19.

FIGURE 1-19

Name	Address	Phone	Specialty	Credit Cards	Hours
Electronics Plus	6443 Elgin St.	555-2330	Electronics	☑	10am to 6pm
				☐	

4. After keying the Hours field entry, a message appears telling you the value you entered isn't appropriate for the field. Click **OK** and delete the data in the Hours field.

5. Close Datasheet view and open the table in Design view.

6. Change the data type for the Hours field to **Text**.

7. Insert a new row above the Hours field and key a new field named **Checks** with the **Yes/No** data type, and **Does the store accept personal checks?** as the description.

8. Save the changes and close Design view.

9. Open the table in Datasheet view and click the check box (for *yes*) in the Checks field.

10. Key **10am to 6pm** in the Hours field.

11. Enter the records shown in Figure 1-20.

FIGURE 1-20

Name	Address	Phone	Specialty	Credit Cards	Checks	Hours
Music Master	2700 Canton	555-9820	Music-CDs	☑	☐	11am to 9pm
Rag Doll	2136 Quaker	555-4560	Ladies clothes	☑	☑	10am to 5:30pm
Vision Computers	6720 Data Drive	555-2300	Computers	☑	☑	10am to 7pm
Athletics X-Press	8904 Richmond	555-7811	Shoes	☑	☑	12pm to 7pm
College Clothiers	3340 University	555-3570	Clothes	☐	☑	12pm to 6pm

12. Change the left and right margins to **.5** inches and print the table.

13. Close the table.

PROJECT 1-3

1. Open the **Stores** table in Design view.

2. Delete the **Checks** field.

3. Change the data type for the Credit Cards field to **Text**.

4. Save the changes and close Design view.

5. Open the table in Datasheet view.

6. Change the left and right margins to **.75"** and print the table.

7. Close the table and database.

PROJECT 1-4

1. Create a new database named **Music**.

2. With the *Music* database open, create a new table named **Pop** using the field names, data types, and descriptions shown in Figure 1-21.

FIGURE 1-21

Field Name	Data Type	Description
Name	Text	Musical artist's name
Title	Text	Title of CD or tape
Year	Number	Year title was released
▶ Type	Text	CD or tape?

Pop : Table

3. Save the table as **Pop**. No primary key is necessary.

4. Switch to Datasheet view and enter the records shown in Figure 1-22.

5. Print and close the table.

Web Site

To find information on your favorite music, artists, concerts, software, instruments, or music education, access Music Search at *http://www.musicsearch.com.* Web sites and addresses change regularly, so if you can't find the information at this site, try another.

FIGURE 1-22

Name	Title	Year	Type
Dire Straits	Money for Nothing	1988	CD
Mariah Carey	Music Box	1993	CD
Van Morrison	Moondance	1970	Tape
Kenny G.	Silhouette	1988	CD
Natalie Merchant	Blind Man's Zoo	1989	CD
Billy Joel	Glass Houses	1980	Tape
▶		0	

PROJECT 1-5

1. With the *Music* database open, open the **Pop** table in Design view.

2. Delete the **Type** field.

3. Save the change.

4. Switch to Datasheet view and add the records as shown in Figure 1-23.

5. Print the table.

6. Close the table and database.

FIGURE 1-23

Name	Title	Year
Pretenders	The Isle Of View	1995
Jackson Browne	Looking East	1996
Genesis	Three Sides Live	1994
▶		0

CRITICAL THINKING

ACTIVITY 1-1

Select a type of collection or personal interest and create a database to organize it. Give the database a name that accurately reflects the data.

Create and design a table for your data using the Table Wizard. Carefully consider what fields your database will need.

To start the Table Wizard, double-click *Create table by using wizard* in the Database window and follow the screens to create your table. In the first screen, choose the Personal category and one of the Sample tables. In the Sample Fields column, select the fields for your new table. When finished with the first screen, click the Next button. In the second screen, enter the name of your table and click Next. On the third screen, choose *Enter data directly into the table* and click the Finish button. The table will appear in Datasheet view. Enter at least two records in the table. Change the margins if necessary and print the table. Close the table and exit Access.

ACTIVITY 1-2

When creating a database with many of the same types of fields, it is helpful to know how to copy the definition of a field. Use the Help feature and search for the steps to copy a field's definition within a table. Write down these basic steps.

MANIPULATING DATA

OBJECTIVES

Upon completion of this lesson, you should be able to:

- Edit a record and undo a change.
- Select records and fields.
- Delete a record.
- Cut, copy, and paste data.
- Change the layout of a datasheet.

⏱ Estimated Time: 1.5 hours

Editing Records

To make editing records easier, Access provides navigation buttons on your screen. The navigation buttons are used to move around the datasheet. These buttons may not be necessary when working with databases as small as those you used in the previous lesson. As databases get larger, however, the navigation buttons become very useful. Figure 2-1 shows the locations of the navigation buttons.

FIGURE 2-1
Navigation buttons

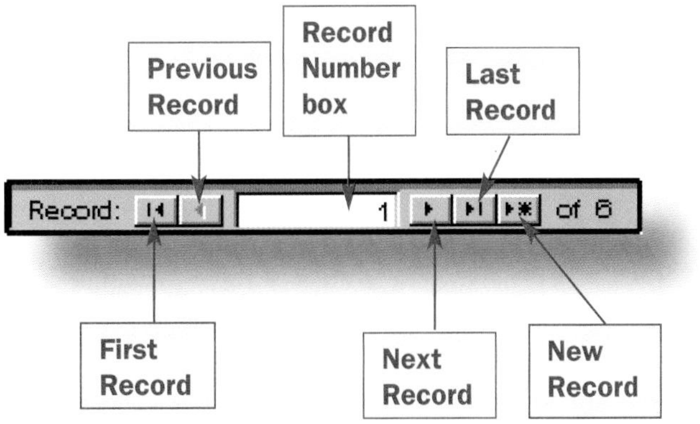

Record: |◄ ◄ [1] ► ►| ►* of 6

Previous Record
Record Number box
Last Record
First Record
Next Record
New Record

The First Record button is used to move quickly to the top of the table and the Last Record button is used to move to the bottom of the table. There are also buttons used to move to the next or previous record. To move to a specific record number, click the Record Number box and key the number of the record in the field. Press Tab to move to the record. To add a new record, click the New Record button.

The current record is indicated by an arrow to the left of the record. The computer keeps track of the current record using a *record pointer*. When you move among records in Datasheet view, you are actually moving the record pointer.

If you use the Tab key to move to a cell, Access highlights the contents of the cell. As in a spreadsheet, you can replace the contents of the cell by keying data while the existing data is highlighted. If you click a cell with the mouse, the insertion point appears in the cell, allowing you to edit the contents.

Undoing Changes to a Cell

There are three ways to undo changes to a cell. If you make a mistake keying data in a cell, you can choose Undo Typing on the Edit menu or click the Undo button on the toolbar. Your last action is reversed. If you have already entered the data in a cell and moved to the next cell (or any cell), choose Undo Current Field/Record on the Edit menu or press the Esc button to restore the contents of the entire record. If you make changes to a record and then move to the next record, you can restore the previous record by choosing Undo Saved Record on the Edit menu.

STEP-BY-STEP ▷ 2.1

1. Open **IA Step2-1** from the student data files.

2. Open the **Calls** table in Datasheet view. The purpose of this table is to keep a log of telephone calls.

3. Click the **Last Record** button at the bottom of the table to move the record pointer to the last record.

4. Click the **First Record** button to move the record pointer to the first record.

5. Click the **Next Record** button to move the record pointer to the next record.

6. In the second record, the time is shown as 11:00 AM when it should be 10:30 AM. Press **Tab** until the **Call Time** field is highlighted.

7. Key **10:30** in the Call Time field and press **Tab**. (The field is formatted for AM.)

8. Move the mouse pointer to the **Subject** field in the third record. Click to place the pointer at the beginning of the field. The entire field will be highlighted.

9. Key **Computers** and press **Tab**.

10. Press **Esc**. The word *Computers* changes back to *Hardware*.

11. The entry in the Notes field of the third record is highlighted. Press **Delete.** The entry is deleted.

12. Click the **Undo** button on the toolbar. The Notes field entry reappears.

13. Leave the table on the screen for the next Step-by-Step.

Selecting Records and Fields

You can quickly select records and fields by clicking the record or field selectors. *Field selectors* are at the top of a table and contain the field name. Figure 2-2 shows the Name field selected. *Record selectors* are located to the left of a record's first field. Clicking in the upper left corner of the datasheet selects all records in the database.

You can select more than one field by clicking the field selector in one field, holding down the Shift key, and clicking the field selector in another field. The two fields, and all the fields in between, will be selected. You can use the same method to select multiple records. You can also select multiple fields or records by clicking and dragging across the field or record selectors.

FIGURE 2-2
Record and field selectors

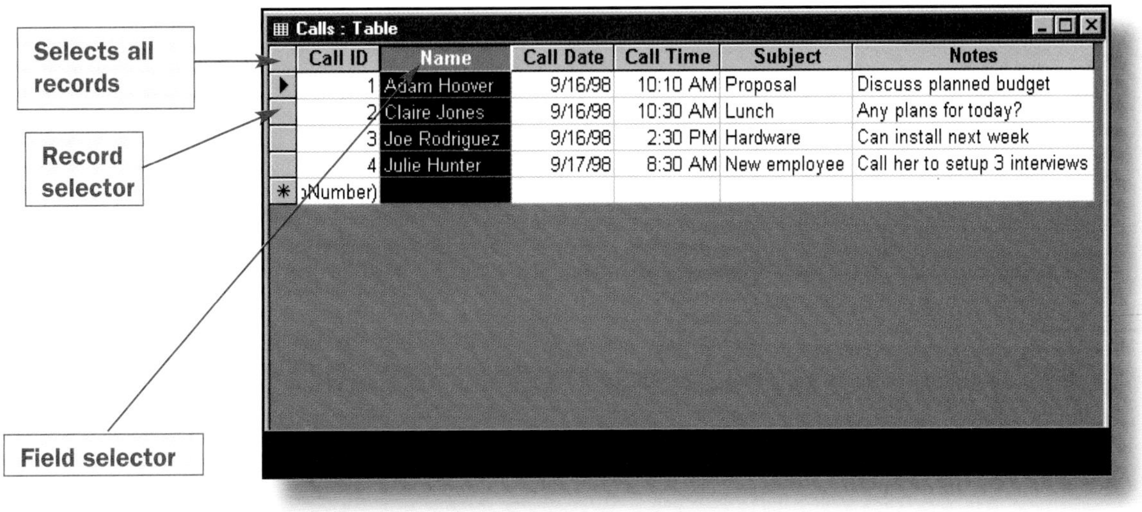

Selects all records →			
Record selector →			
Field selector →			

Calls : Table

	Call ID	Name	Call Date	Call Time	Subject	Notes
▶	1	Adam Hoover	9/16/98	10:10 AM	Proposal	Discuss planned budget
	2	Claire Jones	9/16/98	10:30 AM	Lunch	Any plans for today?
	3	Joe Rodriguez	9/16/98	2:30 PM	Hardware	Can install next week
	4	Julie Hunter	9/17/98	8:30 AM	New employee	Call her to setup 3 interviews
*	(Number)					

STEP-BY-STEP ▷ 2.2

1. Click the **Name** field selector to select the entire column.

2. Click the **Subject** field selector to select the column.

3. Select the **Name** field again.

4. Hold down the **Shift** key and click the **Call Time** field selector. The Name, Call Date, and Call

Time fields are selected, as shown in Figure 2-3.

5. Click the record selector of the **Claire Jones** record. The entire record is selected.

6. Select the **Julie Hunter** record. Leave the table on the screen for the next Step-by-Step.

(continued on next page)

STEP-BY-STEP ⟹ 2.2 CONTINUED

FIGURE 2-3
Selecting multiple columns

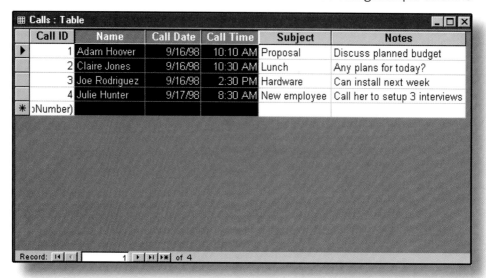

Deleting Records

To delete an entire record, select the record and choose Delete Record on the Edit menu or press the Delete key. You can also click the Delete Record button on the toolbar. A message box appears, as shown in Figure 2-4, warning you that you are about to delete a record. Click Yes to permanently delete the record or No to cancel the deletion. Once you've deleted a record using the Delete Record command, you cannot use the Undo command or Esc key to restore it.

You cannot delete fields in Datasheet view the same way you delete records. As you learned in Lesson 1, you can delete fields in Design view.

Hot Tip

You can delete more than one record by holding down the Shift key, clicking the field selector in each field, and then selecting Delete Record.

FIGURE 2-4
Message warning you that you are about to delete a record

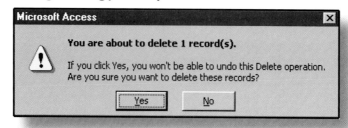

STEP-BY-STEP ▷ 2.3

1. Click the **Previous Record** button to move to the *Joe Rodriguez* record.

2. Click the **Delete Record** button on the toolbar. A message appears, as shown in Figure 2-4, warning you that you are about to delete the record.

3. Click **Yes**. The record is deleted. Notice that the numbers in the Call ID field do not renumber when a record is deleted. The reason is that the number in the Call ID field is automatically assigned when the record is created and does not change. Leave the table on the screen for the next Step-by-Step.

Cutting, Copying, and Pasting Data

The Cut, Copy, and Paste commands in Access work the same way as in other Office applications. You can use the commands to copy and move data within a table or between tables. To cut or copy an entire record, select the record and choose Cut or Copy on the Edit menu or click the Cut or Copy buttons on the toolbar.

Using Cut, Copy, and Paste can sometimes be tricky. You must be aware that data pasted in a table will overwrite the existing data. If you want to copy an entire record and paste it into a table as a new record, use the Paste Append command on the Edit menu. You can also highlight the blank record at the bottom of a table and choose Paste on the Edit menu or the Paste button on the toolbar. When you select a record and choose the Cut command, you will get the same message as when you use the Delete command. The difference is that with the Cut command, you can restore the record to the end of the table by using the Paste or Paste Append command.

Did You Know?

You can move and copy an entire object. In the Database window, select the object (table, query, form, or report) and choose **Cut** or **Copy** on the **Edit** menu. Open the database in which you want to paste the object, and choose **Paste** on the **Edit** menu.

Did You Know?

If you delete data or objects from a database, the database can become fragmented and use disk space inefficiently. Compacting rearranges how the database is stored on disk and optimizes the performance of the database. Access combines compacting and repairing into one process. Specify the database you want to compact and repair, choose **Database Utilities** on the **Tools** menu, and select **Compact and Repair Database**.

STEP-BY-STEP ▷ 2.4

1. Select the **Adam Hoover** record.

2. Click the **Copy** button on the toolbar.

3. Click the **New Record** button, and then click the **Paste** button on the toolbar. The new record appears at the bottom of the database.

(continued on next page)

4. Change the date and time of record **5** to **September 17** at **5:00 PM**.

5. In the **Notes** field, delete the existing text and key **Proposal ready on Monday morning.**

6. Select the **Claire Jones** record.

7. Click the **Cut** button on the toolbar. The message saying that you are about to delete a record appears.

8. Click **Yes**.

9. Select the empty record at the end of the table.

10. Click the **Paste** button on the toolbar. The *Claire Jones* record appears as shown in Figure 2-5.

11. Leave the table on the screen for the next Step-by-Step.

FIGURE 2-5
Using the Cut and Paste buttons to add a record

Calls : Table

	Call ID	Name	Call Date	Call Time	Subject	Notes
	1	Adam Hoover	9/16/98	10:10 AM	Proposal	Discuss planned budget
	4	Julie Hunter	9/17/98	8:30 AM	New employee	Call her to setup 3 interviews
	5	Adam Hoover	9/17/98	5:00 PM	Proposal	Proposal ready on Monday mornii
▶	5	Claire Jones	9/16/98	10:30 AM	Lunch	Any plans for today?
✻	)Number)					

Record: ◄◄ ◄   4   ► ►► ►✻ of 4

Changing Datasheet Layout

Y̲ou can make many changes to the datasheet layout, including changing row height and column width, rearranging columns, and freezing columns.

Changing Row Height

You can adjust the row height in a datasheet, but the adjustment affects all the rows. To change the height, position the pointer on the lower border of a row selector, and it will turn into a double arrow, as shown in Figure 2-6. Using the double arrow, click and drag the row border up or down to adjust the row height.

FIGURE 2-6
Adjusting the row height

	Call ID
✛	1
	4
	5
▶	6
✻	)Number)

You can also specify an exact row height. Choose Row Height on the Format menu and the Row Height dialog box appears, as shown in Figure 2-7. Key a height in points (like font sizes) for the row.

FIGURE 2-7
Row Height dialog box

S TEP-BY-STEP ▷ 2.5

1. Position the mouse pointer on the lower border of the record selector for **Claire Jones**. You will know you have the pointer correctly positioned when it changes to a double arrow.

2. Drag the row border down slightly to increase the height of the row. When you release the mouse button, all rows are affected by the change.

3. Select the **Julie Hunter** record.

4. Choose **Row Height** on the **Format** menu. The Row Height dialog box shown in Figure 2-7 appears.

5. Key **30** in the Row Height box and click **OK**. The row height increases to a height that allows the data in the Subject and Notes field to be read more easily. Leave the table on the screen for the next Step-by-Step.

Changing Column Width

Often, the column widths provided by default are too wide or too narrow for the data in the table. Adjusting column width is similar to adjusting row height. To adjust the column width, place the mouse pointer in the field selector on the border of the column. The pointer changes to a double arrow. Click and drag to the width you want. Unlike rows, which must all have the same height, each field can have a different width.

When you choose Column Width on the Format menu, the Column Width dialog box appears, as shown in Figure 2-8. You can key a specific width or click the Best Fit button. The Best Fit button automatically selects the best width for the data in the column. Another way to choose the "best fit" is to place the mouse pointer on the field border and double-click when it turns into a double arrow.

 Hot Tip

Instead of choosing Column Width on the Format menu, you can right-click the column and select Column Width on the shortcut menu that appears.

FIGURE 2-8
Column Width dialog box

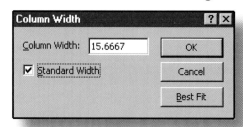

STEP-BY-STEP ▷ 2.6

1. Position the pointer on the right border of the **Notes** field selector.

2. Drag to make the column wide enough to allow all the information to fit in the field.

3. Select the **Call ID** field.

4. Choose **Column Width** on the **Format** menu. The Column Width dialog box appears, as shown in Figure 2-8.

5. Click **Best Fit**. The column narrows.

6. Use the Best Fit option to adjust the width of the **Call Date** field.

7. Select the **Call Time** field.

8. Choose **Column Width** on the **Format** menu. The Column Width dialog box appears.

9. Key **16** in the Column Width box and click **OK**.

10. Change the width of the **Subject** field to **25**.

11. Print the table in landscape orientation. Leave the table on the screen for the next Step-by-Step.

Rearranging Columns

In Datasheet view, Access allows you to rearrange fields by dragging them to a new location. First, select the field you want to move. Then, click and hold down the mouse button on the field selector and drag the field to the new location. A vertical bar follows your mouse pointer to show you where the field will be inserted. Release the mouse button to insert the field in its new location.

STEP-BY-STEP ▷ 2.7

1. Select the **Call Date** field.

2. Click and drag the **Call Date** field to the left until the vertical bar appears between the Call ID and Name fields. Release the mouse button.

The Call Date column appears between the Call ID and Name columns, as shown in Figure 2-9.

3. Leave the table on your screen for the next Step-by-Step.

FIGURE 2-9
Rearranging fields

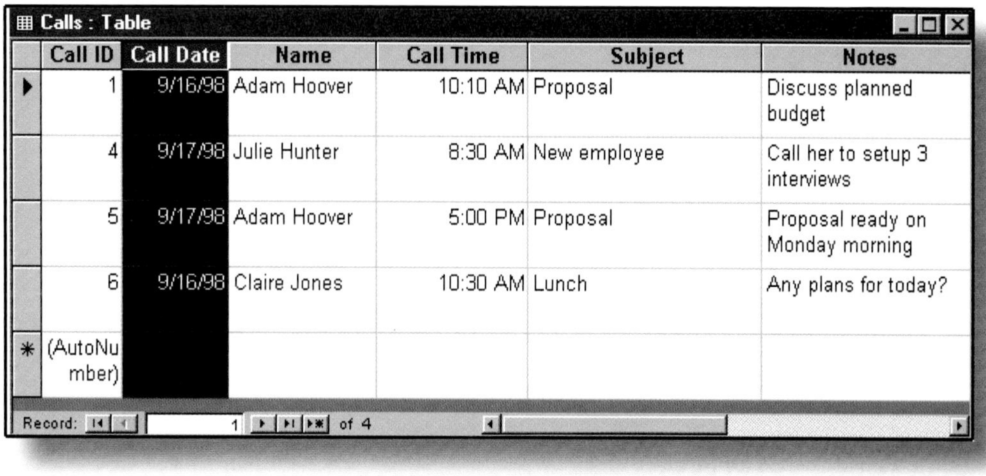

Call ID	Call Date	Name	Call Time	Subject	Notes
1	9/16/98	Adam Hoover	10:10 AM	Proposal	Discuss planned budget
4	9/17/98	Julie Hunter	8:30 AM	New employee	Call her to setup 3 interviews
5	9/17/98	Adam Hoover	5:00 PM	Proposal	Proposal ready on Monday morning
6	9/16/98	Claire Jones	10:30 AM	Lunch	Any plans for today?
* (AutoNumber)					

Record: 1 ▶ ▶I ▶* of 4

Freezing Columns

If a table has many columns, it may be helpful to freeze one or more columns, allowing them to remain on the screen while you scroll to columns that are not currently visible.

To freeze columns, select the column or columns you want to freeze, and choose Freeze Columns on the Format menu. To unfreeze columns, choose Unfreeze All Columns on the Format menu.

STEP-BY-STEP ▷ 2.8

1. Select the **Call ID** field.

2. While holding down the **Shift** key, click the **Name** field. The Call ID, Call Date, and Name fields are all highlighted.

3. Choose **Freeze Columns** on the **Format** menu.

4. Click the horizontal scroll arrow at the bottom right of the table window to scroll to the Notes field. Notice that the frozen fields remain on the screen.

5. Choose **Unfreeze All Columns** on the **Format** menu.

6. Change the left and right margins to **.5"** and print the table in portrait orientation.

7. Choose **Close** on the **File** menu. You will be asked if you want to save changes to the layout of the table.

8. Click **Yes**. The Database window is visible on the screen. Leave the database open for the next Step-by-Step.

Changing Field Properties

When you defined fields for a table in Lesson 1, you specified only the field name, data type, and description. Now that you have created and used fields in a variety of situations, it is time to learn about field properties. ***Field properties*** allow you to further customize a field beyond merely choosing a data type.

You can view and change field properties in a table or form's Design view. Figure 2-10 shows the field properties available; you will learn about the most common ones. The field properties available will vary depending on the field's selected data type.

FIGURE 2-10
Field properties in Design view

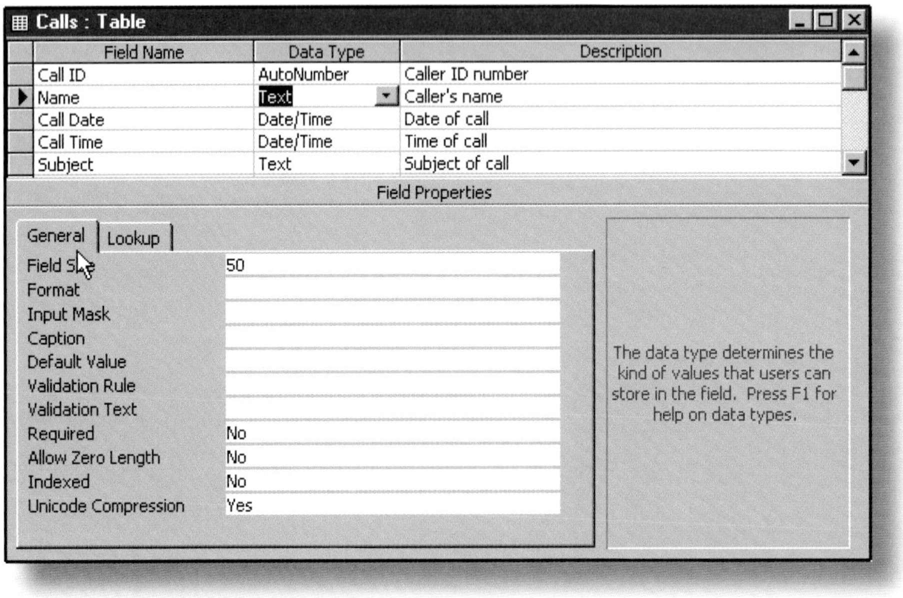

FIELD SIZE

One of the most common field properties is Field Size. In fields of Text type, the Field Size is merely the number of characters allowed in the field. You can specify that the field allow up to 255 characters. The default size is 50.

In fields of Number type, the Field Size allows you to specify what internal data type Access will use to store the number. The available options are Byte, Integer, Long Integer, Single, Double, Replication ID, and Decimal. If you have computer programming experience, the available field sizes may be familiar to you. If the options mean nothing to you, don't worry. There is an easy way to select the appropriate field size. If your field is to store whole numbers only, use the Long Integer field size. If your field will store fractional numbers with decimal places, choose the Double field size.

Did You Know?

If you decrease the size of a field, you may cut off any data over the set number of characters allowed in the field.

FORMAT

Use the Format field property to specify how you want Access to display numbers, dates, times, and text. For example, the default format for dates is *12/29/99*. Using the Format property, you can change the format to *29-Dec-99* or *Sunday, December 29, 1999*. You can also include the time with the date such as *12/29/99 9:15:30 AM*.

INPUT MASK

An input mask allows you to control the data pattern or format allowed in the field. You can also specify characters that will be put into the field automatically. For example, you can specify that a phone number be formatted with area code in parentheses, and the rest of the number split by a hyphen. When you key records, you won't have to key the parentheses or the hyphen; Access will put them in for you automatically. You can use the Input Mask Wizard to set the field's pattern or format for you.

CAPTION

The text you provide in the caption field property will be used *instead* of field names in forms, tables in Datasheet view, reports, and queries. For example, if the field name is *EmailName*, you could enter *E-mail address* in the caption field property. When you create a form that includes the field, the more descriptive name will appear as the field name.

DEFAULT VALUE

Another useful field property is Default Value. Use this field property when you have a field that usually contains the same value. For example, if most of the people in a database of names and addresses live in California, you can enter CA as the Default Value of the State field. The State field will automatically contain CA, unless you change it to another state.

Hot Tip

When you enter an even dollar amount in a formatted field, you only have to key the dollars. For example, you only have to key *3* and press Enter. The 3 you keyed will be formatted automatically to $3.00.

REQUIRED

The Required field property specifies whether you must enter a value in the field. For example, in an employee database, you might specify that each field requires a telephone number. If you try to enter a record without including a telephone number, Access will alert you that you must enter one.

DECIMAL PLACES

Number and Currency fields have a field property called Decimal Places. This property usually adjusts automatically depending on the data in the field. You can specify a number of decimal places here to override the automatic setting.

STEP-BY-STEP ▷ 2.9

1. Open the **Calls** table in Design view.

2. Select the **Name** field.

3. Under the Field Properties section beside *Field Size*, double-click **50** to highlight it. Key **40**.

4. In the *Caption* box, key **Caller's Name**.

5. Click in the *Required* field property box. A down arrow will appear at the right end of the box.

(continued on next page)

6. Click the down arrow and choose **Yes** from the menu.

7. Select the **Call Time** field.

8. Click in the *Format* field property box. A down arrow appears.

9. Click the down arrow. A menu of date and time formats appear.

10. Choose **Long Time**.

11. Choose **Yes** in the *Required* field property.

12. Select the **Notes** field.

13. Change the *Field Size* to **100**.

14. Save the table design. A message may appear stating that some data may be lost be-cause you changed the setting for a field size to a shorter size. Click **Yes** to continue. Another message may appear asking if you want to test the changes. Click **Yes**.

15. Switch to Datasheet view to see the changes to the Call Time field. The Name field now contains the caption you entered. The other changes aren't visible.

16. Adjust the row height, if necessary, so you can see all the record data in each field. Print the table in landscape orientation.

17. Close the table and then close the database by clicking the **Close** button in the Database window.

Summary

In this lesson, you learned:

■ The navigation buttons are used to move around the datasheet. They allow you to move to the first record, the last record, the previous record, or the next record. You can also use a navigation button to add a new record.

■ There are three ways to undo changes to cells. If you make mistakes while keying data in a cell, you can click the Undo button. If you have already entered data and moved to the next cell, press Esc. To reverse all the changes to the previous record, choose Undo Saved Record on the Edit menu.

■ To delete a record, use the Delete Record command. Entire records and fields can be selected by clicking the record and field selectors. Cut, Copy, and Paste are available in Datasheet view to move and copy data. The Paste Append command pastes a record at the end of the database.

■ You can make many changes to a datasheet. You can change the row height and column width. You can also rearrange and freeze columns.

■ Field properties allow you to further customize a field beyond merely choosing a data type. Some of the more common field properties are Field Size, Input Mask, Caption, Default Value, Format, Required, and Decimal Places.

The easiest way to create a form is to use a Form Wizard. Using the Form Wizard, you select the fields and a style for the form. The Form Wizard then creates the form for you.

LESSON 2 REVIEW QUESTIONS

TRUE/FALSE

Circle the T if the statement is true or F if the statement is false.

T   F   1.   If you click a cell with the mouse, the insertion point appears in the cell.

T   F   2.   Holding down the Alt key allows you to select more than one field.

T   F   3.   In Access, you can use the Cut, Copy, and Paste commands.

T   F   4.   Changing the height of one row changes the height of all datasheet rows.

T   F   5.   You can delete records and fields in Datasheet view.

WRITTEN QUESTIONS

Write a brief answer to the following questions.

1.   What is the record pointer?

2.   How do you delete a record in Datasheet view?

3. What does the Paste Append command do?

4. Why would you want to freeze columns in Datasheet view?

5. In what view do you change field properties?

LESSON 2 PROJECTS

PROJECT 2-1

1. Open the **IA Project2-1** database from the student data files.

2. Open the **Employee Information** table in Datasheet view.

3. Go to record 7 and change the address to **4582 104th St**.

4. Go to record 11 and change the birth date to **12/14/61**.

5. Go to record 14 and change the first name to **Alex**.

6. Go to record 1 and change the last name to **Abraham**.

7. Undo your last change.

8. Delete record **5**.

9. Change the width of the **Address** field to **20** and the Zip Code field to **13**.

10. Change all other field widths using **Best Fit**.

11. Change the row height to **15**.

12. Change the left and right margins to **.5"** and print the table in landscape orientation.

13. Close the table. Click **Yes** if prompted to save changes to the layout of the table. Leave the database open for the next project.

PROJECT 2-2

1. Open the **Employee Information** table in Datasheet view.

2. Copy record **4** and paste it at the bottom of the table.

3. In the pasted record, change the First Name to **Mike,** the Title to **Account Executive**, the Birthdate to **9/28/61**, and the Salary to **2950.**

4. Move the **Birthdate** field to between the Zip Code and Department fields.

5. Freeze the **Employee Number**, **Last Name**, and **First Name** fields.

6. Scroll to the right until the **Birthdate** field is beside the **First Name** field.

7. Change the birth date of Hillary Davis to **10/28/68**.

8. Unfreeze the columns.

9. Change the left and right margins to **.5"** and print the table in landscape orientation.

10. Close the table. Click **Yes** if prompted to save changes to the layout of the table. Leave the database open for the next project.

PROJECT 2-3

1. Open the **Employee Information** table in Design view.

2. Format the **Salary** field for currency.

3. Select **Medium Date** from the Format field properties for the **Birthdate** field .

4. Key **Employee Number** as the Caption field property for the **Emp Number** field.

5. Make the **Zip Code** field **Required**.

6. Change the field size of the **Zip Code** field to **10**.

7. Save the table design. A message may appear asking if you want to continue. Click **Yes**. Another message may appear asking if you want to test the changes. Click **Yes**.

8. Switch to Datasheet view and insert the following records at the end of the table.

   ```
   16  Wells  Wendy  2610 21st St. 79832-2610  15-Feb-72  Sales  Secretary  $2,150.00
   17  Abbott  Donna  1824 Saratoga  79833-1900  12-Jan-59  Personnel  Manager  $2,880.00
   ```

9. Widen the **Salary** column and any other fields to show all data and column titles.

10. Change the left and right margins to **.5"** and print the table in landscape orientation.

11. Close the table. Click **Yes** if prompted to save changes to the layout of the table. Close the database.

Web Site

For information on careers, access the Occupational Outlook Handbook at *http://www.bls.gov/dolbls.htm*. Web sites and addresses change constantly. If you can't find the information at this site, try another.

CRITICAL THINKING

ACTIVITY 2-1

SCANS

Open the database you created for the Critical Thinking Activity in Lesson 1. Add two new records using the New Record buton. Select a field and make a change to the data. Delete an entire record. Copy one record and paste it into the table as a new record. If necessary, increase the column width and row height to see all the data. Rearrange the columns. Print and close the table.

ACTIVITY 2-2

You can use the Office Clipboard to collect and paste multiple items from the various Office programs. The Office Clipboard automatically copies multiple items when you do any of the following:

1. Copy or cut two different items in succession in the same program.

2. Copy one item, paste the item, and then copy another item in the same program.

3. Copy one item twice in succession.

Using the Help system, find the steps to collect and paste multiple items. Briefly write down the steps in numbered order.

CREATING AND MODIFYING FORMS

OBJECTIVES

Upon completion of this lesson, you should be able to:

- Create and use forms.
- Modify forms.
- Create a calculated control on a form.
- Compact and repair a database.   ⏱ **Estimated Time: 1.5 hours**

Creating Forms

Datasheet view is useful for many of the ways you work with a database table. Often, however, you may want a more convenient way to enter and view records. For example, the form shown in Figure 3-1 places all of the important fields from the Calls table into a convenient and attractive layout.

FIGURE 3-1

Forms can make entering and editing data easier

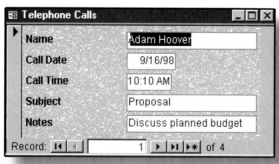

Forms can be created manually by placing fields on a blank form, arranging and sizing fields, and adding graphics. The Form Wizard makes the process easier. Creating a form manually gives you more flexibility, but in most cases the Form Wizard can create the form you need quickly and efficiently.

To create a form, click the Forms button on the Objects bar. Click the New button and the New Form dialog box appears, as shown in Figure 3-2. The New Form dialog box gives you several options for creating a form. In this lesson, you will use the Form Wizard option. The New Form dialog box also asks you to specify the table or query to use as a basis for the form. In more complex databases, you may have to choose among several tables or queries.

You can also create a form using the Form Wizard by double-clicking *Create form by using wizard* in the Database window.

FIGURE 3-2
New Form dialog box

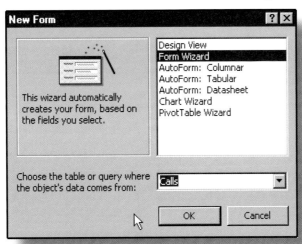

S **TEP-BY-STEP** ▷ **3.1**

1. Open the **IA Step 3-1** database from the student data files. Click the **Forms** button on the Objects bar.

2. Click **New**. The New Form dialog box appears, as shown in Figure 3-2.

3. Choose the **Form Wizard** option and the **Calls** table from the drop-down list.

4. Click **OK**. The Form Wizard dialog box appears, as shown in Figure 3-3. Leave the Form Wizard dialog box on screen for the next Step-by-Step.

(continued on next page)

FIGURE 3-3
Form Wizard dialog box

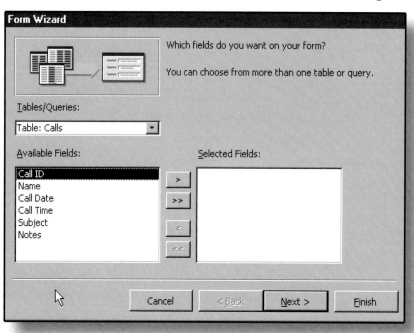

The next step is to choose the fields you want to appear on the form. To add a field to the form, click the field name in the *Available Fields* list and click the > button. To add all of the fields at once, click the >> button. If you plan to include almost all of the fields, click >> to include them all, then use the < button to remove the ones you do not want.

STEP-BY-STEP ⟹ 3.2

1. Click **>>**. All of the field names appear in the *Selected Fields* list.

2. Select the **Call ID** field in the *Selected Fields* list.

3. Click **<**. The **Call ID** field is moved back to the *Available Fields* list.

4. Click the **Next** button. The Form Wizard dialog box changes to ask you to select a layout for the form, as shown in Figure 3-4.

5. Leave the dialog box open for the next Step-by-Step.

FIGURE 3-4

Selecting a layout for a form

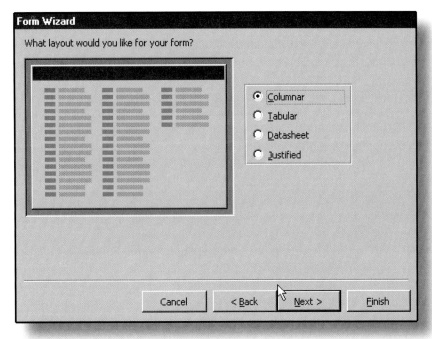

You have a choice of four different layouts for the form: *Columnar*, *Tabular*, *Datasheet*, and *Justified*. The *Columnar* layout is the most common type. The form in Figure 3-1 is an example of a *Columnar* layout. As data is entered, the insertion point moves down the fields.

The *Tabular* layout creates forms similar to Datasheet view. Both layouts display data in a tabular form. The *Tabular* layout gives you the ability to make a more attractive Datasheet view. Figure 3-5 shows an example of a form created using a tabular layout.

FIGURE 3-5

Tabular form layout

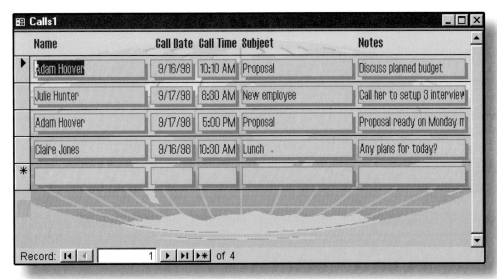

STEP-BY-STEP ▷ 3.3

1. If not already selected, click the **Columnar** option.

2. Click **Next**. This dialog box asks you to choose a style, as shown in Figure 3-6.

3. Leave the dialog box open for the next Step-by-Step.

FIGURE 3-6
Choosing a style for a form

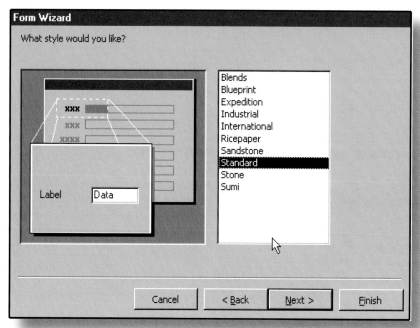

The style you select has no effect on the function of the form. Choosing a style allows you to personalize your form or give it flair. There are several styles from which to choose.

After you choose a style, you will be asked to name the form. The name you provide will appear in the Form section of the Database window. You are also given the option to begin using the form once it is created or to modify the form after the Form Wizard is done.

STEP-BY-STEP ▷ 3.4

1. Choose the **Standard** style from the list. The preview box shows you what this form style looks like. It should look similar to Figure 3-6.

2. Click the other styles to see what they look like.

3. Choose the **Sandstone** style and click **Next**. The final Form Wizard dialog box appears, as shown in Figure 3-7.

4. Key **Telephone Calls** in the title box.

FIGURE 3-7
Naming the form

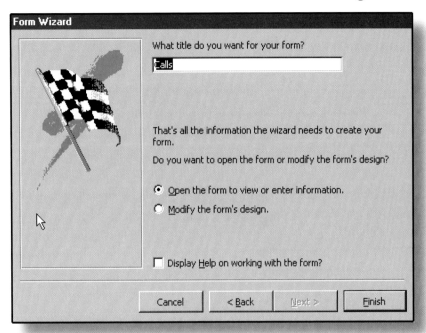

FIGURE 3-8
A custom form

5. Click the **Open the form to view or enter information** button if it's not chosen already.

6. Click **Finish**. Access creates the form, which should look like that shown in Figure 3-8. Leave the form displayed for the next Step-by-Step.

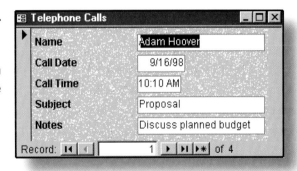

Using Forms

Using a form is basically the same as using Datasheet view. The same keys move the insertion point among the fields. You see the same set of navigation buttons at the bottom of the form, as shown in Figure 3-9. As with Datasheet view, you can move to a specific record by clicking in the Record Number box and entering the number of the record you want to see.

Table 3-1 summarizes the ways to move around when a form is displayed, including keyboard shortcuts.

To add a new record, click the Next Record button until the blank record at the end of the database appears, or click the New Record button. Key the new record. To edit an existing record, display the record and make changes in the fields of the form.

FIGURE 3-9
Navigation controls at the bottom of the form

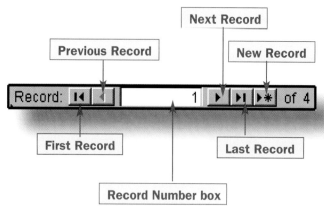

TABLE 3-1
Navigating a form

TO MOVE TO THE...	BUTTON	KEYBOARD SHORTCUT
First record	First Record button	Ctrl+Home
Last record	Last Record button	Ctrl+End
Next record	Next Record button	Page Down
Previous record	Previous Record button	Page Up

After entering or editing records in a form, you do not need to save the changes. Access saves them for you automatically. Remember to always save changes to the form design in Design view.

You can print forms much the same way you print tables. To print all the records in the form, choose Print on the File menu and the Print dialog box appears. In the Print dialog box, choose *All* from the *Print Range* options if you want to print all the records. Access will fit as many forms on each page as possible. To print only one record, display the record on the screen and choose Print on the File menu. Click the *Selected Record(s)* option from the *Print Range* options.

S TEP-BY-STEP ▷ 3.5

1. Click the **New Record** button. A blank record appears in the form.

2. Enter the following information into the form:

   Name: **Excel Travel Agency**
   Call Date: **9/18/98**
   Call Time: **10:21 AM**
   Subject: **Seattle trip**
   Notes: **Flight 412 Departs 7:40 AM/Arrives 1:30 PM**

3. Click in the record number box. Delete the 5, key **4**, and press **Tab**.

4. Highlight the word **today** in the Notes field.

5. Key **Friday**.

6. Display record **5**, and choose **Print** on the **File** menu. The Print dialog box appears.

7. Click the **Selected Record(s)** option from the *Print Range* options, and click **OK**. (The printed form may cut off the data in some of the fields.)

8. Choose **Close** on the **File** menu to close the form. Leave the database open for the next Step-by-Step.

Modifying Forms

Any form, whether created manually or with a Form Wizard, can be modified. You make changes to a form in Design view, which shows the structure of the form. To access Design view, select the form in the Database window, and then click the Design button. The form appears in Design view, as shown in Figure 3-10.

FIGURE 3-10
Design view

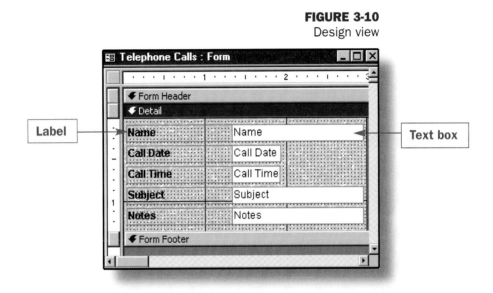

The form is divided into three sections: form header, detail, and form footer. The ***form header*** section displays information that remains the same for every record, such as the title for a form. A form header appears at the top of the screen in Form view and at the top of the first page of the forms when printed. The ***detail*** section displays records. You can display one record on the screen or as many as possible. A ***form footer*** section displays information that remains the same for every record, such as instructions for using the form. A form footer appears at the bottom of the screen in Form view or after the last detail section on the last page of the forms when printed.

The Toolbox, shown in Figure 3-11, has controls that you can use to modify and enhance the sections and objects on a form. The Label and Text Box tools are labeled because they are used frequently. There are three types of controls: bound, unbound, and calculated. A ***bound control*** is connected to a field in a table and is used to display, enter, and update data. An ***unbound control*** is not connected to a field and is used to display information, lines, rectangles, and pictures. The Label control, which is an unbound control, allows you to add text as a title or instructions to a form. Look again at Figure 3-10. Notice that the field name is contained in a Label control, and the field entry is contained in the Text Box control. A Text Box control is tied to, or *bound* to a field in the underlying table, whereas the Label control is not.

FIGURE 3-11
Toolbox

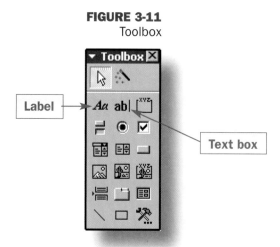

In Design view, you can change the font, size, style, and other attributes of labels and text box data. Simply select the control, and use the buttons on the Formatting toolbar. Or, you can double-click a control to open its Properties dialog box and modify the attributes and other properties listed on the various tabs.

STEP-BY-STEP ▷ 3.6

1. If not already selected, click **Forms** on the Objects bar. Choose the **Telephone Calls** form, and click the **Design** button. The form appears in Design view, as shown in Figure 3-10.

2. If necessary, display the Toolbox by clicking the **Toolbox** button. Click the **Line** button in the Toolbox.

3. Position the pointer in the **Detail** section between the Name label and the data field and click to place a line as shown in Figure 3-12.

4. Position the pointer at the right end of the line until a double arrow appears. Click and drag the right end of the line to the bottom of the form until it is vertical between the field labels and data fields as shown in Figure 3-13.

5. In the Detail section, click twice on the **Call Date** label. The Label properties window opens, as shown in Figure 3-14. If necessary, select the **All** tab.

FIGURE 3-12
Inserting a line

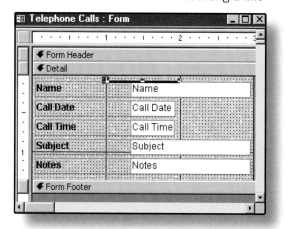

FIGURE 3-13
Repositioning the line object

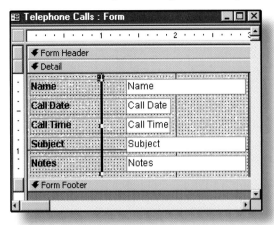

FIGURE 3-14
The Label screen

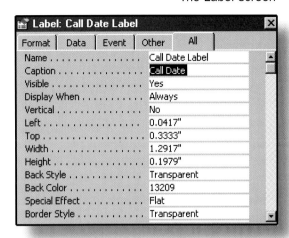

6. Change the caption to **Date** and close the Properties window.

7. Click twice on the **Call Time** label and change the caption to **Time**.

8. Position the pointer on the line between the **Form Header** section and **Detail** section until a double arrow appears as shown in Figure 3-15.

9. Click and drag the line down about a half inch to increase the height of the Form Header section.

10. Click the **Label** button in the Toolbox.

11. Position the pointer in the **Form Header** section and click and drag to draw a text box as shown in Figure 3-16.

12. Key **TELEPHONE CALLS** at the insertion point that appears in the text box.

13. Click outside the text box to view the title. Double-click on the text box to display the Label properties dialog box.

FIGURE 3-15
Resizing the Form Header

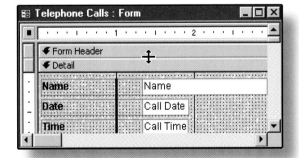

FIGURE 3-16
Inserting a text box

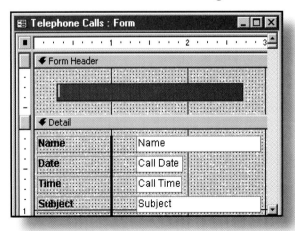

(continued on next page)

14. Scroll through the list of properties until you locate the *Font Name* and *Font Size* properties. Click in the **Font Name** text box, click the down arrow, and select **Arial Black**. Click in the **Font Size** box, click the down arrow, and change the size to **12**. Close the dialog box.

15. Position the pointer on the line at the bottom of the **Form Footer** section until a double arrow appears as shown in Figure 3-17.

16. Click and drag the line down about a half inch to increase the height of the Form Footer section.

17. Click the **Check Box** button in the Toolbox.

18. Position the pointer in the **Form Footer** and click to place a check box as shown in Figure 3-18. Your text box to the right of the check mark will contain a different number from the one showing in the figure.

FIGURE 3-17
Resizing the Form Footer

FIGURE 3-18
Form Footer with check box

19. Double-click the text box to the right of the check mark. The Label properties dialog box appears.

20. Change the caption to **Return Call** and close the dialog box.

21. Click on the right border of the text box and drag to see all of the caption.

22. Choose **Close** on the **File** menu. A message appears asking if you want to save changes. Click **Yes**. You are returned to the Database window.

23. With the name of the form highlighted, click **Open**. The modified form appears on the screen.

24. If necessary, scroll to see all of the records. Go back to **record 1**, select **Print** on the **File** menu, make sure the **Selected Record(s)** option is selected, and click **OK**. Close the form and the database.

Hot Tip

To delete a line or other object on a form, make sure you are in Design view, click on the line or object to select it, and press the **Delete** key or choose **Delete** on the **Edit** menu.

Working with Calculated Controls

A *calculated control* on a form uses an expression to generate the data value for a field. For example, on an Orders form you might use the expression, Unit Cost multiplied by Units Ordered or =*Unit Cost*Units Ordered*, to determine the value in the Total Cost field.

To create a calculated control on a form, open the Properties dialog box for the text box that will contain the calculation. The Properties dialog box will look like that shown in Figure 3-19. In the Control Source text box, key the expression for calculating the field value. You can also key a name for the calculated field in the Name text box, and determine the numerical format in the Format text box. Open the form and the value for the calculated field is calculated for each record.

FIGURE 3-19
Text Box properties dialog box

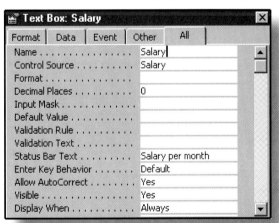

S TEP-BY-STEP ▷ 3.7

1. Open the **IA Step3-7** database from the student data files.

2. Click **Forms** on the Objects bar. Choose the **Employee Bonus** form and click the **Design** button. The form appears in Design view, as shown in Figure 3-20.

3. Position the pointer on the **Salary** text box as shown in Figure 3-20. Click twice to display the Text Box: Salary properties dialog box, as shown in Figure 3-19. If not already selected, choose the **All** tab.

4. Key **Bonus** in the **Name** box.

FIGURE 3-20
Design view

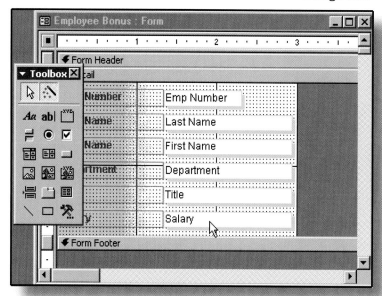

5. Key **=[Salary]*.10** in the **Control Source** box. The bonus field will be 10% of the employee's salary.

6. Click in the **Format** text box, click the down arrow, and choose **Currency**.

7. Close the properties dialog box. Click twice on the **Salary** label box which is to the left of the text box. The Label properties dialog box displays, as shown in Figure 3-21.

FIGURE 3-21
Label properties dialog box screen

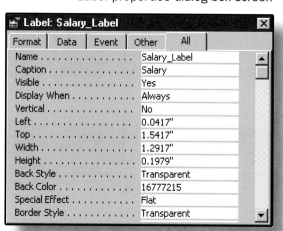

8. Change the **Caption** field to **Bonus** and close the dialog box. Switch to **Form** view by clicking the **View** button.

9. If necessary, scroll to see all the records. Print the form for record **2**. Close the form and leave the database open for the next Step-by-Step.

Working with Hyperlinks

As you learned in Lesson 1, you can define a field in a database table as a hyperlink data type. This type of field actually stores the path to another database object or a specified file, or the address to a Web site.

You can also insert a hyperlink in a form (or the report or page objects in a database) that links you to another object in the database, another file, or a Web site. For example, you might have a form in a company database that you use to enter information regarding employees, like their addresses, start dates, department, responsibilities, etc. You also maintain an Excel spreadsheet that tracks employees' salaries, bonuses, benefits, etc. You could insert a hyperlink in the database form that when clicked, immediately links you to the spreadsheet. The hyperlink provides you with an easy way to gain quick access to more information.

To insert a hyperlink, you must be in the form's Design view. Make sure the pointer is in the section of the form in which you want the hyperlink to appear, and then click the Insert Hyperlink button. In the Insert Hyperlink dialog box, select the file or Web page you want to link to, and then click OK.

Compacting and Repairing a Database

If you delete data or objects from a database, the database can become fragmented and use disk space inefficiently. Compacting rearranges how the database is stored on disk and optimizes the performance of the database. Access combines compacting and repairing into one process.

STEP-BY-STEP ▷ 3.8

1. Click **Tables** on the Objects bar, and open the **Employee Information** table in Datasheet view or Design view. Be sure no one else has the database open before continuing.

2. Choose **Database Utilities** on the **Tools** menu.

3. Click **Compact and Repair Database**.

4. When finished, close the table and database.

 Hot Tip

Follow the steps above to compact and repair a database that is not open. Dialog boxes will display asking you to specify the database to compact and the new file name for the compacted database. If you use the same name, the original file will be replaced with the new compacted file.

Summary

In this lesson, you learned:

- The easiest way to create a form is to use a Form Wizard. Using the Form Wizard, you select the fields and a style for the form. The Form Wizard then creates the form for you.

- Any form, whether created manually or with a Form Wizard, can be modified. You make changes to a form using Design view, which shows the structure of the form.

- The form in Design view is divided into three sections: form header, detail, and form footer. The form header section displays information that remains the same for every record, such as the title for a form. A form header appears at the top of the screen in Form view and at the top of the first page of records when printed. The detail section displays records. You can display one record on the screen or as many as possible. A form footer section displays information that remains the same for every record, such as instructions for using the form. A form footer appears at the bottom of the screen in Form view or after the last detail section on the last page of records when printed.

- The Toolbox has controls that you can use to modify and enhance the sections within a form. There are three types of controls: bound, unbound, and calculated. A bound control is connected to a field in a table and is used to display, enter, and update data. An unbound control is not connected to a field.

- A calculated control on a form uses an expression to calculate the data value for a field.

- If you delete data or objects from a database, the database can become fragmented and use disk space inefficiently. Compacting the database rearranges how the database is stored on disk and optimizes the performance of the database.

LESSON 3 REVIEW QUESTIONS

TRUE/FALSE

Circle T if the statement is true or F if the statement is false.

T F 1. The style you select for a form has an effect on the function of the form.

T F 2. The Toolbox has tools that you can use to modify forms.

T F 3. You make modifications to a form in Datasheet view.

T F 4. If you delete data or objects from a database, the database can become fragmented and use disk space inefficiently.

T F 5. You can change a control's attributes by double-clicking it in Design view, and making changes in the control's Properties dialog box.

WRITTEN QUESTIONS

Write a brief answer to the following questions.

1. What are the four different layouts for a form?

2. How do you move to a specific record using a form?

3. What will happen if you use the same name for a newly compacted database?

4. What view is similar to a Tabular layout for a database?

5. In what view do you change the properties for a control?

PROJECT 3-1

1. Open the **IA Project3-1** database from the student data files. Create a new form with the Form Wizard using the **Employee Information** table.

2. Add the **First Name**, **Last Name**, **Department**, **Title**, and **Birthdate** fields.

3. Use the **Columnar** layout and the **Standard** style.

4. Title the form **Employee Birthdays**.

5. Go to record **3**, Trent Broach, and change the title to **Director of Sales**.

6. Go to record **15**, Donna Abbott, and change the *Birthdate* to **10-Jan-59**.

7. Print record **15**.

8. Close the form and leave the database open for the next project.

PROJECT 3-2

1. Open the **Employee Bonus** form in Design view.

2. Increase the size of the **Form Header** section.

3. Using the Label control, add a label box titled **EMPLOYEE BONUS**.

4. Change the *Font Name* to **Arial Black** and the *Font Size* to **12**.

5. Increase the size of the **Form Footer** section.

6. Using the Check Box control, add a check box titled **Eligible for Stock Plan**. If necessary, increase the size of the text box to see all the title.

7. When finished, save the changes and switch to **Form** view.

8. Open the modified form to view the changes. Display and print record **6**.

9. Close the form and database.

CRITICAL THINKING

SCANS

ACTIVITY 3-1

Open the database you created for the Critical Thinking Activity in Lesson 1. Use the Form Wizard to create a Tabular form that includes the fields of your database table. Choose an attractive style for the form. Add a record to the table using the new form. Print the record and close the form. Close the database.

ACTIVITY 3-2

Using the Help feature, look up the definition of a subform and how it works. Write down a short definition and provide an example of a form and subform relationship used in a business setting. Be sure to mention the name of the field used to link the form and subform.

FINDING AND ORDERING DATA

OBJECTIVES

Upon completion of this lesson, you should be able to:

- Find data in a database.
- Query a database.
- Use filters.
- Sort a database.
- Index a database.
- Establish relationships in a database.
- Create a query from related tables.

🕐 **Estimated Time: 1.5 hours**

Using Find

The Find command is the easiest way to quickly locate data in a database. The Find command allows you to search the database for specified information. There are several options that allow you flexibility in performing the search. These options appear in the Find and Replace dialog box, shown in Figure 4-1.

FIGURE 4-1
Find and Replace dialog box

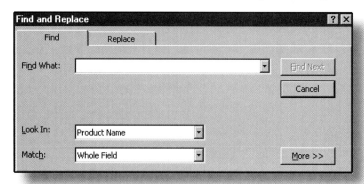

You can access the Find and Replace dialog box by choosing Find on the Edit menu or by clicking the Find button on the toolbar. The Find command is available only when a datasheet or form is displayed.

To search for the data in a particular field, place your insertion point in the field you want to search and click the Find button. The Find and Replace dialog box opens with the *Look In* box containing the field name to search. Key the data for which you are searching in the *Find What* box.

The *Match* text box has a drop-down list that lets you choose what part of the field to search. If you want to match exactly the entire contents of a field, choose *Whole Field*. More commonly, however, you will not want to enter the field's entire contents. For example, if you are searching a database of books for titles relating to history, you might want to search for titles with the word *history* anywhere in the title. In that case, you would choose *Any Part of Field* from the list. You can also specify that the search look only at the first part of the field by choosing the *Start of Field* option. For example, if you need to search a table of names for people whose last name begins with *Mc*, the *Start of Field* option would be convenient.

Click the More button and note that the *Match Case* check box gives you the option of a case-sensitive search. Click the drop-down arrow for the *Search* text box to display a list in which you can specify whether you want to search up from the current record position, down from the current record position, or the entire table.

Click Find Next to display the next record that matches the criteria you've specified. When the entire database has been searched, a message appears stating that the search item was not found.

Hot Tip

Use the Find command when searching for one record at a time. Use the Filter tool when searching for multiple records. You will learn about filters later in this lesson.

STEP-BY-STEP ▷ 4.1

1. Open **IA Step4-1** from the student data files. This database includes a table of products. The products represent the inventory of a small office supply store.

2. Open the **Products** table in Datasheet view.

3. Place the insertion point in the **Product Name** field of the first record.

4. Click the **Find** button. The Find and Replace dialog box appears.

5. Key **Fax Machine** in the **Find What** box.

6. Be sure the **Product Name** field appears in the **Look In** box.

7. Click the down arrow to the right of the **Match** box and choose **Any Part of Field** from the list.

8. Click the **More** button to display more options.

9. Be sure **All** appears in the **Search** box. The *Match Case* and *Search Fields As Formatted* options should not be selected.

10. Click the **Find Next** button. Product 32 is selected, as shown in Figure 4-2.

11. Click **Find Next** again. A message appears telling you that the search item was not found. There is only one fax machine in the product line. Click **OK**.

12. Click **Cancel** to close the Find and Replace box.

13. Close the table and leave the database open for the next Step-by-Step.

(continued on next page)

FIGURE 4-2
Finding data

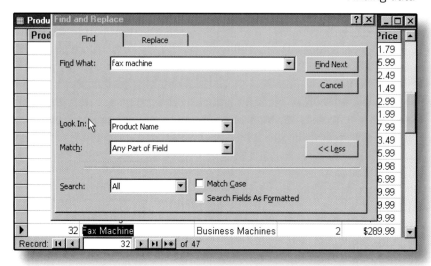

Using Queries

The Find command is an easy way of finding data. Often, however, you will need to locate data based on more complex criteria. For example, you may need to search for products with a value greater than $10. You cannot do that with the Find command. A special operation, called a *query*, will let you combine criteria to perform complex searches. For example, a query could locate products with a value greater than $10 of which fewer than three are in stock.

Queries allow you to "ask" the database almost anything about your data. In addition, you can create queries to display only the fields relevant to the search. For example, if you were querying a database of customers to locate those with a total purchased amount of $10,000 or more, you might want to display only the customers' names and total purchased amounts, rather than all the data in the table.

The first step in creating a query is to open the appropriate database and click Queries on the Objects bar. Then click the New button to create a new query. The New Query dialog box appears, as shown in Figure 4-3. The New Query dialog box gives you the option to create a query manually or to use one of several Query Wizards. In this lesson, you will learn to create a query manually. You use the Design View option in the New Query dialog box to do this.

FIGURE 4-3
New Query dialog box

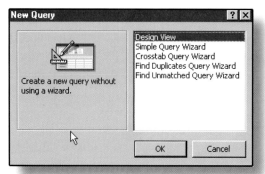

S TEP-BY-STEP ▷ 4.2

1. Click **Queries** on the Objects bar.

2. Click the **New** button. The New Query dialog box appears, as shown in Figure 4-3.

3. Choose **Design View**, if it is not already selected, and click **OK**. The Show Table dialog

box appears from which you select a table to query, as shown in Figure 4-4. Leave the Show Table dialog box on the screen for the next Step-by-Step.

FIGURE 4-4
Show Table dialog box

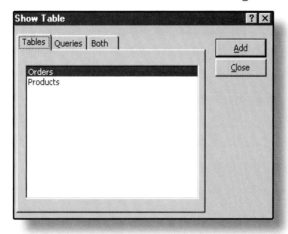

Because databases often include more than one table, you can choose the table you want to use in the Show Table dialog box. The Add button adds the fields from the highlighted table to your new query. After choosing a table and adding fields, click Close to close the Show Table dialog box. The fields you added now appear in a dialog box in the top pane of the query's design window, as shown in Figure 4-5.

FIGURE 4-5
Query window

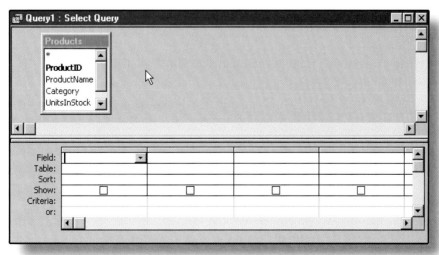

The query window is divided into two parts. The top part of the window shows the available tables and fields (the Products table and its fields are shown in Figure 4-5).

The bottom part of the window contains a grid that allows you to specify the information needed to create a query. To create a query, you must supply three pieces of information: the fields you want to search, what you are searching for (called the *search criteria*), and what fields you want to display with the results. The *Field* row is where you select a field to be part of the query. Click the down arrow to display the available fields. To include more than one field in a query, click in the next column of the *Field* row and choose another field.

The *Sort* row allows you to sort the results of the query. The *Show* checkbox determines whether the field is to be displayed in the query results. Normally, this will be checked. Occasionally, however, you may want to search by a field that does not need to appear in the query results.

For the fields you want to search, enter search conditions in the *Criteria* row. For example, if you want to find only records that contain the words *Office Supplies* in the Category field, you would key "Office Supplies" in the *Criteria* row of the Category field. When keying text in the *Criteria* row, always enclose it with quotation marks.

You can refine a search by using operators. For example, you might want to find all employees in a database table who make more than $30,000 a year, or you might want to search an inventory table for products of which there are less than five in stock. You can use the relational operators listed in Table 4-1 to conduct these types of searches.

TABLE 4-1
Relational operators

OPERATOR	DESCRIPTION
>	Greater than
<	Less than
=	Equal to
>=	Greater than or equal to
<=	Less than or equal to
<>	Not equal

You can also use the *And* or the *Or* operators. If you want to find records that meet more than one criteria, such as employees who make more than $30,000 a year *and* who have been with the company for less than two years, you would use the **And operator**. Simply enter the criteria in the same Criteria row for the fields you want to search.

If you want to find records that meet one criteria or another, you would use the **Or operator**. Enter the criteria in different rows for the fields you want to search.

After choosing the fields and entering search criteria, you should save the query by choosing Save on the File menu and keying a name for the query. To run a query, click the Run button in the query's Design view. Or, you can run a query directly from the Database window. Select the query, and then click the Open button.

 **Hot Tip**

To modify a query, open it in Design view. You can change the fields to be searched, the search criteria, and the fields to be displayed in the query results.

STEP-BY-STEP ▷ 4.3

1. With the **Products** table selected, click **Add**. The fields of the *Products* table appear in the query window. Click **Close** to close the Show Table dialog box.

2. In the query grid, click the down arrow in the **Field** row of the first column and choose **ProductName**, as shown in Figure 4-6.

3. Click the down arrow in the **Field** row of the second column and choose **UnitsInStock** from the menu.

4. In the **Criteria** row of the **Units in Stock** column, key **<3**. This tells Access to display any records with fewer than 3 items in stock.

5. In the third column, choose the **Retail Price** field.

6. In the **Field** row of the fourth column, key **[Retail Price]*.90**.

7. Click in the **Table** row and choose **Products**.

8. Click in the **Field** row again and highlight **Expr1**. Replace *Expr1* by keying **Discount Price**. (Microsoft Access enters the default field name Expr1. Unless replaced by a more appropriate name this is the column heading you will see in Datasheet view.)

9. With the cursor in the **Field** box, *right*-click and choose **Properties** on the shortcut menu. The Field Properties dialog box will display.

10. Click in the **Format** box on the General tab and scroll down to click **Currency**. Close the dialog box.

11. Choose **Save** on the **File** menu. You are prompted for a name for the query.

12. Key **Reorder Query** and click **OK**.

13. Choose **Close** on the **File** menu.

14. To run the query, highlight **Reorder Query** in the Database window and click **Open**. The results of the query appear, as shown in Figure 4-7.

15. Choose **Print** on the **File** menu to print the table with the query applied. Click **OK**.

16. Choose **Close** on the **File** menu to close the results of the query. Leave the database open for the next Step-by-Step.

C ▷ Did You Know?

You can save a table, form, or query as a Web page. Choose **Save As HTML** on the **File** menu. This command will start the *Publish to the Web Wizard*. Follow the steps through the wizard to create your Web page.

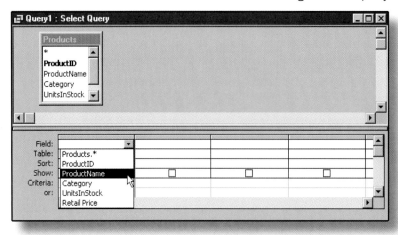

FIGURE 4-6
Selecting fields to query

FIGURE 4-7
Running a query

Product Name	Units In Stock	Retail Price	Discount Price
Heavy Duty Stapler	2	$16.99	$15.29
Letter Sorter	2	$7.99	$7.19
Speaker Phone	2	$99.99	$89.99
Fax Machine	2	$289.99	$260.99
Cash Register	0	$269.99	$242.99
Photocopier	1	$699.00	$629.10
Typewriter	2	$129.99	$116.99
Computer Desk	2	$299.00	$269.10
Oak Office Desk	1	$399.00	$359.10
Bookshelf	2	$99.99	$89.99
Guest Chair	2	$159.00	$143.10

Filters

Queries are very powerful and flexible tools. In many cases, however, less power is adequate. *Filters* provide a way to display selected records in a database more easily than using queries. Think of a filter as a simpler form of a query. A filter "filters out" the records that do not match the specified criteria. When you use a filter, all of the fields are displayed, and the filter cannot be saved for use again later.

There are four types of filters: Filter By Form, Filter By Selection, Filter Excluding Selection, and Advanced Filter/Sort. The Filter By Form allows you to select records by keying the criteria into a form. To use Filter By Selection (the fastest and easiest option), you highlight a value or part of a value in a field as the criteria for the selection. The Filter Excluding Selection excludes the value you highlight as the criteria for the selection. To duplicate a query or create a more complicated selection use the Advanced Filter/Sort option.

To create a filter, a table must be open. Select Filter on the Records menu and then select one of the filter types from the submenu. If you select the Advanced Filter/Sort option, a Filter window like the one in Figure 4-8 appears. Notice that the Filter window is very similar to the query window. (Since there is only one table in this database, it's automatically added to the top part of the window.) Also notice that there is no *Show* row in the grid—all fields are displayed when you use a filter. In the grid, you select only those fields for which you want to enter criteria. When you have included all of the field specifications, choose Apply Filter/Sort on the Filter menu or click the Apply Filter button on the toolbar.

INTRODUCTION TO MICROSOFT ACCESS

If you select Filter by Form, only the field names in the datasheet are displayed. When you click in a field, the filter arrow appears, as shown in Figure 4-9. Click the arrow and choose a data value from the list of all data values entered in the field. When finished, apply the filter. To create a filter by Selection you must first highlight the criteria in the table. Click Filter by Selection on the submenu and the filtered records display.

FIGURE 4-8

Design view for an advanced filter

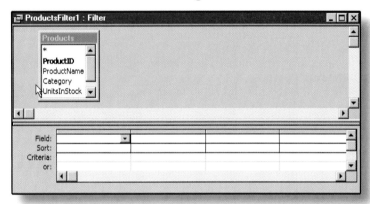

FIGURE 4-9

Filter by form

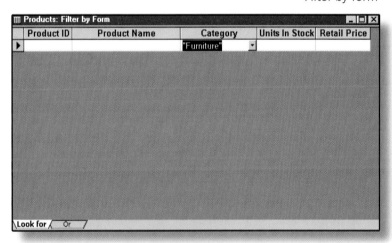

STEP-BY-STEP ▷ 4.4

1. In the Database window, click **Tables** on the Objects bar.

2. Open the **Products** table in Datasheet view.

3. Choose **Filter** on the **Records** menu, then select **Advanced Filter/Sort** on the sub-

menu. The Filter window appears, as shown in Figure 4-8.

4. Click the down arrow in the **Field** row of the first column and choose **Category** from the menu.

(continued on next page)

5. Key **"Furniture"** in the **Criteria** field of the first column. Include the quotation marks.

6. Click the **Apply Filter** button on the toolbar. The filter is applied, and only the products in the Furniture category are displayed, as shown in Figure 4-10.

7. Print the table with the filter applied.

8. Click the **Remove Filter** button to remove the filter and display all records.

9. Choose **Filter** on the **Records** menu, then select **Filter by Form** on the submenu. A form appears, as shown in Figure 4-9.

10. Click the down arrow in the **Category** field. (Furniture was the criteria in the previous filter.)

11. Choose **Desk Accessories** from the list of options.

12. Click the **Apply Filter** button on the toolbar. The filter is applied, and only the products in the Desk Accessories category are displayed, as shown in Figure 4-11.

13. Print the table with the filter applied.

14. Click the **Remove Filter** button.

15. To create a Filter by Selection, highlight **Calculator** in the **Product Name** field for record 27.

16. Choose **Filter** on the **Records** menu, then select **Filter by Selection** on the submenu. The filter is applied, and only the calculator products are displayed, as shown in Figure 4-12.

17. Print the table with the filter applied.

18. Click the **Remove Filter** button. Leave the table on the screen for the next Step-by-Step.

FIGURE 4-10
A filter displaying the Furniture category

Product ID	Product Name	Category	Units In Stock	Retail Price
39	Computer Desk	Furniture	2	$299.00
40	Oak Office Desk	Furniture	1	$399.00
41	Bookshelf	Furniture	2	$99.99
42	Executive Chair	Furniture	3	$259.99
43	Guest Chair	Furniture	2	$159.00
44	Desk Chair	Furniture	3	$129.99
45	4-Drawer Filing Cabinet	Furniture	4	$139.99
46	2-Drawer Filing Cabinet	Furniture	3	$79.99
47	Folding Table (8')	Furniture	4	$46.00
(AutoNumber)				

Record: 1 of 9 (Filtered)

FIGURE 4-11
A filter displaying the Desk Accessories category

FIGURE 4-11
A filter displaying the Desk Accessories category

Product ID	Product Name	Category	Units In Stock	Retail Price
22	Letter Tray	Desk Accessories	4	$2.99
23	Desk Accessory Set	Desk Accessories	3	$21.99
24	Letter Sorter	Desk Accessories	2	$7.99
25	Drawer Tray	Desk Accessories	5	$3.49
26	Rotary Card File	Desk Accessories	3	$25.99
* (utoNumber)				

FIGURE 4-12
A filter displaying the Calculator products

Product ID	Product Name	Category	Units In Stock	Retail Price
27	Scientific Calculator	Business Machines	3	$19.98
28	Basic Calculator	Business Machines	7	$6.99
29	Printing Calculator	Business Machines	3	$29.99
* (utoNumber)				

Sorting

Sorting is an important part of working with a database. Often you will need records to appear in a specific order. For example, you may normally want a mailing list sorted by last name. But when preparing to mail literature to the entire mailing list, you may need the records to appear in ZIP code order. Access provides buttons on the toolbar to quickly sort the records of a table.

To sort a table, open the table and place the insertion point in the field by which you want to sort. Then click either the Sort Ascending or Sort Descending button. An *ascending sort* arranges records from A to Z or smallest to largest. A *descending sort* arranges records from Z to A or largest to smallest.

STEP-BY-STEP ▷ 4.5

1. The **Products** table should be open in Datasheet view. Suppose you want to sort the records from least in stock to most in stock. Place the insertion point in the first record of the **Units In Stock** field.

2. Click the **Sort Ascending** button. The records appear in order by Units In Stock.

3. Suppose you want to sort the records from most expensive to least expensive. Place the insertion point in the first record of the **Retail Price** field.

4. Click the **Sort Descending** button. The products are sorted from most to least expensive.

5. Print the table and leave it open for the next Step-by-Step.

Sorting using the Sort Ascending and Sort Descending buttons is quick and easy. However, you will sometimes need to sort by more than one field. For example, suppose you want to sort the Products table by Category, but within each category you want the items to appear from most to least expensive. To perform this kind of sort, you must create a filter.

To use a filter to sort, create a filter as you normally do, but select an ascending or descending sort for the desired field or fields by clicking the down arrow in the *Sort* row. If the filter window has information left over from a previous sort or filter, you may need to click the cells with existing data and press the Backspace key to clear them.

STEP-BY-STEP ▷ 4.6

1. Choose **Filter** on the **Records** menu, and then choose **Advanced Filter/Sort** on the submenu.

2. Choose the **Category** and **Retail Price** fields as shown in Figure 4-13. Click the down arrow in the **Sort** row and choose **Ascending** for the Category field, and **Descending** for the Retail Price field. You may need to clear some existing data from the filter window.

3. Click the **Apply Filter** button.

4. Scroll through the datasheet to see that the records have been sorted according to the specifications in the filter.

5. Print the table with the filter applied.

6. Leave the table and filter window open for the next Step-by-Step.

FIGURE 4-13
Sorting by more than one field

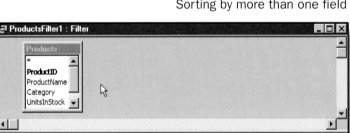

To filter and sort at the same time, you add the information for both to the same filter window. Choose Filter on the Records menu and select Advanced/Filter Sort. In the filter window select the field to which you want to apply a filter and the field to be sorted. Click the Apply Filter button on the toolbar.

S TEP-BY-STEP ▷ 4.7

1. Choose **Filter** on the **Records** menu, and then choose **Advanced Filter/Sort** on the submenu.

2. Suppose you want to display only the products with a retail price greater than $150. Key **>150** in the **Criteria** row of the **Retail Price** column. Leave the Category column as is.

3. Click the **Apply Filter** button. Only seven of the records meet the filter criteria and they are sorted by retail price within the categories, as shown in Figure 4-14.

4. Print the table with the filter applied.

5. Click the **Remove Filter** button to remove the filter. All of the records appear again.

6. Close the table. If prompted to save the design of the table, click **No**. Leave the database open for the next Step-by-Step.

FIGURE 4-14

Filtering and sorting records

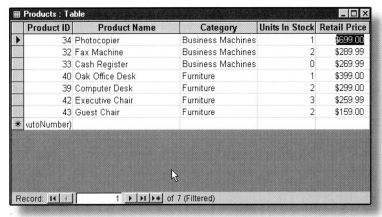

Indexing

I*ndexing* is an important part of database management systems. In small databases, indexes do not provide much benefit. Large databases, however, rely on indexing to quickly locate data. In an Access database, you can specify that certain fields be indexed. Access can find data in an indexed field faster than it can find data in a field that is not indexed.

To index a field, go to Design view. For each field in Design view, you can specify whether you want the field to be indexed.

If indexing improves speed, why not index all of the fields? The reason is that each indexed field causes more work and uses more disk space. Before indexing a database, you should be sure that the benefit of indexing a field outweighs the negatives caused by indexing. As a general rule, index fields only in large databases, and index only those fields that are regularly used to locate records.

Setting a Primary Key

When you save a newly created table in a database, a message appears asking if you want to create a **primary key**, which is a special field that assigns a unique identifier to each record. You can have Access create the primary key for you, in which case, each record is automatically assigned a unique number. Or, you can set the primary key to an existing field within the table. The existing field should contain a unique value such as an ID number or part number. Primary keys must be set before creating table relationships, which are covered in the next section.

To designate a field as the primary key, open the table in Design view. Choose the field you want to set as the primary key by clicking the row selector. Click the Primary Key button on the toolbar. A primary key icon will now appear next to the primary key field.

S TEP-BY-STEP ▷ 4.8

1. In the **IA Step4-1** database, open the **Products** table in **Design** view.

2. Click the **row selector** for the **Product ID** field.

3. Click the **Primary Key** button on the toolbar. A key icon appears next to the **ProductID** field, as shown in Figure 4-15.

4. Close the table and a message appears asking you to save changes to the table. Click **Yes**. Leave the database open for the next Step-by-Step.

FIGURE 4-15
Setting the primary key

Products : Table		
Field Name	Data Type	Description
ProductID	AutoNumber	
ProductName	Text	
Category	Text	
UnitsInStock	Number	

Relationships

By defining **relationships** between the different tables within a database, you can create queries, forms, and reports to display information from several tables at once. You can create a relationship between tables that contain a common field. For example, you might have a table that contains the name, telephone number, and other data on real estate agents. A second table might contain information, including the name of the listing agent, on properties for sale. You could set up a relationship between the two tables by joining the fields containing the agents' names. Then, you could create forms, queries, and reports that include fields from both tables.

The common fields must be of the same data type, although they can have different field names. In most relationships, the common field is also the primary key in at least one of the tables. It is referred to as the foreign key in the other table(s).

To ensure valid relationships between tables and prevent invalid data from being entered, Access utilizes *referential integrity* rules. These also help ensure that related data is not accidentally deleted or changed. To enforce referential integrity between tables, choose the Enforce Referential Integrity option when creating the relationship. If you break one of the rules with the related tables, Access displays a message and doesn't allow the change.

A *one-to-many relationship*, as illustrated in Figure 4-16, is the most common type of relationship. In a one-to-many relationship, a record in Table A can have matching records in Table B, but a record in Table B has only one matching record in Table A. In Figure 4-16, the Realtor field is the primary key in the Realtors table and the foreign key in the Houses table.

You define a relationship by clicking Relationships on the Tools menu or clicking the Relationships button on the toolbar. Add the tables you want to relate to the Relationships window. Next, you drag the key field from one table to the key field in the other table.

FIGURE 4-16
One-to-many relationship

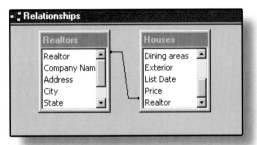

STEP-BY-STEP 4.9

1. The **IA Step4-1** Database window should still be open. Click **Relationships** on the **Tools** menu or click the **Relationships** button on the toolbar. If the Show Table dialog box does not appear, as shown in Figure 4-17, click **Show Table** on the **Relationships** menu.

2. Choose the **Products** table and click **Add**. Repeat this step for the **Orders** table.

3. When finished, click **Close**. The Relationships window should appear as shown in Figure 4-18.

4. Click the **ProductID** field in the **Products** table. Drag and drop it on the **Product ID** field in the **Orders** table. (*Remember:* The common fields don't have to have the same field name; they

just need to be of the same data type.) The Edit Relationships dialog box will appear as shown in Figure 4-19.

5. Check to be sure the Product ID field appears for both the Products and Orders tables. Click the **Enforce Referential Integrity** check box.

6. Click **Create**. The Relationships window appears as shown in Figure 4-20.

7. Close the Relationships window and a message appears asking if you want to save changes to the layout of Relationships. Click **Yes** to save the changes. Leave the database open for the next Step-by-Step.

(continued on next page)

FIGURE 4-17
Show Table dialog box

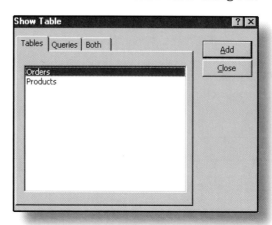

FIGURE 4-18
Relationships window

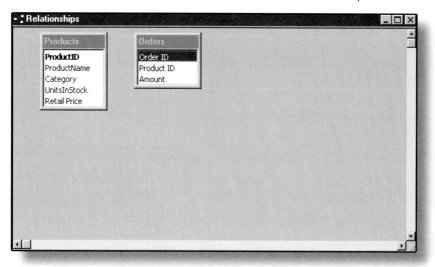

FIGURE 4-19
Edit Relationships dialog box

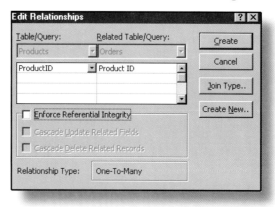

FIGURE 4-20
Table relationships

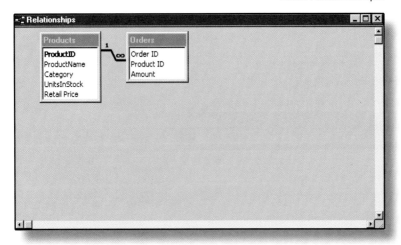

To print a database relationship, click Relationships on the Tools menu to display the Relationships window. Click Print Relationships on the File menu and a report listing the table relationships will display. Choose Print on the File menu or save the report for future reference.

STEP-BY-STEP ▷ 4.10

1. With the **IA Step4-1** Database window open, click **Relationships** on the **Tools** menu. The Relationships window appears (see Figure 4-20).

2. Click **Print Relationships** on the **File** menu. A report listing the table relationships will display as shown in Figure 4-21.

3. Click **Print** on the **File** menu and the Print dialog box appears. Click **OK** to print the report.

4. Close the Report window. A message displays asking if you want to save changes to the design of the report. Click **No**.

5. Close the Relationships window. Leave the database open for the next Step-by-Step.

FIGURE 4-21
Table relationships report

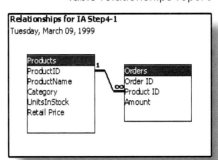

Viewing Related Records

To view the related records between two tables you can add a *subdatasheet*. To insert a subdatasheet, open the table with the primary key in Datasheet view, and choose Subdatasheet on the Insert menu. In the Insert Subdatasheet window, choose the related table and click OK. The table with the primary key will reappear. Click the expand indicator icon (+) to the left of each row to display a subdatasheet of related records.

STEP-BY-STEP ▷ 4.11

1. Open the **Products** table in Datasheet view.

2. Click **Subdatasheet** on the **Insert** menu. The Insert Subdatasheet dialog box will appear as shown in Figure 4-22.

3. Choose the **Orders** table and click **OK**. The Products table will reappear.

4. Click the expand indicator button (**+**) to the left of Product ID number **3** to display a subdat-

sheet of related records as shown in Figure 4-23.

5. Click the indicator button again to close the subdatasheet. Close the **Products** table. A message displays asking if you want to save the changes to the Products table. Click **Yes** to save. Leave the database open for the next Step-by-Step.

FIGURE 4-22
Insert Subdatasheet dialog box

FIGURE 4-23
Subdatasheet of related records

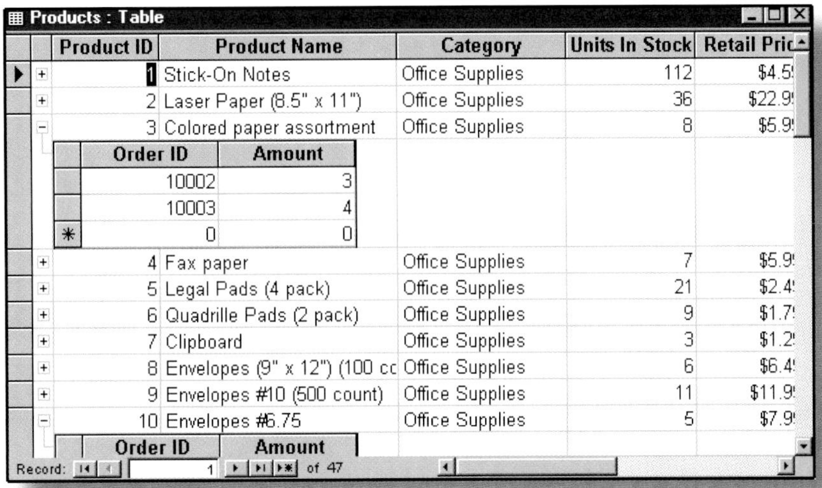

Creating a Multitable Query

After defining relationships in a database, you can create a ***multitable query*** to display the information from the related tables at once. For example, you might want to view customer information with the orders placed by the customers. To do this you would need data from both the Customers and Orders tables.

Except for a few additional steps, you will create a multitable query using the same procedure you've used to create queries. After opening the appropriate database, choose Queries on the Objects bar, and then click the New button to create a new query. The New Query dialog box appears. Choose the Design View option to create a query manually. In the Show Table dialog box, choose to add the related tables to the query. The fields in the related tables will appear in small boxes in the top part of the query window, as shown in Figure 4-24.

In the lower pane of the query window, specify the information needed from both tables to create the query. After choosing the fields and entering the search criteria, save the query.

FIGURE 4-24
Query window

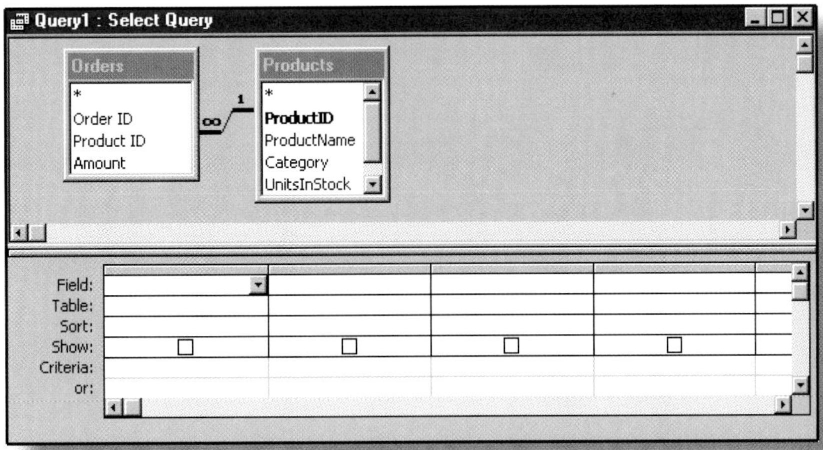

I A - 7 7

1. Click **Queries** on the Objects bar. Click the **New** button. The New Query dialog box appears.

2. Choose **Design View**, if it is not already selected, and click **OK**. The Show Table dialog box appears to allow you to choose the related tables for the query.

3. Select the **Orders** table, if necessary, and then click **Add**. The fields of the Orders table appear in the query window.

4. Select **Products** in the Show Table dialog box and click **Add**. The fields of the Products table appear in the query window.

5. Close the Show Table dialog box. The query window should look like Figure 4-24.

6. Click the down arrow in the **Field** row of the first column and choose **Orders.Order ID**, as shown in Figure 4-25.

7. Click the down arrow in the **Field** row of the second column and choose **Orders.Product ID**.

8. In the third column, choose **Products.Product Name**.

9. In the fourth column, choose **Orders.Amount**.

10. In the fifth column, choose **Products.Retail Price**.

11. Choose **Save** on the **File** menu, and enter **Invoice Query** as the name for the query. Click **OK**.

12. Click the **Run** button. The results of the query appear, as shown in Figure 4-26.

13. Choose **Print** on the **File** menu to print the table with the query applied. Click **OK**.

14. Choose **Close** on the **File** menu to close the query. Close the database.

FIGURE 4-25
Select fields to display in the query results

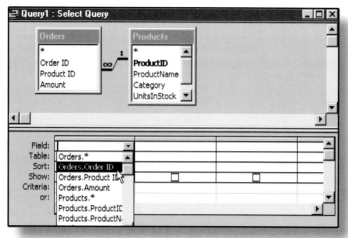

FIGURE 4-26

Results of a multitable query

Order ID	Product ID	Product Name	Amount	Retail Price
10000	10	Envelopes #6.75	2	$7.99
10001	31	Answering Machine	1	$49.99
10001	24	Letter Sorter	1	$7.99
10002	46	2-Drawer Filing Cabinet	1	$79.99
10002	11	3-ring binders (1")	10	$1.49
10002	3	Colored paper assortment	3	$5.99
10003	25	Drawer Tray	2	$3.49
10003	17	3-hole punch	1	$9.99
10003	3	Colored paper assortment	4	$5.99
10004	32	Fax Machine	1	$289.99
10004	20	Date Stamp	2	$2.49
10005	26	Rotary Card File	1	$25.99
10005	4	Fax paper	3	$5.99

Record: 1 of 13

Summary

In this lesson, you learned:

■ The Find command is the easiest way to locate data in the database. The Find command searches the database for specified information.

■ Queries allow more complex searches. A query allows you to search records using multiple and complex criteria and allows you to display selected fields. You can save a query and apply it again later.

■ A filter is similar to a query; however, it displays all fields and cannot be saved. A filter can be used to sort records, or records can be sorted directly in a table without the use of a filter. Using a filter to sort records allows you to sort by more than one record.

■ Indexing is an important part of database management systems. Indexing allows records to be located more quickly, especially in large databases.

■ By defining relationships between the different tables within a database, you can create queries, forms, and reports to display information from several tables at once. A relationship is set up by matching data in key fields.

TRUE/FALSE

Circle the T if the statement is true or F if the statement is false.

T F 1. The Find command can search for data in all fields.

T F 2. The Find Next button in the Find dialog box finds the next record that matches the criteria you've specified.

T F 3. A query automatically displays all fields in the table.

T F 4. Filters cannot be saved for later use.

T F 5. An ascending sort arranges records from *Z* to *A*.

WRITTEN QUESTIONS

Write a brief answer to the following questions.

1. What is the easiest way to quickly locate data in a database?

2. What are the three pieces of information you must supply when creating a query?

3. What menu is used to access the command that creates a filter?

4. What button is used to sort records from largest to smallest?

5. What view allows you to index a field?

LESSON 4 PROJECTS

PROJECT 4-1

1. Open the **IA Project4-1** database file from the student data files.

2. Open the **Houses** table in Datasheet view.

3. Use the **Find** command to locate the first house with wood exterior.

4. Use the **Find** command to locate any remaining houses with wood exterior.

5. Close the table.

6. Create a query that displays houses with two bedrooms. Have the query display only the Address, Bedrooms, and Price fields. Save the query as **2 Bedrooms**.

7. Run the query and print the results. Close the query. Leave the database open for the next project.

PROJECT 4-2

1. Open the **Houses** table in the **IA Project4-1** database in Datasheet view.

2. Sort the table so that the houses are displayed from most expensive to least expensive.

3. Change the column width to **Best Fit** for all the columns.

4. Print the results of the sort in landscape orientation.

5. Create a filter to display only the houses listed with **Brad Gray** as the agent. You do not have to sort the records.

6. Print the results of the filter in landscape orientation.

7. Remove the filter to show all the records in the table. Leave the database open for the next project.

PROJECT 4-3

1. With the **Houses** table in the **IA Project4-1** database open, create a filter that displays three-bedroom houses only, sorted from least to most expensive.

2. Print the results of the filter in landscape orientation.

3. Remove the filter to show all records in the table.

4. Create a filter that displays only houses with two-car garages and brick exterior.

5. Print the results of the filter in landscape orientation.

6. Remove the filter to show all records in the table. Leave the database open for the next project.

PROJECT 4-4

1. With the **Houses** table in the **IA Project4-1** database open, use the **Find** command to locate the houses that were listed during December.

2. Create a query that displays the houses listed with **Nina Bertinelli** or **John Schultz** as the agent. Have the query display only the **Address**, **List Date**, **Price**, and **Agent** fields and sort the **Price** field from most to least expensive. Save the query as **Bertinelli/Schultz**.

3. Run the query and print the results. Close the query.

4. Open the **Houses** table and create a filter that sorts the houses from most to least bathrooms and the price from least to most expensive.

5. Print the results of the filter in landscape orientation.

6. Remove the filter to show all records in the table.

7. Close the table and the database.

CRITICAL THINKING

ACTIVITY 4-1

SCANS

You are a Realtor with three new clients who are ready to buy homes. List on paper each client's requirements in a home. For example, buyer #1 might want a three-bedroom house with a brick exterior and the maximum price is $90,000.

Using the **IA Project4-1** database and the **Houses** table, create a filter or query to locate the information for each client and print the results.

ACTIVITY 4-2

SCANS

Referential integrity is a set of rules that Access uses to check for valid relationships between tables. It also ensures that related data is not accidentally deleted or changed. Using the Help system, determine what conditions must be met before you can enforce referential integrity. Write a brief essay that explains the importance of referential integrity in a relational database, and why users of the database objects would benefit from it.

REPORTS AND MACROS

OBJECTIVES

Upon completion of this lesson, you should be able to:

■ Create a report using a Report Wizard.

■ Modify a report.

■ Create and run a macro.

🕐 **Estimated Time: 1.5 hours**

Reports

Databases can become large as records are added. Printing the database from Datasheet view may not always be the most desirable way to put the data on paper. Creating a *database report* allows you to organize, summarize, and print all or a portion of the data in a database. You can even use reports to print form letters and mailing labels. Figure 5-1 shows two examples of database reports. Database reports are compiled by creating a report object.

FIGURE 5-1
Database reports

Products by Units in Stock Tiffany Matthews

UnitsInStock	Product Name	Product ID	Category	Retail
	0 Cash Register	33	Business Machines	$22
	1 Oak Office Desk	40	Furniture	$39
	Photocopier	34	Business Machines	$59
	2 Bookshelf	41	Furniture	$8
	Computer Desk	39	Furniture	$29
	Fax Machine	32	Business Machines	$24
	Guest Chair	43	Furniture	$19
	Heavy Duty Stapler	15	Office Supplies	$1
	Letter Sorter	24	Desk Accessories	$
	Speaker Phone	30	Business Machines	$9
	Typewriter	35	Business Machines	$14
	3 2-Drawer Filing Cabinet	46	Furniture	$8
	Clipboard	7	Office Supplies	$
	Desk Accessory Set	23	Desk Accessories	$1
	Desk Chair	44	Furniture	$18
	Executive Chair	42	Furniture	$25
	Printing Calculator	29	Business Machines	$2
	Rotary Card File	26	Desk Accessories	$2
	Scientific Calculator	27	Business Machines	$1
	Surge Protector	37	Computer Supplies	$1
	4 4-Drawer Filing Cabinet	45	Furniture	$14
	Answering Machine	31	Business Machines	$4
	Disk Storage Box	38	Computer Supplies	$
	Folding Table (8')	47	Furniture	$4
	Letter Tray	22	Desk Accessories	$
	Scissors	16	Office Supplies	$
	Tape Dispenser	19	Office Supplies	$
	5 Drawer Tray	25	Desk Accessories	$
	Envelopes #6.75	10	Office Supplies	$
	6 Envelopes (9" x 12") (10	8	Office Supplies	$
	Standard Stapler	14	Office Supplies	$
	7 3-hole punch	17	Office Supplies	$
	Basic Calculator	28	Business Machines	$
	Date Stamp	20	Office Supplies	$
	Fax paper	4	Office Supplies	$
	8 Colored paper assortme	3	Office Supplies	$
	9 3-ring binders (2")	12	Office Supplies	$
	3.5" HD Diskettes (Box o	36	Computer Supplies	$

Page

Employees by Department

Department	Last Name	First Name	Salary
Advertising			
	Abernathy	Mark	$2,375.00
	Barton	Brad	$2,590.00
	Denton	Scott	$2,600.00
	Doss	Derek	$2,200.00
Marketing			
	Martinez	Christine	$1,780.00
	Powell	Lynne	$2,970.00
	Powers	Sarah	$1,500.00
Personnel			
	Davis	Lee	$2,680.00
Public Relations			
	Smith	Shawna	$2,950.00
Sales			
	Best	Trent	$2,800.00
	Broach	Margie	$2,450.00
	Collins	Greg	$2,750.00
	Collins	Dave	$2,620.00
	Davis	Hillary	$2,620.00
	Sims	Jennifer	$1,550.00
	West	Debbie	$3,100.00

Page 1 of 1

Printing a database from Datasheet view is a form of a report. Printing from Datasheet view, however, offers you much less flexibility than creating a report and printing it. In this lesson, you will learn how to create report objects.

Creating a Report

The report database object lets you create reports that include selected fields, groups of records, and even calculations. As with other Access objects, you can create a report object manually or use the Report Wizard. In this lesson, you will create a report using the Report Wizard.

To create a report, click Reports on the Objects bar, and click the New button. The New Report dialog box appears, as shown in Figure 5-2.

In the New Report dialog box, you choose the method to create the report. To use a Report Wizard, choose *Report Wizard* from the list. Click the down arrow to select the table or query Access will use to create a report. Choose a table if you want to include the entire table in the report. Choose a query to include only certain data in the report. In many cases, you will want to create a query before creating a report.

FIGURE 5-2
New Report dialog box

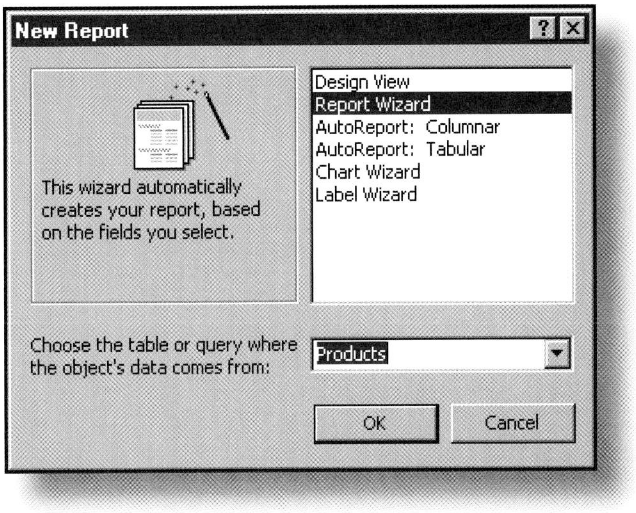

STEP-BY-STEP ▷ 5.1

1. Open **IA Step5-1** from the student data files.

2. Click the **Reports** button on the Objects bar.

3. Click **New**. The New Report dialog box appears, as shown in Figure 5-2.

4. Choose **Report Wizard** from the list.

5. Click the down arrow and choose the table **Products** from the drop-down list. Click **OK**. The Report Wizard dialog box appears, as shown in Figure 5-3.

6. Leave the dialog box on the screen for the next Step-by-Step.

(continued on next page)

FIGURE 5-3
Starting the Report Wizard

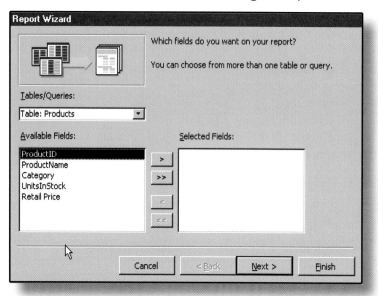

CHOOSING FIELDS FOR THE REPORT

You select fields for the report in the Report Wizard dialog box shown in Figure 5-3. You select fields the same way you did when creating a form using the Form Wizard.

STEP-BY-STEP 5.2

1. Highlight **ProductName** in the *Available Fields* list. Click **>**. The ProductName field is now listed in the *Selected Fields* box.

2. The Category field is now highlighted in the *Available Fields* list. Click **>** three times to move the **Category**, **UnitsInStock**, and **Retail Price** fields to the *Selected Fields* box. Your screen should appear similar to Figure 5-4.

3. Click **Next**. The Report Wizard now gives you the option to group the report. Leave the dialog box on the screen for the next Step-by-Step.

Hot Tip

The >> button moves all fields in the *Available Fields* list to the *Selected Fields* box.

FIGURE 5-4
Choosing fields

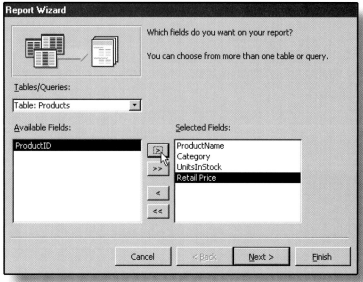

GROUPING AND SORTING THE REPORT

Grouping a report allows you to break it into parts based on the contents of a field. For example, you could organize a customers report into parts that group the customers by city. In the report you are creating now, you will group the report by product category. To group a report, choose the field(s) by which you want to group from the Report Wizard dialog box shown in Figure 5-5.

FIGURE 5-5
Grouping a report by fields

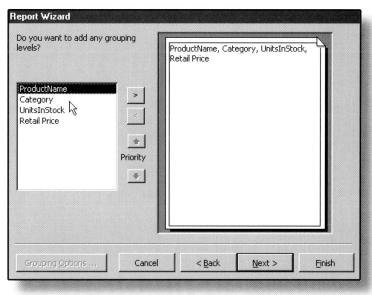

You can group by more than one field. When you group by more than one field, however, you must give the fields priority. For example, you could group customers by state first, then by city within each state.

Sorting the report goes hand-in-hand with grouping. The dialog box shown in Figure 5-6 allows you to specify fields by which the report will be sorted. As you can see, you can sort by multiple fields. Sorting orders the records in a group based on the chosen field or fields. For example, you could group a customers report by city and then sort it by company name. The records for each city would be listed in alphabetic order by company name.

FIGURE 5-6
Sorting a report

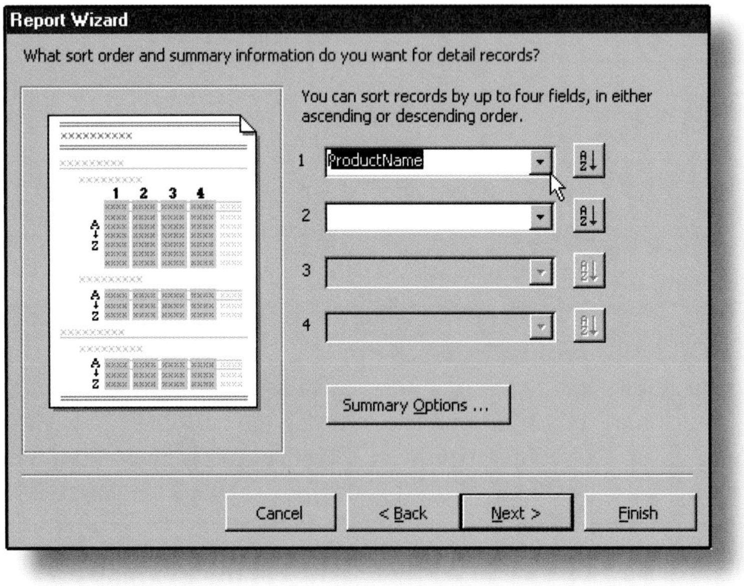

STEP-BY-STEP ▷ 5.3

1. Highlight **Category** and click **>**. Your screen should appear similar to Figure 5-7.

2. Click **Next**. The Report Wizard asks you which fields you want to sort by, as shown in Figure 5-6.

3. Choose **ProductName** as the first sort field by clicking the down arrow next to the number 1 box. For this report, you will sort by one field only. Leave the sort screen displayed for the next Step-by-Step.

FIGURE 5-7

Report grouped by product category

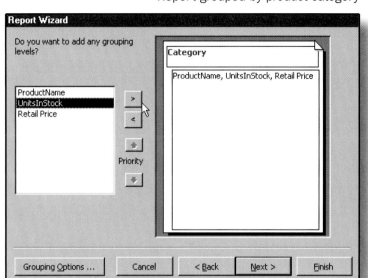

SUMMARY OPTIONS

One of the most useful features of reports is the ability to create summaries within it. Each group of records in a report can be followed by totals, averages, or other summary information. The Summary Options dialog box allows you to specify summaries for fields in the report.

STEP-BY-STEP ▷ 5.4

1. Click the **Summary Options** button. The Summary Options dialog box appears.

2. For the **UnitsInStock** field, click the **Sum** option. The report will total the UnitsInStock field.

3. For the **Retail Price** field, click the **Min** and **Max** options.

4. Choose the **Calculate percent of total for sums** option. (Access takes the total UnitsIn-

Stock for each category and calculates a percentage of the Grand Total.) Your screen should appear similar to Figure 5-8.

5. Click **OK** to close the Summary Options dialog box.

6. Click **Next**. The Report Wizard asks you to choose a layout and page orientation. Leave the Report Wizard on the screen for the next Step-by-Step.

(continued on next page)

FIGURE 5-8
Summary Options dialog box

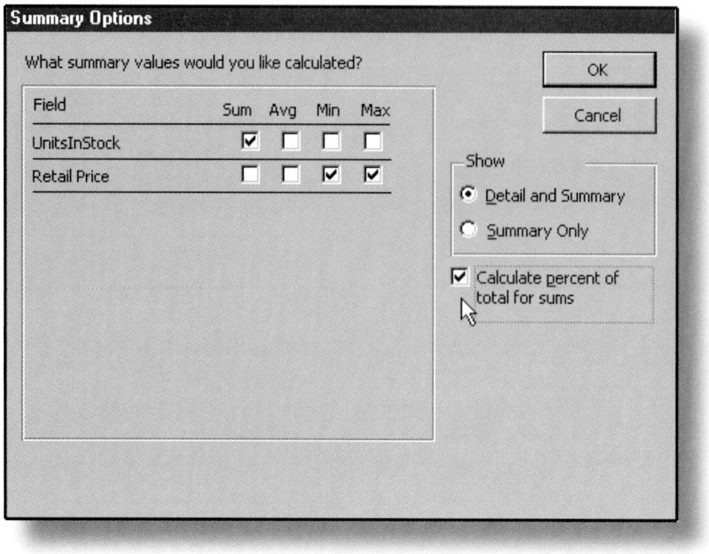

LAYOUT AND ORIENTATION

Next, you'll choose the layout and orientation for your report, as shown in Figure 5-9. The layout options let you choose how you want data arranged on the page. When you choose a layout, a sample is shown in the preview box. Choose from *Landscape* or *Portrait* orientation and click Next.

The next dialog box, shown in Figure 5-10, allows you to choose a style for the report. The style options are designed to give you some control over the report's appearance. The style you choose tells the reader of the report something about the data being presented. Some reports may call for a formal style, while others may benefit from a more casual style. When you choose a style, a sample is shown in the preview box.

FIGURE 5-9
Layout options

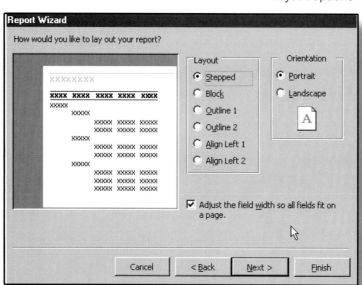

FIGURE 5-10
Style options

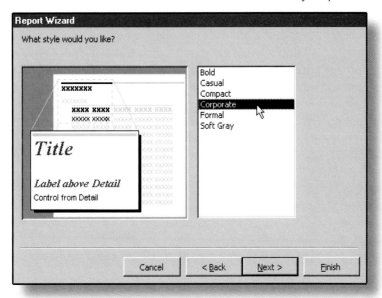

STEP-BY-STEP ▷ 5.5

1. Choose the **Outline 2** layout. The sample layout is shown in the preview box. Click the other options to look at the other layouts. When you have seen all of the available options, choose **Stepped** as the layout.

2. Choose **Portrait** as the page orientation, if it is not already selected.

3. Click **Next**.

4. Choose the **Casual** style. The sample style is shown in the preview box. Click on the other options to look at the other styles. When you have seen all of the available options, choose **Corporate** as the style.

5. Click **Next**. The final Report Wizard dialog box appears. Leave the Report Wizard on the screen for the next Step-by-Step.

Did You Know?

You can create a chart in either a form's or report's Design view. Click **Chart** on the **Insert** menu. On the form or report, click where you want the chart to appear. Follow the steps in the Chart Wizard to create the chart based on the tables and the fields you select.

NAMING THE REPORT

The final step is naming the report, as shown in Figure 5-11. Use a name that gives an indication of the report's output. A report name can be up to 64 characters including letters, numbers, spaces, and some special characters. For example, if a report from a database of customers prints only the customers with companies in your city, you might name the report *Local Customers*.

In addition to naming the report, this dialog box presents you with options for what you want to be displayed when the Report Wizard completes its work. Most of the time you will want to preview the report you just created, so that is the default option. After Access creates the report, it is shown on your screen in Preview mode. You may instead choose to make modifications to the report. You will get a brief look at how modifications are made later in this lesson.

After creating a report, you do not need to save it. Access saves it for you automatically with the title you entered in the Report Wizard. You will, however, need to save any modifications made later to the design of the report.

FIGURE 5-11
Naming the report

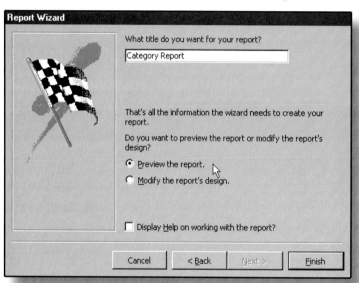

S TEP-BY-STEP ▷ 5.6

1. Key **Category Report** as the title of the report.

2. Make sure the option to preview the report is selected and click **Finish**. The report appears in a window, as shown in Figure 5-12.

3. Scroll through the report to see the various categories.

4. Click the **Print** button to print the report.

5. Choose **Close** on the **File** menu. The report will be saved automatically. Leave the Database window open for the next Step-by-Step.

 Did You Know?

To add a graphic to a report, open it in Design view, and click the **Image** button in the Toolbox. Click where you want to place the graphic in the report and the Insert Picture dialog box displays. Select the file where the picture is located. When finished, click **OK**. Access creates an image control that will display the graphic.

FIGURE 5-12
Previewing a report

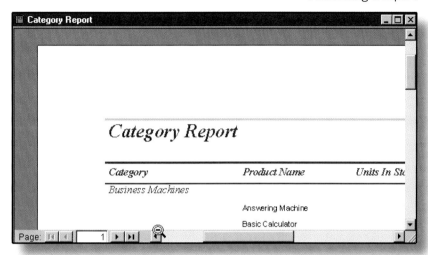

Modifying a Report

Any report, whether created manually or with the Report Wizard, can be modified. You make changes to a report using Design view, which shows the structure of a report. To open a report in Design view, select the report in the Database window, and then click the Design button. Figure 5-13 shows a report in Design view.

FIGURE 5-13
A report in Design view

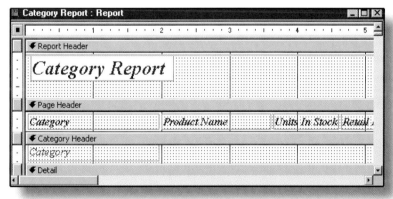

Like a form, the report is divided into sections, each identified by a band. Each section controls a part of the report and can be modified. Table 5-1 summarizes the purpose of each of the sections in the report.

TABLE 5-1
Report sections

SECTION	DESCRIPTION
Report Header	Contents appear at the top of the first page of the report.
Page Header	Contents appear at the top of each page of the report.
Category Header	Contents appear at the top of each group. Because your report is grouped by Category, the band is called Category Header.
Detail	Specifies the fields that will appear in the detail of the report.
Category Footer	Contents appear at the end of each group. The summary options appear in this band.
Page Footer	Contents appear at the end of each page of the report.
Report Footer	Contents appear at the end of the report.

Like a form, the sections in a report contain controls that represent each object on the report. These objects include field names, field entries, a title for the report, or even a graphical object, such as a piece of clip art. You can modify the format, size, and location of the controls in Design view to enhance the appearance of the data on the report.

In Design view, you can change the font, size, style, and other attributes of labels and text box data. Simply select the control, and use the buttons on the Formatting toolbar. Or you can double-click a control to open its Properties dialog box, and then change attributes and other properties.

The Toolbox, shown in Figure 5-14, has tools that you can use to modify reports. The Label tool, for example, allows you to add text.

FIGURE 5-14
Toolbox

STEP-BY-STEP ▷ 5.7

1. If not already selected, click **Reports** on the Objects bar. Choose the **Category Report** and click the **Design** button. The report appears in Design view, as shown in Figure 5-13.

2. Click the **Label** button in the Toolbox. (If the Toolbox is not displayed, *right*-click on the

   report and choose **Toolbox** on the shortcut menu.)

3. In the **Report Header**, position the pointer to the right of the *Category Report* text, and click and drag to draw a text box as shown in Figure 5-15.

4. Key your name at the insertion point that appears in the text box. Click outside the text box to view the text.

5. Double-click the text box to display its properties dialog box, as shown in Figure 5-16. If not already selected, click the **All** tab.

6. Scroll through the list of properties until you locate the *Font Name* and *Font Size* properties. Click in the **Font Name** text box, click the down arrow, and select **Mistral** (or a comparable font). Then, click in the **Font Size** text box, click the down arrow, and choose **14**. Close the properties dialog box.

7. Scroll down to the **Report Footer** section. Position the pointer on the **Grand Total** label box as shown in Figure 5-17, and double-click to open its properties dialog box. If not already selected, click the **All** tab.

8. Change the *Caption* to **Total Units in Stock**. Change the *Font Size* to **12**. Close the dialog box.

9. In the **Detail** section, double-click the **Retail Price** box to open its properties dialog box, as shown in Figure 5-18. If not already selected, choose the **All** tab.

10. Click in the **Name** text box and key **Discount Price**. Click in the **Control Source** text box and key **=[Retail Price]*.90**. Change the *Format* property to **Currency**. Then, close the dialog box.

11. In the **Page Header** section, double-click the **Retail Price** label box to open its properties dialog box.

12. Change the *Caption* to **Discount Price** and close the dialog box.

13. With the **Discount Price** label still highlighted, increase the label size by dragging the handle on the right border to the right until you see the entire caption.

14. Click the **View** button to switch to **Print Preview**. If a message appears asking if you want to save changes, click **Yes**.

15. If necessary, scroll to the right to see your name on the report.

16. Choose **Print** on the **File** menu. In the Print dialog box, click **Pages** from the *Print Range* options. Specify that you want to print only page 1 by keying **1** in the *From* box and **1** in the *To* box. Click **OK**.

17. Close the report and leave the database open for the next Step-by-Step.

C **Hot Tip**

To delete a text box, click on the text box and press the **Delete** key or choose **Delete** on the **Edit** menu. To move a text box, click inside the box and drag. To resize a text box, click on the edge of the text box and drag.

(continued on next page)

FIGURE 5-15
Inserting text

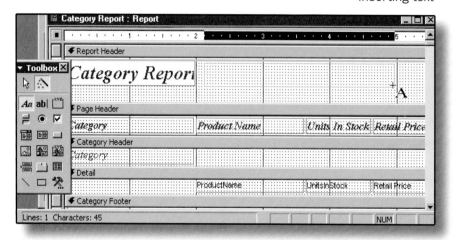

FIGURE 5-16
Label properties dialog box

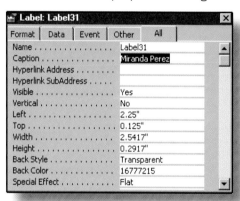

FIGURE 5-17
Modifying the Grand Total label

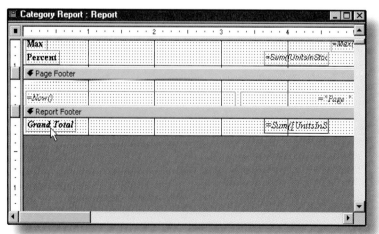

FIGURE 5-18
Text Box properties dialog box

Macros

One of the nice features of database management systems such as Access is the ability to automate tasks that are performed often. This is done by creating an object called a macro. A ***macro*** is a collection of one or more actions that Access can perform on a database. You can think of a macro as a computer program you create to automate some task you perform with the database.

Creating macros can be challenging, and there are many details to learn before you can become an expert. In this book you will get a taste of how macros work by creating a macro and running it.

Creating a Macro

To create a macro, click Macros on the Objects bar, and click the New button. The Macro window appears, allowing you to specify the actions to be performed by the macro. Figure 5-19 shows a macro in Design view with an example of actions that a macro can perform. The macro will perform the actions specified in the Action list.

FIGURE 5-19
Macro in Design view

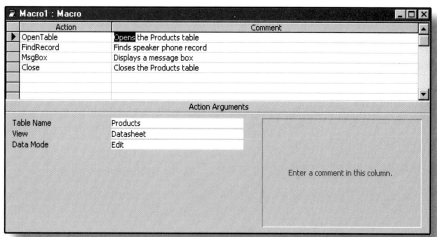

1. Click **Macros** on the Objects bar.

2. Click **New**. A blank macro window appears.

Leave the window open for the next Step-by-Step.

Adding Actions to a Macro

You can choose an action by clicking the down arrow in the *Action* column cells. There are many available actions, some of which perform advanced operations. You can key an explanation of the action in the *Comment* column. The lower portion of the Macro window shows the action arguments for the chosen action. Action arguments contain detailed information that Access needs in order to perform the specified action. For example, if you choose the *OpenTable* action in the *Action* column, you would specify which table to open, such as the Products table, in the *Action Arguments* section.

Different actions require different detailed information in the *Action Arguments* section, as you will see in the next Step-by-Step. You will create a macro that will open the Products table, find the first speaker phone in the table, present a message box and beep, and close the table.

1. Click the arrow in the **Action** column of the first blank row to display the list of available actions.

2. Scroll down and choose **OpenTable** from the menu.

3. In the **Comment** section, key **Opens the Products table**.

4. In the **Action Arguments** section, place the insertion point in the **Table Name** box. An arrow appears. Notice the box to the right of the *Action Arguments* contains an explanation of the data to be specified.

5. Click the arrow and choose **Products** from the list.

6. Leave the remaining *Action Arguments* at the default settings.

7. Place the insertion point in the second row of the **Action** column. Click the drop-down list arrow.

8. Scroll down and choose **FindRecord** from the list.

9. In the **Comment** section, key **Finds speaker phone record**.

10. In the **Action Arguments** section, key **Speaker Phone** in the **Find What** box.

11. In the **Match** box, choose **Any Part of Field** from the drop-down list.

12. Leave the next two action arguments at the default settings.

13. In the **Search As Formatted** box, choose **Yes** from the drop-down list.

14. In the **Only Current Field** box, choose **No** to search all the fields in each record.

15. In the **Find First** box, choose **Yes**, if it's not chosen already. Your screen should look similar to Figure 5-20.

16. Place the insertion point in the third row of the **Action** column, scroll down, and choose **MsgBox** from the list.

17. Key **Displays a message box** in the **Comment** section.

18. In the Action Arguments section, key **Record Found** in the **Message** box.

19. Choose **Yes** in the **Beep** box, if it is not already chosen.

20. Choose **Information** in the **Type** box.

21. Key **Results:** in the **Title** box.

22. Place the insertion point in the fourth row of the **Action** column and choose **Close** from the list.

23. Key **Closes the Products table** in the **Comment** section.

24. In the **Action Arguments** section, choose **Table** in the **Object Type** box.

25. Choose **Products** in the **Object Name** box.

26. Leave the window open for the next Step-by-Step.

FIGURE 5-20
Specifying Action Arguments

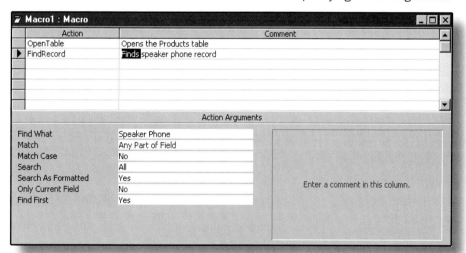

Saving and Running a Macro

After creating a macro, you will need to name and save it. This process is similar to the way you named and saved other database objects. Choose Save on the File menu and key a name. To close the macro, choose Close on the File menu. When you want to run a macro, highlight it in the Database window and click Run.

 Extra Challenge

Modify the Speaker Phone macro to find the scientific calculator record. Save and run the macro.

1. Choose **Save As** on the **File** Menu. The Save As dialog box appears.

2. Key **Speaker Phone** as the macro name and click **OK**.

3. Choose **Close** on the **File** menu to close the macro window. You are returned to the Database window.

4. Select **Macro** on the Objects bar. Highlight the **Speaker Phone** macro, if it is not already highlighted. Click the **Run** button. The *Products* table opens, the computer beeps, and the message box generated by the macro appears, as shown in Figure 5-21.

5. Click **OK** to close the message box. The table closes because of the Close action in the macro.

6. Open the **Speaker Phone** macro in Design view.

7. Highlight the row with the **MsgBox** action and choose **Delete** on the **Edit** menu.

8. Choose **Rows** on the **Insert** menu.

9. Click the down arrow in the **Action** column. Scroll down to choose the **PrintOut** action.

10. Key **Prints speaker phone record** in the **Comment** section.

11. In the **Action Arguments** section, choose **Selection** from the **Print Range** drop-down list.

12. Choose **Save** on the **File** menu to save the design changes.

13. Close the macro window.

14. Highlight the **Speaker Phone** macro, if it is not already highlighted. Click the **Run** button.

15. The *Products* table opens, the Speaker Phone record prints, and the table closes.

16. Close the database.

Hot Tip

If your computer does not beep when the message box appears, click the volume icon in the lower right-hand corner of your screen. In the Volume box, click the **Mute** box to remove the check mark. Rerun the macro to hear the beep.

FIGURE 5-21
Macro message box

Summary

In this lesson, you learned:

- Database reports allow you to organize, summarize, and print all or a portion of the data in a database. Database reports are compiled by creating a report object.

- The easiest way to create a report object is to use the Report Wizard. When using the Report Wizard, you first choose the table you want to base the report on and what fields of that table you want to include in the report. You can also choose to group the records and sort them.

- The Report Wizard also allows you to choose a style for your report. The style can give a report a casual or formal look.

- Reports are modified using Design view. Each report is divided into sections. Each section controls a different part of the report and can be modified.

- Macros automate tasks you perform often. The Macro window allows you to create a macro object.

LESSON 5 REVIEW QUESTIONS

TRUE/FALSE

Circle T if the statement is true or F if the statement is false.

T F 1. Database reports are prepared by creating a report object.

T F 2. The Report Wizard always includes all fields in a report.

T F 3. Like file names, report names can contain only eight characters.

T F 4. Action arguments contain detailed information about an action.

T F 5. To run a macro, highlight it in the Database window and click Run.

WRITTEN QUESTIONS

Write a brief answer to the following questions.

1. What are the two ways to create a report?

2. How does sorting affect a group?

3. What are sections in a report?

4. How do you use the Label tool to add text to a report?

5. When creating a macro, what action displays a message box?

LESSON 5 PROJECTS

PROJECT 5-1

1. Open **IA Step5-1** from the student data files. This is the database you used in this lesson.

2. Use the Report Wizard to create a report using all the fields in the **Products** table. Group the report by **UnitsInStock** and sort it by **ProductName**.

INTRODUCTION TO MICROSOFT ACCESS

3. Choose the **Block** layout, **Portrait** orientation, and **Compact** style.

4. Title the report **Products by Units in Stock**. Select the option to preview the report.

5. Close the report after previewing.

6. Modify the report in Design view. Use the label tool to insert your name in the Report header. Save the changes.

7. Print the report.

8. Close the report and the database.

PROJECT 5-2

1. Open **IA Project5-2** from the student data files.

2. Use the Report Wizard to create a report. Use the **Employee Information** table and choose the **Last Name**, **First Name**, **Department**, and **Salary** fields.

3. Group the records by **Department** and sort by **Last Name**.

4. Choose the **Stepped** layout, **Portrait** orientation, and **Corporate** style.

5. Title the report **Employees by Department**. Select the option to preview the report.

6. Save the report.

7. Print and close the report. Leave the database open for the next project.

PROJECT 5-3

1. With the **IA Project5-2** database open, create a new macro that will open the **Employee Birthdays** form in Form view and find the **Shapiro** record. For the **FindRecord Action Arguments**, select **Any Part of Field** in the **Match** box, **No** in the **Match Case** box, **All** in the **Search** box, **Yes** in the **Search As Formatted** box, **No** in the **Only Current Field** box, and **Yes** in the **Find First** box. Then, have the macro print the Shapiro record only (*Print Range = Selection*), and close the Employee Birthdays form.

2. Save the macro as **Print Form Record** and close it.

3. Run the macro. Leave the database open for the next project.

PROJECT 5-4

1. Create a new macro in the **IA Project5-2** database that will open the **Managers** query in Datasheet view and find the **Marketing** record. (For the **FindRecord Action Arguments**, select **Any Part of Field** in the **Match** box, **No** in the **Match Case** box, **All** in the **Search** box, **Yes** in the **Search As Formatted** box, **No** in the **Only Current Field** box, and **Yes** in the **Find First** box. Then, have the macro print the Marketing record (Selection) only, and close the **Managers** query.

2. Save the macro as **Print Marketing Manager** and close it.

3. Run the macro. Close the database.

CRITICAL THINKING

ACTIVITY 5-1

SCANS

Using the **IA Activity5-1** database file in the student data files and the **Houses** table, create a report listing all the information in the table. Also, create a macro that will open the **2 Bedrooms** query, find all of the two bedroom houses, print the results (*Print Range = All*), and close the query. Save the macro as **2 Bedroom Houses for Sale**. Run the macro and close the database.

ACTIVITY 5-2

SCANS

Using the Help feature, look up the definition of a *subreport*. In your own words, write a brief essay that defines a subreport and provide an example of when you might use a subreport. For your example, assume you have a database containing tables on customers and product sales.

ACTIVITY 5-3

SCANS

A *switchboard* is a form in a database that contains buttons representing macros you've created to open, close, and manage the objects in the database. Use the Help system to find out more about switchboards and how to create them. Write a brief essay explaining how you would use a switchboard in a database that you maintain.

INTEGRATING ACCESS

OBJECTIVES

Upon completion of this lesson, you should be able to:

- Integrate Access with other Office applications.

- Create a form letter.

- Use query options to print only selected form letters.

- Create and print mailing labels.   ⏱ **Estimated Time: 1.5 hours**

Sharing Data

Because Office is an integrated suite of programs, you can easily move and copy data between applications. You can export an Access table to an Excel worksheet, or you can merge records in a table with a Word document. In this lesson, you'll learn how to share data between Access and other applications.

Word to Access

Suppose you have been given a list of names and addresses in a Word file. The names need to be entered into a database. You can easily paste the information into an Access table, where you can then edit and sort it, and create forms, queries, reports, and pages from it. If the text from Word is set up as a table or is separated by tabs, Access will automatically create the fields and enter the data as records. If the text is in a single block, all of the text will be pasted into the currently highlighted field.

Access to Word

You can also paste table records from an Access database into a Word document. The data is formatted with tabs when it enters the Word document. This feature could be used to create a table in Word, based on data from Access. Merging database records with a Word document is another method for integrating Access and Word, and is discussed later in this lesson.

Access to Excel

There are times when you might want to paste Access data into an Excel worksheet. Excel provides powerful calculation and data analysis features that can easily be applied to database records that are exported to an Excel workbook file. Each record in the table appears as a row in the worksheet, and each field is converted to a column.

Excel to Access

You can also paste data from an Excel worksheet into an Access database table. A worksheet is set up as columns and rows, much like a database table. The cells cut or copied from the worksheet will appear in the database beginning with the highlighted entry.

You could also use the Import Spreadsheet Wizard to insert Excel data in an Access table. Open the database file, select the Get External Data command on the File menu, and then select Import on the submenu. An Import dialog box opens, where you select the file you want to import. The Wizard then guides you through the process of placing the spreadsheet data in a table.

STEP-BY-STEP ▷ 6.1

1. Open the **IA Step6-1** database from the student data files.

2. Choose **Get External Data** on the **File** menu, and select **Import** on the submenu. The Import dialog box appears, similar to that shown in Figure 6-1.

3. Click the down arrow in the *Files of type* box and choose **Microsoft Excel** from the list.

4. Select the **New Products** Excel workbook from the student data files.

5. Click **Import**. The Import Spreadsheet Wizard dialog box opens, as shown in Figure 6-2. Notice the data from the New Products worksheet appears in the grid.

6. Click **Next** and a second wizard dialog box opens, asking if the first row of the spreadsheet contains the column headings.

7. Click **Next** since the first row does contain the column headings and the option is already selected. A third wizard dialog box appears asking where you would like to store your data.

8. The **In a New Table** option should already be selected. Click **Next** and a fourth wizard dialog box appears as shown in Figure 6-3.

9. Scroll to the right in the grid to view all the field columns in the table. Then, click **Next**. This wizard dialog box asks you to let Access add a primary key to the table.

10. Choose **No primary key** and click **Next**.

11. Key **New Products** in the *Import to Table* box. Click **Finish**.

12. A message appears stating that the wizard is finished importing the file. Click **OK**.

13. The New Products table should be listed in the Database window. Open the table in Datasheet view. Print the table.

14. Close the table and the database.

Hot Tip

Backing up files on your computer should be a regular practice. To back up a database, you must close it first, and make sure that no other users have it opened. Using Windows Explorer, My Computer, Microsoft Backup, or other backup software, copy the database file to a backup medium, such as a floppy disk, a zip disk, tape, etc. To restore the database, simply copy the backup database file to the appropriate folder or disk.

FIGURE 6-1
Import dialog box

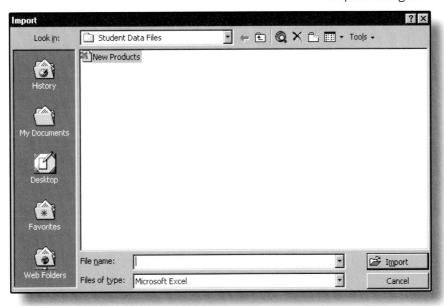

FIGURE 6-2
Import Spreadsheet Wizard dialog box

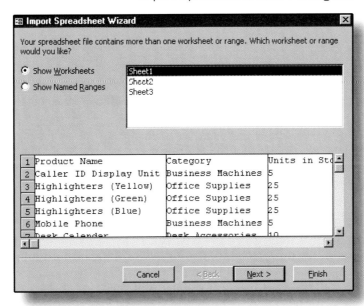

(continued on next page)

FIGURE 6-3
Import Spreadsheet Wizard lets you tailor Excel data

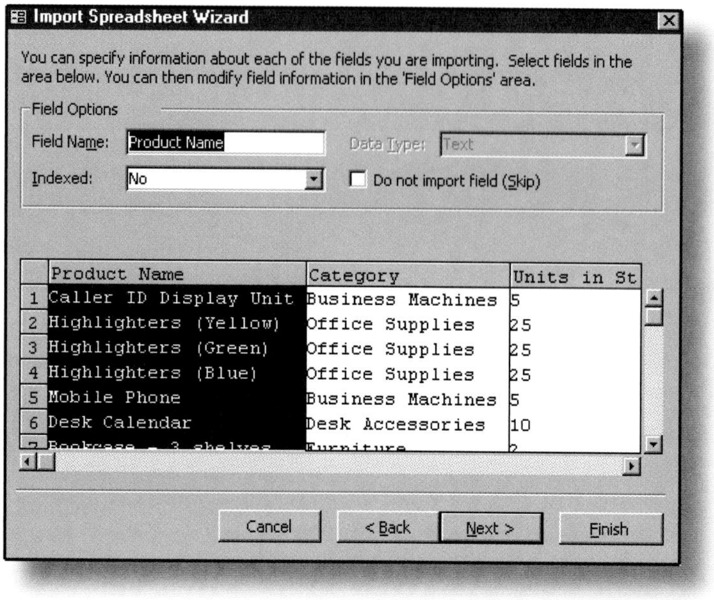

Form Letters

Another way to integrate Access and Word is through form letters. A *form letter* is a word processor document that uses information from a database in specified areas to personalize a document.

For example, you might send a letter to all the members of a professional organization using a form letter. In each letter, the information is the same but the names of the recipients will be different. One letter may begin "Dear Mr. Hartsfield" and another "Dear Ms. Perez."

Creating a Form Letter

To create form letters, you integrate information from a data source, such as an Access database, with a document from Word, called the main document. The *main document* contains the information that will stay the same in each form letter. The *data source* contains the information that will vary in each form letter. You insert the field names, or *merge fields*, in the main document where you want to print the information from the data source. The merge fields you place in the Word document are enclosed in angle brackets (<< Field Name >>). When the main document and the data source are merged, the merge fields in the main document are replaced with the appropriate information from the data source to create personalized form letters.

Word provides a Mail Merge Helper that makes it easy to create a form letter. To access the Mail Merge Helper dialog box, shown in Figure 6-4, choose the Mail Merge command on Word's Tools menu. You will complete three steps in the Mail Merge Helper dialog box. To specify the main document, click Create in step 1, click Form Letters, and then click Active Window. The active document (the one displayed on the screen) is now the main document. To specify a data source, click Get Data in step 2, and click Open Data Source. When the Open Data Source dialog box appears, choose the file you want to use as the data source. If you want to query the database before merging, click the Query Options button in step 3. When you are ready to merge, click Merge.

FIGURE 6-4
Mail Merge Helper

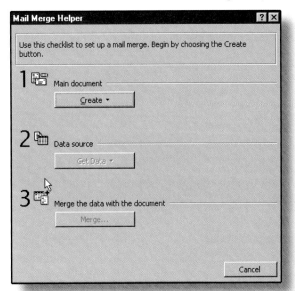

The Mail Merge toolbar, shown in Figure 6-5, contains buttons to make the merging process easier. This toolbar is located above the ruler and below the formatting toolbar, but does not appear until you use the Mail Merge Helper. To insert merge fields, position the insertion point in the place in the main document where you want to insert information from the data source. Then click Insert Merge Field on the Mail Merge toolbar and click the appropriate field name from the data source. Insert all the merge fields you want until your main document is complete. Click the Merge to New Document button and the data from the database is inserted into the merge fields to create the form letters.

FIGURE 6-5
Mail Merge toolbar

S TEP-BY-STEP ▷ 6.2

1. Open **Access** and the **Lakewood parents** database from the student data files. Open the **Fourth Grade** table.

2. Enlarge the table's window, if necessary, so all the fields and records are visible.

3. Open **Word** and the **Lakewood letter** document from the student data files.

4. Choose **Mail Merge** on the **Tools** menu. The Mail Merge Helper dialog box appears, as shown in Figure 6-4.

(continued on next page)

5. Click **Create**, and then choose **Form Letters**.

6. Click **Active Window**.

7. Click **Get Data**, and then choose **Open Data Source**. The Open Data Source dialog box appears.

8. Click the down arrow to the right of the **Files of type** list box. Click **MS Access Databases**.

9. Open the **Lakewood parents** database from the student data files. The Microsoft Access dialog box appears, as shown in Figure 6-6.

10. With the **Tables** tab displayed, highlight **Fourth Grade** and click **OK**.

11. When the Microsoft Word dialog box appears, as shown in Figure 6-7, click **Edit Main Document.** The *Lakewood letter* document appears on the screen.

12. Place the insertion point on the second line after the date.

13. Click the **Insert Merge Field** button on the Mail Merge toolbar.

14. Choose **Title** from the drop-down list.

15. Insert the rest of the merge fields shown in Figure 6-8 using the same method. (Be sure to add spaces where necessary and include a comma between the City and State merge fields.)

16. When finished, click the **Merge to New Document** button on the Mail Merge toolbar. The data from the database is inserted into the merge fields to create the form letters in a new file.

17. Scroll down the file to see the form letters.

18. Save the file as **Lake forms** and close it. Leave the **Lakewood letter** document open for the next Step-by-Step.

FIGURE 6-6
Microsoft Access dialog box

FIGURE 6-7
Microsoft Word dialog box

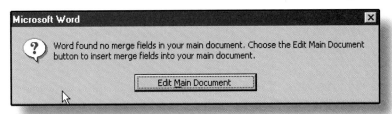

FIGURE 6-8
Inserted merge fields

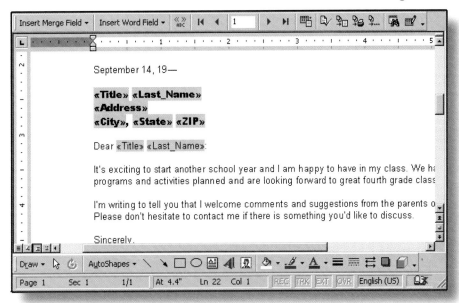

Using Query Options and Printing Form Letters

After the form letters have been created, they are ready to print. If you don't want to print every letter, you can click the Query Options button in the Mail Merge Helper. The Query Options dialog box will appear and you can then filter out only the records you want to merge and print.

STEP-BY-STEP 6.3

1. The **Lakewood letter** document should be open on your screen. Save it as **Lakewood letter 2**.

2. Click the **Mail Merge Helper** button on Word's Mail Merge toolbar. The Mail Merge Helper dialog box appears.

3. Click the **Query Options** button in Step 3. The Query Options dialog box appears.

4. You want to print only the letters to the parents of Ashlynn McNeal and Rafael Wade. In the **Field** box, click the down arrow and choose **Last Name**.

(continued on next page)

5. The *Comparison* box should read *Equal to*. In the **Compare to** box, key **McNeal**.

6. In the **And** box, click the down arrow and choose **Or**.

7. In the second **Field** box, click the down arrow and choose **Last Name**.

8. The *Comparison* box should read *Equal to*. In the **Compare to** box, key **Wade**. The Query Options dialog box should appear similar to Figure 6-9.

9. Click **OK**. The Mail Merge Helper dialog box reappears.

10. Click **Merge**. The Merge dialog box appears, as shown in Figure 6-10.

11. Click **Merge**. The two form letters you wanted to print are created in a new file.

12. Save the file as **Print form**.

13. Print the form letters by choosing **Print** on the **File** menu.

14. Click **OK**.

15. Close **Print form**. Save **Lakewood letter 2** and close it. Leave the **Fourth Grade** table and **Lakewood parents** database open.

FIGURE 6-9
Query Options dialog box

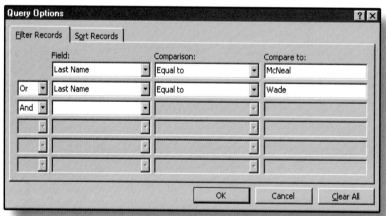

FIGURE 6-10
Merge dialog box

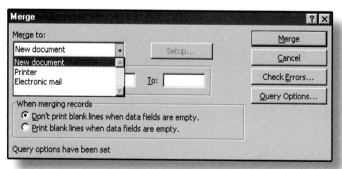

Mailing Labels

Office makes it easy to create mailing labels from any data source that has name and address information. In this activity, creating mailing labels involves integrating the Word and Access applications. Creating mailing labels is very similar to creating form letters. The main difference is that mailing labels place information from more than one record on the same page. This is because mailing labels usually come in sheets that have as many as 30 labels per page.

To create mailing labels, you will be using the Mail Merge Helper again. This time, choose Mailing Labels on the Create menu in the Mail Merge Helper dialog box. After specifying a main document and a data source, you can choose the label options you want, insert merge fields that contain the address information, and print your mailing labels.

S TEP-BY-STEP ▷ 6.4

1. Open a new Word document.

2. Choose **Mail Merge** on the **Tools** menu. The Mail Merge Helper dialog box appears.

3. Click **Create** and then click **Mailing Labels**.

4. Click **Active Window**.

5. Click **Get Data** and then click **Open Data Source**. The Open Data Source dialog box appears.

6. Click the down arrow to the right of the **Files of type** box. Click **MS Access Databases**.

7. Select **Lakewood parents** from the student data files, and click **Open**. The Microsoft Access dialog box appears.

8. With the Tables tab displayed, highlight **Fourth Grade** and click **OK**.

9. When the Microsoft Word dialog box appears, click **Set Up Main Document**. The Label Options dialog box appears, as shown in Figure 6-11.

10. From the **Printer Information** options, be sure **Laser and ink jet** is chosen, and then select the **Tray** option that you wish to use with your printer.

11. The **Label products** box should have **Avery standard** chosen. In the **Product number** box, scroll down to highlight **5160 - Address**.

12. Click **OK**. The Create Labels dialog box appears.

13. Click the **Insert Merge Field** button and insert merge fields into the **Sample label** box, as shown in Figure 6-12. (Be sure to add spaces where necessary and include a comma between the City and State merge fields.)

14. Click **OK**. The Mail Merge Helper reappears.

15. Click **Merge**. The Merge dialog box appears.

16. Click **Merge**. The labels are displayed in a new file.

17. Save the file as **Mailing Labels**.

18. Print the labels.

19. Close **Mailing Labels**. Close the unsaved document without saving changes. Exit Word and Access.

(continued on next page)

FIGURE 6-11
Label Options dialog box

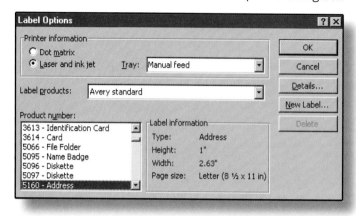

FIGURE 6-12
Create Labels dialog box

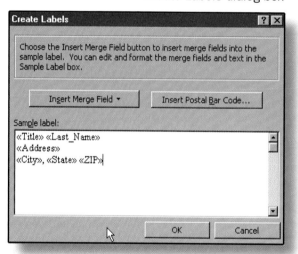

Summary

In this lesson, you learned:

■ Because Office is an integrated suite of programs, you can easily move and copy data between applications. No matter which applications you are using, the data is automatically formatted so that it can be used in the destination file.

■ A form letter is a word processor document that uses information from a database in specified areas to personalize a document. To create form letters, you insert merge fields in the main document that are replaced with information from the data source.

■ Creating mailing labels is very similar to creating form letters. The Mail Merge Helper and Mail Merge toolbar make it easy to create form letters or mailing labels.

LESSON 6 REVIEW QUESTIONS

TRUE/FALSE

Circle T if the statement is true or F if the statement is false.

T F 1. A merge field is a field name in the main document where you want to print the information from the data source.

T F 2. When moving and copying data with the Office suite of programs, the data is automatically formatted so it can be used in the destination file.

T F 3. The data source contains the information that stays the same in each form letter.

T F 4. The Mail Merge toolbar contains buttons to make the merging process easier.

T F 5. Click the Merge to New Document button to insert the data into the merge fields and create the form letters.

WRITTEN QUESTIONS

Write a brief answer to the following questions.

1. Which button do you click to filter out only the records to merge and print in a form letter?

2. Creating mailing labels involves integrating which two Office applications?

3. What is the Main Document in a form letter?

4. After opening a new Word document, what option do you choose on the Tools menu to create mailing labels?

5. What is a form letter?

LESSON 6 PROJECTS

PROJECT 6-1

1. Open **IA Project6-1** from the student data files, and then open the **Employee Information** table.

2. Open **Word** and the **Dinner letter** document from the student data files.

3. Use the Mail Merge Helper to create a form letter by merging the **Dinner letter** document with data from the **Employee Information** table. Insert the merge fields as shown in Figure 6-13. When finished merging, scroll down to see the form letters.

4. Save the new document as **Dinner form** and close it.

5. Leave the **Dinner letter** open for the next project.

FIGURE 6-13

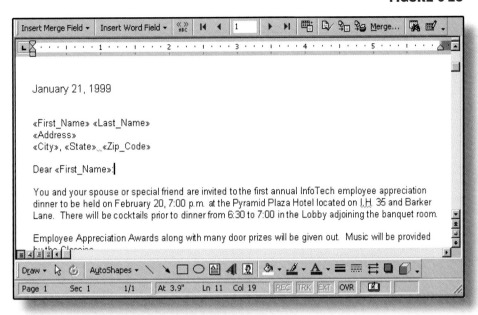

PROJECT 6-2

1. The Dinner letter should be open on your screen. Save it as **Dinner letter 2**.

2. Use the Mail Merge Helper to create a query to merge only the employees in the Public Relations department.

3. Save the new document as **PRForm**.

4. Print the form letters.

5. Close **PRForm**. Save **Dinner letter 2** and close. Leave the **Employee Information** table open.

PROJECT 6-3

1. Open a new Word document.

2. Use the Mail Merge Helper to create mailing labels. Merge the **Employee Information** table from the **IA Project6-1** database. Choose **Avery standard** in the **Label products** box. In the **Product number** box, scroll down to highlight **5160 – Address**.

3. Insert the merge fields as shown in Figure 6-14.

4. When finished, save the file as **Employee Labels**.

5. Print the labels.

6. Close **Employee Labels**. Close the unsaved document without saving changes. Exit Word and Access.

FIGURE 6-14

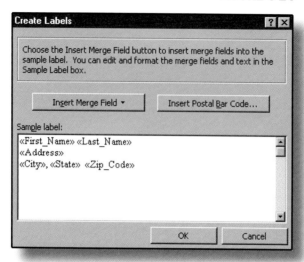

CRITICAL THINKING

ACTIVITY 6-1

SCANS

Teachers need to send consent forms to each student's parents at the beginning of the year. This allows the students to participate in field trips or special activities away from the school. Create a consent form by merging the **Consent letter** with data from the **Third grade** table in the **Washington parents** database. The letter and database are stored in the student data files. Save the new document as **Consent form**. Merge and print letters for only the students with last names of **Davis**, **Hope**, **Shihab**, and **Ellis**. Save the new document as **Late form**.

ACTIVITY 6-2

Using the Help feature, look up the steps for adding a hyperlink to a form or report in a database. Write down the basic steps. Give an example of why you might add a hyperlink to either an Inventory, Customer, or Vendor database.

COMMAND SUMMARY

FEATURE	MENU COMMAND	TOOLBAR BUTTON	LESSON
Close	File, Close	☒	1
Close a Table	File, Close	☒	1
Column Width	Format, Column Width		2
Compact and Repair a Database	Tools, Database Utilities, Compact and Repair Database		2
Copy Record	Edit, Copy	📋	2
Cut Record	Edit, Cut	✂	2
Database (create)	File, New		1
Datasheet View	Open	▦	1
Delete Record	Edit, Delete Record	✖	2
Delete Row	Edit, Delete Row	➡	1
Design View	Highlight name of Object, Design	📐 Design	1
Exit Access	File, Exit		1
Field Properties	Tables, Design	📐 Design	2
File, create	File, New, General tab, Database	▯	1
Filter, apply	Filter, Apply Filter/Sort	▽	3
Filter, create	Records, Filter		3
Filter, remove	Filter, Remove Filter/Sort	▽	3
Find Data	Edit, Find	♏	3
First Record		◄	2
Form, create	Forms, New		2

FEATURE	MENU COMMAND	TOOLBAR BUTTON	LESSON
Form, modify	Forms, Design		2
Freeze Column	Format, Freeze Columns		2
Index Field	General tab, Indexed		3
Insert Merge Field			5
Insert Row			1
Last Record			2
Macro, create	Macro, New		4
Mailing Labels, create	Tools, Mail Merge, Create, Mailing Labels		5
Mail Merge Helper	Tools, Mail Merge		5
Merge to New Document			5
New Record			2
Next Record			2
Open Existing Database	File, Open		1
Paste Record	Edit, Paste		2
Previous Record			2
Print	File, Print		1
Query, create	Queries, New, Design View		3
Relationships, define	Tools, Relationships		3
Relationships, print	File, Print Relationships		3
Report, create	Reports, New		4
Report, modify	Reports, Design		4
Row Height	Format, Row Height		2
Save	File, Save		1

FEATURE	MENU COMMAND	TOOLBAR BUTTON	LESSON
Sort Ascending	Records, Sort, Sort Ascending	A/Z↓	3
Sort Descending`	Records, Sort, Sort Descending	Z/A↓	3
Start Access	Start, Programs, Microsoft Access		1
Subdatasheet	Insert, Subdatasheet		3
Table, create	Table, New		1
Table, modify	Highlight name of Table, Design	Design	1
Undo Changes in Cell	Edit, Undo Typing	↜	2
Undo Changes in Previous Cell	Edit, Undo Current Field/ Record or Esc key		2
Unfreeze All Columns	Format, Unfreeze All Columns		2

REVIEW QUESTIONS

TRUE/FALSE

Circle T if the statement is true or F if the statement is false.

T F 1. A record appears as a column in Datasheet view.

T F 2. The navigation buttons are used to move around the datasheet.

T F 3. Queries allow the most complex searches.

T F 4. Sections are shown in Modify Report view.

T F 5. In the Label Options dialog box, you choose the data source you will be using for the mailing labels.

WRITTEN QUESTIONS

Write a brief answer to the following questions.

1. What data type is used to store dollar amounts?

2. What option makes Access choose the width of a column?

3. What button is used to cause the result of a filter to be displayed?

4. What is a macro?

5. In what document are merge fields inserted?

APPLICATION 1

1. Open the **IA App1** database from the student data files.

2. Open the **Stores** table in Datasheet view.

3. Move the **Hours** column between the **Specialty** and **Credit Cards** fields.

4. Move record **4** to the bottom of the table.

5. Close the table. Click **Yes** if prompted to save changes to the table.

6. Open the **Stores** table in Design view.

7. Insert a field between the **Specialty** and **Credit Card** fields. Name the field **Last Visit** with the **Date/Time** data type, and **Date of last visit** in the description field.

8. Choose **Medium Date** for the format of the **Last Visit** field.

9. Change the field size of the **Specialty** field to **25**.

10. Make the **Name** field **Required**.

11. Save the table design. A message may appear asking if you want to continue. Click **Yes**. Another message may appear asking if you want to test the changes. Click **Yes**.

12. Switch to Datasheet view and print the table in landscape orientation.

13. Close the table.

APPLICATION 2

1. The **IA App1** database should still be open. Create a new form with the Form Wizard using the **Stores** table.

2. Add the **Name**, **Specialty**, **Credit Cards**, and **Hours** fields.

3. Use the **Tabular** layout and the **Standard** style.

4. Title the form **Store Form**.

5. Insert the following record:

Name	Specialty	Credit Cards	Hours
Sports Authority	**Sporting Goods**	**Yes**	**9am to 9pm**

6. Print all the records in the form.

7. Close the form and the database.

APPLICATION 3

1. Open **IA App3** from the student data files.

2. Open the **Employee Information** table in Datasheet view.

3. Sort the table so that the employees's salaries are listed from lowest to highest.

4. Change the left and right margins to **.5"** and print the results of the sort in landscape orientation.

5. Create a query that displays the employees with a title of manager. Have the query display only the **Last Name**, **First Name**, **Department**, **Title**, and **Salary** fields. Save the query as **Managers**.

6. Run the query and print the results. Close the query.

APPLICATION 4

1. The **IA App3** database should still be open. Open the **Employee Information** table, and use the Find command to locate the employees with a title of Account Executive.

2. Create a filter to display only the employees in the Sales department.

3. Change the left and right margins to **.5"** and print the results of the filter in landscape orientation.

4. Show all the records in the table.

5. Close the table and the database.

APPLICATION 5

1. Open the database you created in the Lesson 1 Critical Thinking Activity.

2. Create a report that prints the information from your database. If possible, group the report by some field in your database.

3. Give the report an appropriate name and print it.

4. Close the database.

APPLICATION 6

1. Open the **IA App6** database from the student data files.

2. Create a macro to open the **Products** table in Datasheet view, print all the pages, and close the table.

3. Save the macro as **Print Products Table**.

4. Run the macro.

5. Close the database.

You work at the Java Internet Café, which has been open a short time. The café serves coffee, other beverages, and pastries, and offers Internet access. Seven computers are set up on tables along the north side of the store. Customers can come in and have a cup of coffee and a Danish, and explore the World Wide Web.

All membership fees for March were due on March 1. A few members have not paid their monthly dues. Your manager asks you to write a letter to the members as a reminder.

JOB 1

SCANS

1. Open **Word** and the **Payment Late Letter** from the student data files.

2. Save the document as **Payment Late Merge Letter**.

3. Open Excel and the **Computer Prices** workbook from the student data files.

4. In the spreadsheet, copy the range **A1** through **B11**, and paste it between the first and second paragraphs of the **Payment Late Merge Letter**. Make sure there is one blank line before and after the spreadsheet data.

5. Close **Computer Prices** without saving, and exit Excel.

6. Open **Access**, open the **Java members** database from the student data files, and then open the **Membership** table.

7. Scott Payton just paid his membership fee. Key **$10.00** in the March Paid field of his record.

8. Add the following new member to the end of the database:

   Ms. Halie Shook, 1290 Wood Crest Apt. 224, Boulder, CO 80302, March Paid = $10

9. Save the table and switch to Word.

10. Use the **Mail Merge Helper** to create form letters using the open database and Word document. Insert the merge fields as shown in Figure UR-1.

11. Use **Query Options** to create a query to merge the form letters for records with **0** in the **March Paid** field. (There should be three form letters.)

12. Merge the data into a new document.

13. Save the new document as **Payment form letter**.

14. Print the three form letters.

15. Close **Payment form letter**.

16. Save and close **Payment Late Merge Letter** and exit **Word**.

17. Close **Java members** and exit Access.

FIGURE UR-1

Java Internet Café

2001 Zephyr Street
Boulder, CO 80302-2001
303.555.JAVA JavaCafe@Cybershop.com

March 15, ----

«Name»
«Address»
«City_State_Zip»

Our records show that you have not paid your $10 membership fee, which was due March 1. We hope you plan to continue your membership with us. Membership lowers your hourly access fees and includes an e-mail account as explained below.

JOB 2

You need to create mailing labels for the form letters you printed yesterday.

1. Open a new Word document.

2. Use the **Mail Merge Helper** to create mailing labels for the three letters you printed yesterday.

3. Use the **Active Window** as the Main Document and the **Java members** database as the Data Source.

4. Choose the **5162 - Address** labels.

5. Insert the merge fields **Name**, **Address**, and **City_State_Zip** on the sample label.

6. Use **Query Options** to create a query to merge only the records with **0** in the **March Paid** field. Merge the data into a new document.

7. Highlight the labels and change the font size to **14** pt.

8. Save the labels document as **Late labels**.

9. Print the labels and close.

10. Close the unsaved document without saving changes and exit Word.

11. Close **Java Members** and exit Access.

ADVANCED MICROSOFT® ACCESS

lesson 1   1 hr.

Modifying Table Design

lesson 2   1 hr.

Relationships in Tables and Queries

lesson 3   1 hr.

Advanced Form Features

lesson 4   1.5 hrs.

Analyzing Data

lesson 5   1.5 hrs.

Advanced Queries

lesson 6   1.5 hrs.

Advanced Report Features

lesson 7   1 hr.

Importing and Exporting Data

lesson 8   1.5 hrs.

Creating Macros and Switchboards

lesson 9   1 hr.

Working with Web Features

lesson 10   1 hr.

Using Advanced Access Tools

⏱ Estimated Time for Unit: 12 hours

MODIFYING TABLE DESIGN

OBJECTIVES

Upon completion of this lesson, you should be able to:

- Understand the use of input masks.
- Select the correct input mask.
- Enter data with input masks.
- Use validation rules and text.
- Set required properties.
- Set lookup fields.

⏱ Estimated Time: 1 hour

Introduction

Microsoft Access is a powerful database application that lets you store, organize, and manipulate vast amounts of data. You should already be familiar with the primary objects that comprise a database: tables, forms, queries, reports, and macros. In the next 10 lessons, you'll learn more about each of these objects, plus other features that help you manage and control your database records.

In this lesson, you will learn more about the various data types you can apply when defining fields in a table. You will also explore the properties associated with particular fields. The lesson will discuss the use of input masks in setting up data types for fields. You will also learn about applying validation rules to data and how to create a lookup field.

Choosing an Input Mask

An *input mask* is a predetermined format for certain types of data entered in a field. For example, if you need to enter phone numbers in the format (XXX) XXX-XXXX, it might get tiresome typing both parentheses and the dash. Instead, you can apply Access's Phone Number input mask and then all you need to type is the numbers. The input mask inserts the parentheses and hyphen in the correct positions.

To create an input mask, you must be in the table's Design view. Select the field you want to create the input mask for and then click in the Input Mask text box in the Field Properties pane. The Build button (an ellipsis) appears at the end of the text box, as shown in Figure 1-1.

FIGURE 1-1
Applying an input mask

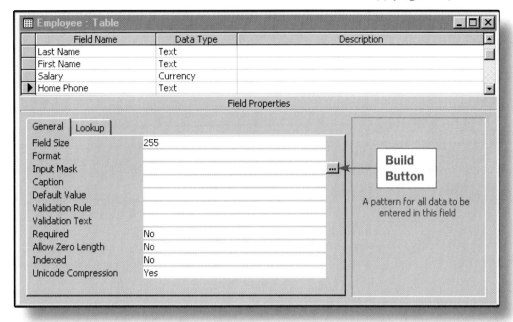

Click the Build button. A message box displays, requesting that you save the table before continuing. Click Yes to save the table. Access will then start the Input Mask Wizard, as shown in Figure 1-2. There are 10 common input mask formats from which you can choose.

FIGURE 1-2
Input Mask Wizard

Select an input mask and then click in the Try It box to see an example of how your data will look. If you want to edit the mask, click the Edit List button to create a custom input mask. Once you select the mask you need, click the Next button to go to the next step in the Input Mask Wizard, as shown in Figure 1-3.

FIGURE 1-3
Second step in the Input Mask Wizard

Input Mask Wizard

Do you want to change the input mask?

Input Mask Name: Phone Number

Input Mask: !(999) 000-0000

What placeholder character do you want the field to display?

Placeholders are replaced as you enter data into the field.

Placeholder character: _ ▼

Try It:

Cancel   < Back   Next >   Finish

This step of the wizard asks you if you need to make changes to this mask. You may also select the placeholder for your number. The default is the underscore. The placeholder simply identifies in the table that there is an input mask assigned to the field. The placeholder is replaced by the data you enter in the field. Click the Next button and the Input Mask Wizard dialog box shown in Figure 1-4 appears.

In this step of the wizard, you decide how to store the data. For example, you may want a date field stored in the format *mm-dd-yy*. Just select this format and Access will store newly entered dates with this format. Most often, data will be stored with the symbols. Click the Next button and the final Input Mask Wizard dialog box appears, as shown in Figure 1-5. Clicking the Finish button will create your mask.

You can create an input mask when you define a field or after the field has been defined and data entered in it.

Hot Tip

When you apply an input mask to an existing field that already contains data, Access typically asks you to check the existing data with the new rules. Click **Yes** to apply the input mask. However, Microsoft Technical Support reports that there are some inconsistencies when the input mask formats actually change existing data.

FIGURE 1-4
Determining how to store data in the Input Mask Wizard

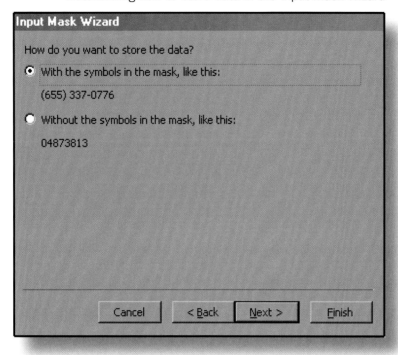

FIGURE 1-5
Final Input Mask Wizard dialog box

C

1. Open the **AA Step1-1** database from the student data files.

2. Open the **Employees** table in Design view.

3. Select the **Home Phone** field name.

4. In the Field Properties pane, click in the **Input Mask** text box.

5. Click the **Build** button to start the Input Mask Wizard.

6. Select the **Phone Number** input mask, if necessary. Click **Next**.

7. You will not change the input mask. Click **Next**.

8. If necessary, select the **With the symbols in the mask, like this** option. Click **Next**.

9. Click **Finish** to apply your mask. Your screen should look similar to Figure 1-6. (After you save the table design, Access will add additional punctuation.)

FIGURE 1-6
Applying the phone number input mask

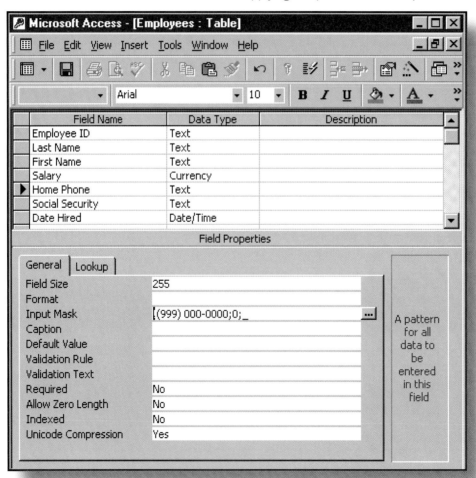

10. Let's create another input mask. Select the **Social Security** field name.

11. In the Field Properties pane, click in the **Input Mask** text box.

12. Click the **Build** button to start the Input Mask Wizard.

13. Click **Yes** to save the table.

14. Click the **Social Security Number** input mask. Click **Next**.

15. You will not change the input mask. Click **Next**.

16. If necessary, select the **With the symbols in the mask, like this** option. Click **Next**.

17. Click **Finish** to apply your mask. Click **Save**. Your screen should look like Figure 1-7.

18. Switch to Datasheet view. Remain in this screen for the next Step-by-Step.

FIGURE 1-7
Applying the Social Security input mask

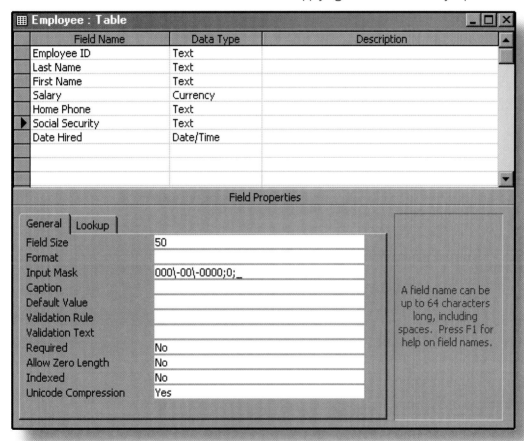

Entering Data with Input Masks

After you have applied an input mask to a field, the format will be applied automatically as you enter new records.

STEP-BY-STEP ▷ 1.2

1. Go to the **Home Phone** field of record **5** and select the value currently entered.

2. Type **8175557373**. When you start to type, underscores appear. This indicates that a mask has been applied to the field.

3. Press **Tab** to go to the **Social Security** field.

4. Type **000000005**. Notice how the input mask inserts the hyphens where appropriate.

5. Click in a different record to save the changes.

6. Adjust the column widths in the table as you feel appropriate. Then print the table in landscape orientation. Close the table and remain in this screen for the next Step-by-Step.

Setting Validation Rules

You can enhance the efficiency of data entry by setting validation rules. *Validation rules* are properties applied to a field that either require certain values to be entered or prevent them from being entered in a field. For example, validation rules can require that data entered in a salary field not exceed a certain dollar amount, such as $50,000. This can help prevent data entry errors and increase accuracy and conformity.

When you set a validation rule on a field, you are given the option to create a message that explains the validation rule to the data entry person. The validation text is displayed in a message box that appears when data entered into the cell does not meet the validation rule. Using the above example, if a dollar amount greater than $50,000 is entered in the salary field, the validation message might be "Salary amounts cannot exceed $50,000."

> **Hot Tip**
>
> Validation rules will be applied only to new data that is entered into a field.

STEP-BY-STEP ▷ 1.3

1. Click **Tables** on the Objects bar and double-click **Create table in Design view**.

2. Define two fields for the table: The first field should be named **Product Description** and should be the **Text** data type. The second

field should be named **Product Price** and should be the **Currency** data type.

3. Click the **Save** button, enter **Product Sales** as the table name, and click **OK**.

4. Select **No** if asked to create a primary key field.

5. Select the **Product Price** field name.

6. In the Field Properties pane, click in the **Validation Rule** box and enter **<50**. This will restrict any product price that is equal to or more than $50 from being entered.

7. Click in the **Validation Text** box and enter **All product prices are less than $50**.

8. Click the **Save** button and then switch to Datasheet view.

9. Enter the following records:

Product Description	Product Price
Dog Carrier - Small	$27.50
Dog Carrier - Large	$500.00

10. When you press **Enter**, you should see a message box that displays the validation text as shown in Figure 1-8. Click **OK**.

FIGURE 1-8
Message box

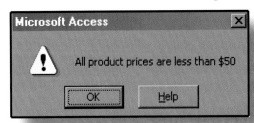

11. Enter **$47.50** for the Product Price and press **Enter**. Notice that Access accepts this amount since it is less than $50. Remain in this screen for the next Step-by-Step.

Setting Required Properties

For some fields, you may want to apply the Required property, which means that the field cannot be left blank when records are entered. For example, you might set up a table so that a customer's phone number must be entered in the phone number field. Access will not move to another record until data is entered in this field.

S TEP-BY-STEP ▷ 1.4

1. Switch to Design view, if necessary.

2. Select the **Product Description** field and then click in the **Required** property text box.

3. Click the down arrow that appears at the end of the *Required* text box and click **Yes**.

4. Click the **Save** button. Access displays a dialog box that asks if you want to test the existing field information with the new required property selection. Click **Yes**.

5. Click the **View** button to switch to Datasheet view.

6. Go to the first empty **Product Price** field.

7. Key **$43.00** for the Product Price and press **Enter**.

8. You will see a warning box as shown in Figure 1-9 that explains that the Product Description field cannot contain a Null value. Click **OK** to close the warning box.

(continued on next page)

FIGURE 1-9
Warning box

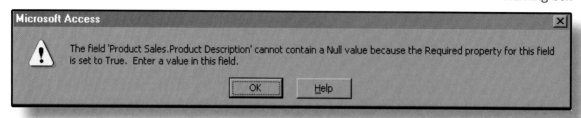

Microsoft Access

⚠ The field 'Product Sales.Product Description' cannot contain a Null value because the Required property for this field is set to True. Enter a value in this field.

[OK]   [Help]

9. Click in the **Product Description** field for the record you are adding and enter **Cat Carrier - Medium**.

10. Close the table.

Creating Lookup Fields

You can define a *lookup field* in a table as a field that actually "looks up" and pulls data from a field in another table or query in the database. Looking up data from existing tables can help prevent data entry errors. You create a lookup field by using the Lookup Wizard. Or you can click the Lookup tab in the Field Properties pane and specify the table or query containing the data you want to look up.

In the following Step-by-Step, you will create a table that has only one field. This field will contain several shipping options. After this table is created, you will open an existing table and "look up" data in the new table in order to insert values in the existing table.

STEP-BY-STEP ▷ 1.5

1. Create a new table in Design view.

2. Define a field named **Shipping Terms** of **Text** data type.

3. Click the **Save** button, enter **Shipping Terms** as the table name, and click **OK**.

4. Select **No** if asked to create a primary key field.

5. Click the **View** button to switch to Datasheet view.

6. Enter the following shipping terms as new records:

Record 1	Net 10th
Record 2	COD
Record 3	Cash Only
Record 4	1% in 10 Days

7. Close the **Shipping Terms** table.

8. Open the **Product Sales** table in Design view.

9. Define a new field named **Shipping Terms** with the **Text** data type.

10. With the **Shipping Terms** field selected, click the **Lookup** tab in the *Field Properties* pane.

11. Click in the **Display Control** box.

12. Click the down arrow at the end of the *Display Control* box and click **List Box**.

13. Click in the **Row Source** box.

14. Click the down arrow at the end of the Row Source text box and click **Shipping Terms**.

15. Click the **Save** button and switch to Datasheet view.

16. Add a new record: Enter Cat Carrier - Small in the Product Description field and **$23.50** in the Product Price field.

17. In the **Shipping Terms** field, click the down arrow. Your screen should look similar to Figure 1-10. Choose **1% in 10 Days**.

18. Enter **Net 10th** as the shipping term for the remaining records.

19. Adjust the column widths in the table, if necessary. Then print the table and close the database.

FIGURE 1-10
Lookup field

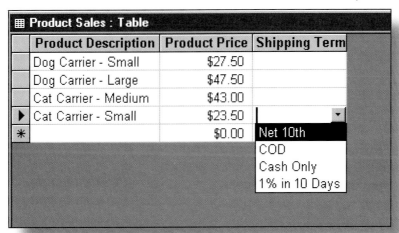

Summary

In this lesson, you learned:

- Input masks are used to save data entry time and improve accuracy of the data entered.

- After the input mask is created, data entered into the field will display the new format. In most instances, an input mask created on an existing field will apply the formatting changes to values already entered in the field.

- Validation rules can help prevent data entry errors by indicating when incorrect data is entered.

- When you apply the required property to a field, Access requires that a value be entered in the field before it lets you complete the record entry. Access will not allow another field to be selected until the field with required properties has data entered.

- A lookup field lets you pull or "look up" data from another table or query in the same database.

LESSON 1 REVIEW QUESTIONS

WRITTEN QUESTIONS

Write a brief answer to the following questions.

1. How many input masks are provided in the Input Mask Wizard?

2. To which data types can you add an input mask?

3. What does the Input Mask Wizard do?

4. When you assign an input mask to a field that already contains data, what happens to that data?

5. Why would you want to assign an input mask to a field?

6. Explain the difference between a validation rule and validation text.

7. Explain the purpose of the Required field property.

8. What is the benefit of creating a lookup field?

9. Explain the steps for creating a lookup field.

10. Explain the steps for setting a Required property field to Yes.

LESSON 1 PROJECTS

PROJECT 1-1

1. Open the database **AA Project1-1** from the student data files.

2. Open the **Employees** table.

3. Enter an input mask for the Social Security field.

4. Make this field a Required field.

5. Print the table in landscape orientation.

6. Save and close the database.

PROJECT 1-2

1. Open the database **AA Project1-2** from the student data files.

2. Open the **Employees** table.

3. Make the **Employee ID** field a Required field and create an input mask for the **Phone Number** field.

4. Print the table.

5. Save and close the database.

CRITICAL THINKING

ACTIVITY 1-1

SCANS

You are the office manager for the Sadie Products Corporation. After viewing the company's existing database, **AA Activity1-1**, you realize that a new table needs to be created for recording sales information.

1. Define the following fields in the table:

   Customer ID
   Employee ID
   Product ID
   Quantity Sold

2. Save the table as **January Sales**.

3. For the Employee ID field, apply the lookup property so that you can pull data from the **Employees** table, using the **List Box** display control.

4. Create input masks for the fields that you think they would apply to.

ACTIVITY 1-2

SCANS

You should be familiar with how to change the Field Size property in a table. However, there are a number of different Field Size properties associated with fields that are defined as Number types. These include *byte*, *long integer*, *single*, and *double*. Use the Access Help system to find information on the different types of Number field size properties. Write a brief essay explaining the type of data to which you would apply these properties.

A A - 1 5

RELATIONSHIPS IN TABLES AND QUERIES

OBJECTIVES

Upon completion of this lesson, you should be able to:

- Understand relationships in tables.
- Create relationships among multiple tables.
- Enforce referential integrity.
- Create a query using related tables.

⏱ Estimated Time: 1 hour

Introduction

In this lesson, you will learn how to create relationships between tables. When tables are related, or joined, you have the ability to create forms, queries, and reports that pull fields and records from all tables in the relationship.

Understanding Table Relationships

Most databases contain more than one table. And more than likely, one or more of the tables contain identical data in at least one field. For example, a business might have a table containing customer names, customer ID numbers, and addresses, and another table that contains customer ID numbers and purchases or orders. If two or more tables contain a common field like the customer ID numbers in the preceding example, you can link these fields to create a relationship between the tables. Then you can create queries, forms, and reports using the data from the tables in the relationship.

There are three types of relationships that can be created in Access: a one-to-many relationship, a one-to-one relationship, and a many-to-many relationship. A *one-to-many relationship* exists when you relate a table whose common field is a primary key field to a table that does not have the common field as a primary key field. As you know, a *primary key* is a field that contains a value that uniquely identifies the record. Each value in this field must be unique. A *foreign key* is a field that refers to the primary key field in a related table.

Table 2-1 illustrates the one-to-many relationship. The Salesperson Number field in the Salesperson table is a primary key field. This field is a primary key field because you want only one ID number assigned to each salesperson. In the Invoice table, you would not want the Salesperson Number to be a primary key field because each salesperson will make many sales and you would need to enter the Saleperson Number for each sale.

TABLE 2-1
One-to-many relationship

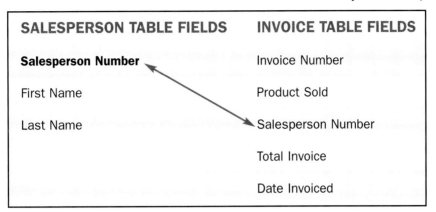

SALESPERSON TABLE FIELDS	INVOICE TABLE FIELDS
Salesperson Number	Invoice Number
First Name	Product Sold
Last Name	Salesperson Number
	Total Invoice
	Date Invoiced

It's important to remember that related fields are not required to have the same field name. However, related fields must be of the same data type.

When you set up a relationship between or among tables, you will be asked if you want to enforce referential integrity. *Referential integrity* simply refers to having Access check new data as it is entered into related fields. For example, as data is entered into the Salesperson Number field in the Salary table (shown in Table 2-1), Access will check to see if this is a correct number in the Salesperson Number field in the Salesperson table. If the Salesperson number that is being entered into the Salary table is not found in the Salesperson table, then Access will display an error message. This will alert the person entering the data to reenter the correct Salesperson ID number into the Salary table. This feature improves the accuracy and consistency of data entered.

Concept Builder

Remember, if a table has a primary key field, each record must have unique (nonmatching) information in this field.

STEP-BY-STEP 2.1

1. Open the database **AA Step2-1** from the student data files.

2. Click the **Relationships** button on the toolbar. Then select **Show Table** on the **Relationships** menu. The Show Table dialog box appears, as shown on Figure 2-1.

3. Select **Marketing Department** and then click **Add**. The Marketing Department table window is added to the Relationships window.

Hot Tip

You can also double-click on a table in the Show Table dialog box to add it to the Relationships window.

4. Select the **March Orders** table and click **Add**.

5. Click the **Close** button to close the Show Table dialog box. Your screen should look similar to Figure 2-2. Remain in this screen for the next Step-by-Step.

(continued on next page)

A A - 1 7

FIGURE 2-1
Show Table dialog box

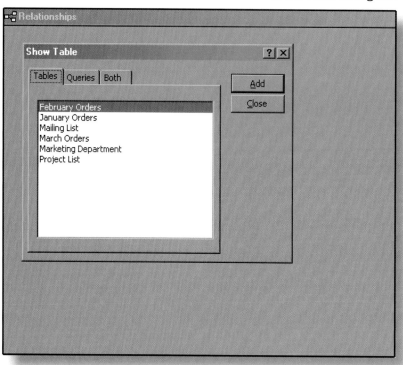

FIGURE 2-2
Relationships window with tables displayed

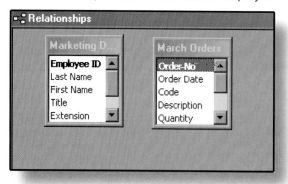

Defining Relationships Between Tables

To define a relationship between selected tables in the Relationships window, you drag a field from the primary table to the field in the related table that contains the same data. Once you release the mouse button, the Edit Relationships dialog box appears, as shown in Figure 2-3. The Edit Relationships dialog box displays options for enforcing referential integrity. Referential integrity can only be enforced between tables in the same database.

If you choose to enforce referential integrity, two options in the dialog box become available. The first option, *Cascade Update Related Fields*, allows for updates to occur between the primary table and the related table in the joined fields. For example, to change a salesperson's number, you would change it in the primary table and Access would automatically change that field information in the related table.

The second option, *Cascade Delete Related Records*, lets you delete a record in the primary table. Upon deleting the record in the primary table, Access will delete the record in the related table. Access finds the correct record or records by the joined field.

FIGURE 2-3
Edit Relationships dialog box

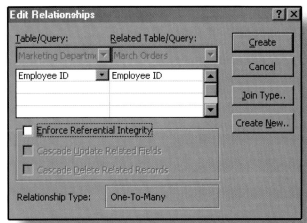

STEP-BY-STEP ▷ 2.2

1. If necessary, scroll the March Orders table to display the **Employee ID** field.

2. Select the **Employee ID** field in the **Marketing Department** table. From the bold type, you can tell that this is the primary key.

3. In the Edit Relationships dialog box, click the check box beside **Enforce Referential Integrity**.

4. Click **Create**. Your screen should look similar to Figure 2-4. Remain in this screen for the next Step-by-Step.

FIGURE 2-4
Relationship established

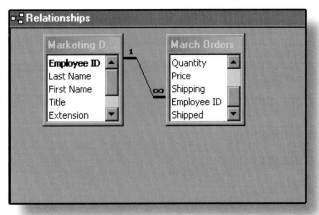

A A - 1 9

Notice the symbols on the relationship line connecting the two tables in Figure 2-4. The 1 indicates the primary table, and the infinity symbol (∞) indicates the related table. These symbols refer to the type of relationship that has been created. In this example, the 1 means that the Employee ID number can only appear one time in the Employee ID field in the Marketing Department table. However, since each employee can make many sales in March, the Employee ID can appear more than once in the March Orders table; thus, the infinity symbol. Therefore, this relationship is a one-to-many relationship.

STEP-BY-STEP ▷ 2.3

1. Close the **Relationships** dialog box.

2. Click **Yes** to save the layout changes.

3. Open the **March Orders** table. This is the related table.

4. Click the **New Record** button. Enter the following information:

Field Name	Information
Order No.	3050
Order Date	3/15/00
Code	DB-BB
Description	Beginning Databases
Quantity	155
Price	$19.00
Shipping	$2.00
Employee ID	S555
Shipped	No

Hot Tip

You can press Ctrl+; to enter the current date.

5. Press **Enter**. Access cannot add the record to the table because there is no Employee ID *S555* in the primary table, Marketing Department. You should see a message box as shown in Figure 2-5.

6. Click **OK** to close the message box.

7. Click in the **Employee ID** field of the new record you just entered and key **N205**. Press **Enter**. Close the table.

8. Remain in this screen for the next Step-by-Step.

FIGURE 2-5
Message box

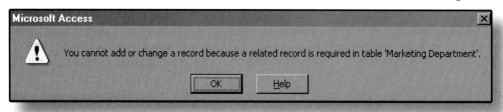

In the preceding Step-by-Step, it is important to understand why the message box appeared. If you need to enter a record in the March Orders table for an employee who is not yet recorded in the Marketing Department table, Access will display the message about adding or changing a record. A record for the employee must first be entered in the Marketing Department table.

STEP-BY-STEP ▷ 2.4

1. Open the **Marketing Department** table.

2. Click the **New Record** button and add the following record. Once you've entered the record, your screen should look similar to Figure 2-6.

Field Name	Information
Employee ID	S555
Last Name	Walters
First Name	William
Title	Marketing Rep
Extension	229
Date Hired	3/15/00
Salary	$62,000

 **Hot Tip**

If you close the table and reopen it, the records will be sorted according to the primary key field. In this Step-by-Step, records are sorted by Employee ID.

3. Close the **Marketing Department** table and remain in this screen for the next Step-by-Step.

FIGURE 2-6
Adding a record

Employee ID	Last Name	First Name	Title	Extension	Date Hired	Salary
N125	Loyal	Sally	Marketing Rep	338	10/12/97	$54,800.00
N175	Limosine	John	Marketing Assistant	442	5/7/97	$32,000.00
N205	Kemper	Bertha	Marketing Assistant	265	5/7/95	$46,000.00
N440	Lopez	Karen	Marketing Manager	410	11/26/90	$45,200.00
N445	Woodard	Katheryn	Marketing Assistant	932	12/3/97	$39,000.00
N522	Robinson	Harold	Secretary	543	3/6/92	$30,000.00
N550	Gordon	Kelly	Marketing Rep	435	5/2/97	$35,000.00
N660	Anderson	David	Marketing Rep	876	2/27/95	$43,500.00
N750	Joshua	John	Marketing Rep	564	4/20/95	$43,390.00
S330	Martin	Annie	Secretary	912	1/5/94	$38,500.00
S525	Taylor	Helen	Marketing Rep	234	8/9/89	$34,450.00
S535	Williamson	Kori	Marketing Assistant	654	3/11/97	$29,000.00
S555	Walters	William	Marketing Rep	229	3/15/00	$62,000.00
S604	Smith	Jeff	Marketing Rep	411	4/7/90	$41,800.00
S605	Johnson	Jennifer	Marketing Rep	287	1/25/89	$48,000.00
S880	Davidson	Zach	Marketing Rep	581	7/10/89	$56,040.00

Marketing Department : Table

Now that the record for this employee is entered in the Marketing Department table, you enter any orders for him in the March Orders table.

1. Open the **March Orders** table.

2. Click the **New Record** button, and enter the following information:

Field Name	Information
Order No.	3051
Order Date	3/15/00
Code	DB-BD
Description	Beginning Publishing
Quantity	193
Price	$15.95
Shipping	$3.00
Employee ID	S555
Shipped	No

3. Adjust column widths in the table, if necessary. Print the table in landscape orientation and then close it. Remain in this screen for the next Step-by-Step.

Adding Tables to a Relationship

You can have more than two tables in a relationship. For example, in the previous Step-by-Steps, you created a relationship between the Marketing Department table and the March Orders table by joining their Employee ID fields. You can add another table to the relationship, as long as it contains a field that is also contained in either the Marketing Department or March Orders tables, or both.

Hot Tip

You can edit or delete relationships by *right*-clicking the join line between tables and choosing either the Edit or Delete options on the shortcut menu.

1. Click the **Relationships** button. The current table relationship is displayed in the Relationships window.

2. Click the **Show Table** button.

3. Select the **February Orders** table, click **Add**, and then select the **January Orders** table and click **Add**.

4. Click **Close** to close the dialog box.

5. In the **Marketing Department** table, drag the **Employee ID** field to the **Employee ID** field in the **February Orders** table, click the **Enforce Referential Integrity** check box, and click **Create**. Repeat this procedure for the **January Orders** table. Your screen should look similar to Figure 2-7.

6. Close the **Relationships** window.

7. Select **Yes** to save the relationships. Remain in this screen for the next Step-by-Step.

FIGURE 2-7
Multiple table relationship

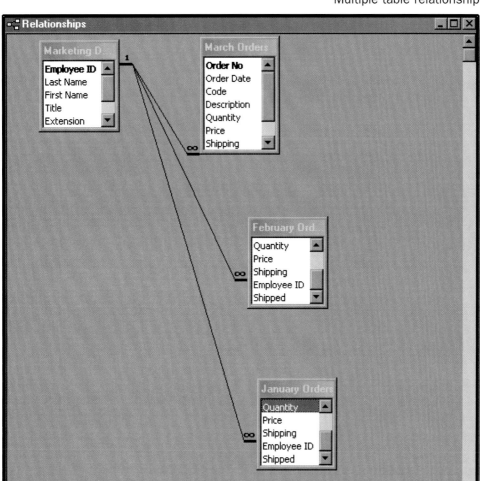

Setting and Removing Joins in a Query

After you've created a relationship between tables, you can pull information from the related tables in a query, form, or report. Using related tables in forms and reports is discussed in later lessons.

If your tables are not joined in a relationship, you can define the relationship in the query itself. As you probably remember, when you are in the query's Design view, a window containing the field names of the table you are querying appears in the top pane. When you select more than one table to query, a window for each table will appear in the top pane. To join tables, simply drag the field names as you did in the Relationships window.

If you need to remove the line joining the tables, thereby removing the relationship, simply click the line and then press Delete.

S TEP-BY-STEP ▷ 2.7

1. In the Database window, click **Queries** on the Objects bar. Then double-click **Create query in Design view**.

2. Double-click the **Marketing Department** table and then double-click the **January Orders** table to add them to the query window.

3. Click **Close** to close the Show Table dialog box.

4. You will see a line appear between the **Marketing Department** and **January Orders** tables because you created a relationship between these tables in the previous Step-by-Step. Let's practice deleting a relationship in queries and then you'll reestablish the relationship.

5. To delete this relationship line, simply click on the line and press **Delete**.

6. Place the mouse pointer over the **Employee ID** field in the **Marketing Department** table

and drag it to the **Employee ID** field in the **January Orders** table. You will see a line appear between the two tables, as shown in Figure 2-8. Notice how the 1 and ∞ symbols do not appear. You would need to open the Relationships window in order to select the one-to-many relationship. Access assumes this type of relationship in a query.

7. Double-click the **Order No** and **Quantity** fields from the **January Orders** table and the **Last Name** field from the **Marketing Department** table.

8. Sort the **Last Name** field in **Ascending** order.

9. Save the query as **Qry-January Orders by Rep** and then click the **Run** button to run the query.

10. Adjust the column widths and then print the results of the query. Close the query and then close the database.

FIGURE 2-8
Relationship created in a query

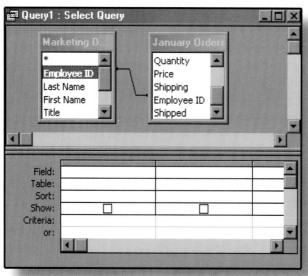

Establishing One-to-One Relationships

In a **one-to-one relationship**, each record in Table A can have only one matching record in Table B and each record in Table B can have only one matching record in Table A. This is because the common fields in these tables are both primary key fields. Table 2-2 illustrates the one-to-one relationship. Notice that in the Salesperson table, the Salesperson Number is a primary key field. This means that each salesperson is assigned his or her own individual number. In the Salary table, the Salesperson Number is also a primary key field for obvious reasons. You do not want a salesperson's number duplicated in this table or that individual will receive two paychecks!

TABLE 2-2
One-to-one relationship

SALESPERSON TABLE FIELDS	SALARY TABLE FIELDS
Salesperson Number	**Salesperson Number**
First Name	Position
Last Name	Salary

S TEP-BY-STEP ▷ 2.8

1. Open the **AA Step2-8** database from the student data files.

2. Open each table to view the fields and records. Close the tables after viewing them.

3. Click the **Relationships** button.

4. Double-click the **Employee Information** table and the **Benefits Package** table to add them to the Relationships window.

5. Click the **Close** button to close the **Show Table** dialog box.

6. Place your mouse pointer over the **Employee Number** field in the **Employee Information** table.

Press and hold the mouse button down and drag to the **Employee Number** field in the **Benefits Package** table.

7. In the Edit Relationships dialog box, notice that the relationship is identified at the bottom as a *One-To-One*. Access recognizes that this is a one-to-one relationship.

8. Click **Create** to create the relationship. Then, click **Save** to save the relationship.

9. Close the Relationships window. Then, close the database.

Establishing Many-to-Many Relationships

A *many-to-many relationship* exists when a record in Table A has many matching records in Table B, and a record in Table B has many matching records in Table A, *and* a record in either Table A or Table B has many matching records in Table C.

Figure 2-9 shows an example of this type of relationship. Table A contains order information, with fields named Order Number (primary key), Customer Name, and Employee Number. Table B contains production information, with fields named Product ID (primary key), Product Name, and Selling Price. Table C contains different information on orders, with fields named Order Number (foreign key that refers to Table A), Product ID (foreign key that refers to Table B), and Selling Price.

FIGURE 2-9
Many-to-many relationship

Table A

Order Number	Customer Name	Employee Number
2000	Bill's Print Shop	1600
2001	Juarez Accounting	2300

Table C

Order Number	Product ID	Selling Price
2000	25	$ 14.95
2000	32	$ 17.95
2001	25	$ 14.95

Table B

Product ID	Product Name	Selling Price
25	Paper – Copy	$ 14.95
32	Paper - Laser	$ 17.95
37	Toner Cartridge	$ 32.45

S TEP-BY-STEP ▷ 2.9

C

1. Open the **AA Step2-9** database from the student data files.

2. Open each table to view the fields and records. Close the tables after viewing them.

3. Click the **Relationships** button.

4. Double-click the **Orders**, **Order Details**, and **Products** tables to add them to the Relationships window.

5. Click the **Close** button to close the **Show Table** dialog box.

6. Place your mouse pointer over the **Product ID** field in the **Products** table. Press and hold the mouse button down and drag to the **Product ID** field in the **Order Details** table.

7. In the Edit Relationships dialog box, notice that the relationship is identified at the bottom as an *Indeterminate*. Access recognizes that this is *not* a one-to-one or one-to-many relationship.

8. Click **Create** to create the relationship. Then, click **Save** to save the relationship.

9. Place your mouse pointer over the **Order Number** field in the **Orders** table. Press and hold down the mouse button and drag to the **Order Number** field in the **Order Details** table.

10. Click **Create** to create the relationship. Then, click **Save** to save the relationship.

11. Close the Relationships window, and then close the database file.

Summary

In this lesson, you learned:

■ Creating a relationship between tables allows you to use information from both tables in forms, queries, and reports. In order to create a relationship, the tables must contain a common field of data.

■ There are three basic types of relationships: one-to-many, one-to-one, and many-to-many. A one-to-many relationship exists when you relate a table with a primary key field to a table where the common field is not a primary key field. Information in the primary table's key field will appear only once in the table, whereas information in the common field in the related table can appear many times because it is not a primary key field. A one-to-one relationship exists when the common field is a primary key field in both tables. A many-to-many relationship can exist between three or more tables.

■ Referential integrity refers to having Access check new data as it is entered into related fields. This feature helps the accuracy and consistency of data entered.

■ You can create relationships in a query's Design view. You can also delete relationships in the query window by clicking the join line and pressing Delete.

LESSON 2 REVIEW QUESTIONS

WRITTEN QUESTIONS

Write a brief answer to the following questions.

1. Why would you want to link tables together in a database?

2. In creating relationships, what is a primary table?

3. Explain what referential integrity does.

4. What is a one-to-many relationship?

5. List the steps for joining two tables in a query and explain why this feature is useful.

MATCHING

Match the correct term in Column 2 to its description in Column 1.

Column 1		**Column 2**
_____ 1.	Requires unique data to be entered into every record.	**A.** Referential integrity
_____ 2.	Field whose data type is the same in each table in a relation-ship, but whose field name can vary.	**B.** One-to-many relationship
_____ 3.	Checks data entry in a related table against data in the primary key table to be certain data exists in both tables.	**C.** One-to-one relationship
		D. Primary key field
_____ 4.	In this type of relationship, a table with a primary key field is related to a nonprimary key field in another table.	**E.** Common field
_____ 5.	In this type of relationship, the common field in related tables is the primary key field in the tables.	

PROJECT 2-1

1. Open the database **AA Project2-1** from the student data files.

2. Create a one-to-many relationship between the **Products** and **Transactions** tables by linking the common field.

3. Enforce referential integrity and save the relationship.

4. Create a query in Design view using the **Transactions** table and the **Customers** table. You will need to create a relationship between the tables using the Customer ID field in each table.

5. Add the **Transaction Number**, **Company Name**, **Quantity**, **Date Ordered**, and **Date Shipped** fields to the query in that order. The Company Name field is in the Customers table; the rest of the fields are in the Transactions table.

6. Save the query as **Qry-Transactions by Customer** and then run the query.

7. Adjust column widths, if necessary. Print the query results and then close the database.

CRITICAL THINKING

ACTIVITY 2-1

SCANS

You are an Office Manager at Bayside Supplies. After a conversation with the owner of the company, you have determined that you need a printout of your customers and their transactions for the year. Using the **AA Activity2-1** database in the student data files, create and print a query with this information.

ACTIVITY 2-2

SCANS

You have created a database that contains a number of tables. One of these tables is named Customers and another table is named Purchases. There is a Customer Number field in the Customers table that identifies each customer with an individual number. The Purchases table has a Customer Number field as well. You want to create a relationship between the two tables. Write a brief essay that explains which relationship you would choose for these tables and why. Use Access's Help system to find this information, if necessary.

ADVANCED FORM FEATURES

Upon completion of this lesson, you should be able to:

- Add a subform to a form.

- Add a record to a subform.

- Modify the properties of a subform.

- Create and modify a form in Design view.

⏱ Estimated Time: 1 hour

A database form is a tool used primarily for data entry. You should already know how to create a basic form and modify its design. In this lesson, you will learn more about customizing and designing forms. You will also learn how to work with subforms.

Creating a Subform

As you know, you create a form from a database table or query. You can use any of the fields in the table or query to build your form. And you can create any number of forms using the same table or related tables. *Subforms* are useful when you want to show records from one table that are related to a specific record in the main form.

For example, say you have a table containing data on each of your customers. The fields in this table might include the customer's name, address, phone number, and a customer identification number. You have another table in the database that tracks orders. The fields in this table might include the product ordered, transaction amount, customer name, and the customer identification number. Now, as you go through your list of customers, you want to know how many orders they have put in over the past year. Since there is a common field between these two tables, the customer identification number, Access will allow you to view information from both tables at one time in a form that contains a subform. For example, your main form would include the information from the customers table and the subform would include information from the orders table. The main form and subform are displayed together on your screen. You can think of a subform as a form within a form. An example of a subform is shown in Figure 3-1.

You might also want to use subforms to simply combine information from separate forms. For example, let's say you've created a form from a table that contains personnel information. The fields are Employee ID, First Name, and Last Name. You've created a second form from a table that contains salary information. The fields are Employee ID, Department and Current Salary. Rather than creating a third form to combine this information, you can add the Department and Current Salary fields to the form

FIGURE 3-1
Main form with a subform

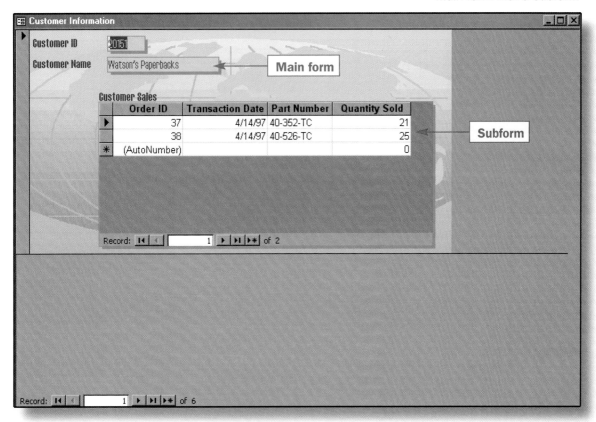

that contains personnel information. The form with the personnel information would be the main form. The subform shows the Department and Current Salary fields.

Main forms and subforms maintain the individual formats and styles you have applied to them. A subform has its own set of scroll bars and navigation buttons.

To add a subform to a main form, open the main form in Design view. Click the Subform/Subreport button in the Toolbox. Then click in the area of the main form where you want the subform to appear. Typically, you'll want the subform to appear in the Detail section of the form. Once you've clicked in the desired location, the Subform/Subreport Wizard starts, providing you with step-by-step instructions on how to create the subform.

Hot Tip

If the Toolbox is not displayed in Design view, select Toolbox on the View menu.

STEP-BY-STEP ▷ 3.1

1. Open the **AA Step3-1** database from the student data files.

2. Click **Forms** on the Objects bar and then double-click the **Customer Information** form.

(continued on next page)

3. View the information in the form and then switch to Design view.

4. Enlarge the **Detail** section so that it's about 3" deep. If necessary, display the Toolbox.

5. Click the **Subform/Subreport** button in the Toolbox. Then, position the crosshair at the intersection of the 1" marks on the horizontal and vertical rulers and click. The SubForm Wizard displays, as shown in Figure 3-2.

6. Make sure that the **Use existing Tables and Queries** option is selected and then click

If the SubForm Wizard does not start after clicking the Subform/Subreport button, make sure the **Control Wizards** button is selected in the Toolbox.

Next. The SubForm Wizard asks you which fields you want to include on the subform. See Figure 3-3.

7. Click the down arrow of the *Tables/Queries* box and choose the **Book Sales** table.

FIGURE 3-2
SubForm Wizard

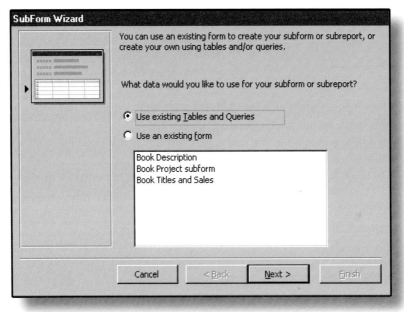

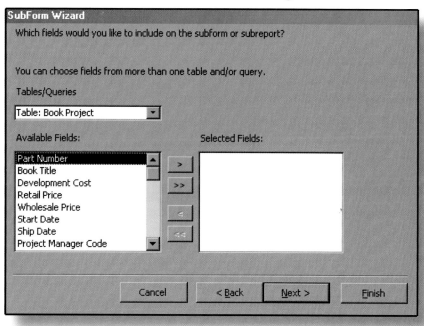

FIGURE 3-3
Selecting fields for the subform

8. Double-click the **Order ID**, **Transaction Date**, **Part Number**, and **Quantity Sold** fields to place them in the *Selected Fields* box. Then click **Next**. The SubForm Wizard asks you to define which fields link the main form to the subform. See Figure 3-4.

9. The **Choose from a list** option should be selected. In the list, select **Show Book Sales for each record in Customer using Customer ID**. Then click **Next**. The final SubForm Wizard dialog box displays. Figure 3-5 shows the dialog box with a new name entered for the subform.

10. Enter **Customer Sales** for the Subform name and click **Finish**. The main form/subform should look similar to that shown in Figure 3-6. If a dialog box

containing the fields for either table appears, click its **Close** button. Adjust the size of the subform by dragging one of its sizing handles, so you can see all the sections and controls.

11. Switch to Form view. Notice that the column widths in the subform are not wide enough to accommodate some of the field names. Adjust the widths as necessary by double-clicking the border between the field names.

12. Click the **Save** button. Scroll through the records in the main form and notice how the subform records change accordingly.

13. Print the form for record **1**. Remain in this screen for the next Step-by-Step.

(continued on next page)

FIGURE 3-4
Defining the linking field(s)

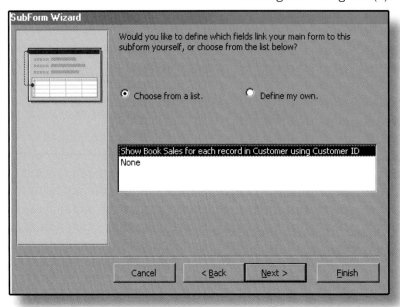

FIGURE 3-5
Naming the subform

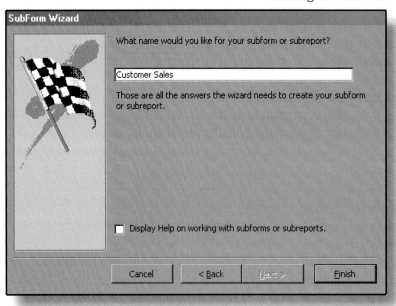

FIGURE 3-6
Main form and subform in Design view

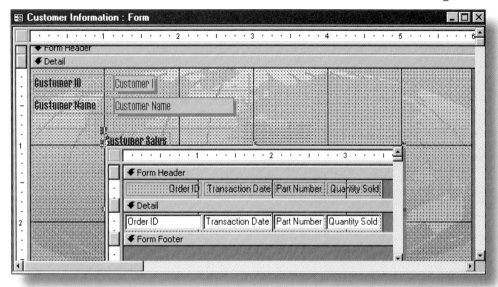

Let's review the parts of this main form and subform. The main form displays a customer record with the customer's ID and name. The subform displays the related records for this customer. When you select the navigation button to advance to the next record in the main form, you will see the orders related to that customer on the subform.

Adding a Record in the Subform

You can add a record to the subform. Access will also let you add records to the main form just as you can to any Access form.

STEP-BY-STEP ▷ 3.2

1. In the main form, go to the record for **Hector's Good Reading**.

2. In the subform, enter **2/5/2000** in the **Transaction Date** field.

    **Hot Tip**

   The Order ID field is an Auto-Number field, so Access will assign the number automatically for you.

3. Enter **41-241-TC** for the Part Number and then enter **75** for the Quantity.

4. If necessary switch to Design view and enlarge the subform so you can see all the records in the subform.

5. Switch to Form view and print the form for the **Hector's Good Reading** record only. Remain in this screen for the next Step-by-Step.

Modifying a Subform

You can control the basic appearance and operation of a form and a subform by changing its properties. For example, there are scroll bars and record navigation buttons that appear in both the main form and subform. You might decide to remove the scroll bars from the subform if all records in the subform can be viewed in the space provided.

STEP-BY-STEP ▷ 3.3

1. Switch to Design view. Click the gray box in the upper-left corner of the window, to the left of the horizontal ruler. (The color of this box may be different if you have chosen a color scheme other than Windows standard.) This selects the entire form.

2. Click the **Properties** button on the toolbar. Select the **All** tab.

3. Click in the **Scroll Bars** text box. This displays a drop-down arrow. Click the arrow and select **Neither**.

4. Click in the text box for **Navigation Buttons**. Click the drop-down arrow and select **No**. The Properties dialog box should look similar to Figure 3-7.

5. Close the **Properties** dialog box and then switch to Form view. Your screen should appear similar to Figure 3-8.

6. Save the form and then close it. Close the database.

FIGURE 3-7
Properties dialog box

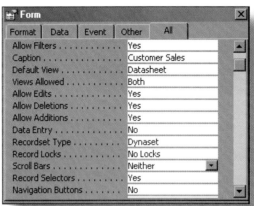

FIGURE 3-8
Adjusting form properties

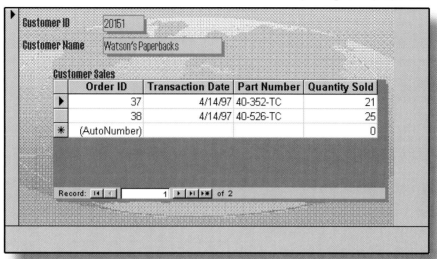

	Order ID	Transaction Date	Part Number	Quantity Sold
▶	37	4/14/97	40-352-TC	21
	38	4/14/97	40-526-TC	25
✳	(AutoNumber)			0

Customer ID 20151
Customer Name Watson's Paperbacks
Customer Sales
Record: ◄◄ ◄ 1 ► ►I ►✳ of 2

Creating and Modifying a Form in Design View

As you probably know, you can create a form using the Form Wizard, or by designing it from scratch in the Design view. Forms are developed primarily to streamline data entry. That's why Access provides you with a number of tools and options for designing forms that are user-friendly. You can re-arrange the order of fields, change field names, add and delete fields, and insert graphics and pictures, in order to customize the appearance of the form and maximize data entry time and effort.

S TEP-BY-STEP ▷ 3.4

1. Open the **AA Step3-4** database from the student data files.

2. Click **Forms** on the Objects bar.

3. Double-click **Create form in Design view**.

4. Place your mouse pointer in a blank area outside the Detail section of the form but within the Form window, and *right*-click. Choose **Properties** on the shortcut menu.

5. In the dialog box, select the **All** tab if necessary. Click in the **Record Source** text box, click the down arrow, and select **Orders**. You will use the Orders table to create the form.

6. Close the Form Properties dialog box. A window containing the fields in the Orders table should be displayed.

7. Place your mouse pointer over the **Order Number** field and drag it to the intersection of

(continued on next page)

the 1 inch marks on the horizontal and vertical rulers. Then, drag the **Customer Name** field and position it beneath the Order Number field. Finally, drag the **Employee Number** and position it below the Customer Name field.

8. Now, customize the form's header section. Open the **View** menu and then select **Form Header/Footer**. You should now see these sections in the Design view.

9. Click the **Label** button in the Toolbox and then click in the **Form Header** section.

10. Key **Orders** and press **Enter**. You should see selection handles around this box. If not, click on the label box to select it.

11. Click the **Bold** button on the Formatting toolbar. Then, click the down arrow on the **Font Size** button and choose **16**. To automatically increase the size of the label box, double-click on the middle right selection handle.

12. To insert a graphic, click the **Unbound Object Frame** button in the Toolbox and draw a box in

the upper left corner of the Detail section that's about 1 inch tall and 2 inches wide. The Insert Object dialog box should open.

13. Click **Microsoft Clip Gallery** in the Object Type list box and click **OK**.

14. Choose any piece of clip art you like and click **OK**.

15. To modify the graphic so it fits in the box you drew, *right*-click on it and choose **Properties** on the shortcut menu.

16. With the **All** tab selected, click in the **Size Mode** text box, click the down arrow, and choose **Zoom**. Close the Properties dialog box and view the results.

17. Save the form as **Orders**. Print the form for the first record.

18. Close the **Orders** form and then close the database.

Summary

In this lesson, you learned:

■ A subform is simply a form within a form. This allows you to view, add, or make changes to information in more than one form at one time.

■ After you create a subform, you can easily add or edit records within the subform as you would any form.

■ You can create a form from scratch in Design view. Access provides you with great flexability in designing and modifying a form so that data entry time and effort are truly maximized.

■ You can change properties of a form or a subform. For example, you may not want the scroll bars or record navigation buttons to appear in a subform. For some users, these features may be distracting since there are scroll bars and record navigation buttons on the main form. And since the subform will change to a related record if you select another record in the main form, having additional scroll bars and record navigation buttons may not be necessary.

LESSON 3 REVIEW QUESTIONS

WRITTEN QUESTIONS

Write a brief answer to the following questions.

1. What is a subform?

2. Why would you want to use a subform?

3. How can you change the column width in a subform?

4. How can you add a new record to a subform?

5. How do you open the Properties dialog box for the entire form?

6. List three form properties that you can change with regard to navigation.

7. Describe the differences between a main form and subform.

8. Can a record be added to a main form even though it has a subform? If so, why is this possible?

9. If there are more records than can be displayed in the subform, how can you view the additional records?

10. How does Access recognize that there is a common field between a main form and a subform?

LESSON 3 PROJECT

PROJECT 3-1

1. Open the database **AA Project3-1** from the data files.

2. Create a one-to-many relationship between the **Marketing Department** table and the **January Orders** table using the **Employee ID** field as the common field.

3. Create a form using the Form Wizard for the **Marketing Department** table. Include the **Employee ID**, **Last Name**, and **First Name** fields on the form. Choose the Columnar layout and select a style of your choice. Name the form **Marketing Department Sales**.

4. Create a subform in the Marketing Department Sales form using the **January Orders** table. Include the **Order No**, **Order Date**, **Description**, **Quantity**, and **Price** fields in the subform. Accept the default name of **January Orders subform** for the subform.

5. Modify the main form to hide its scroll bars.

6. Make any other changes to the design of the forms that you think will make them more attractive.

7. Print the form for record **4**. Then close the form and the database.

CRITICAL THINKING

ACTIVITY 3-1

SCANS

You have just taken over as the database administrator for the Last Resort Sales Company. You view the existing database file, named **AA Activity3-1** on the student data files. You decide to create a main form/subform, using the **Employees** table for the main form and the **Personnel Information** table for the subform. You want a form that displays the employee's ID, last name, first name, and telephone number.

ACTIVITY 3-2

SCANS

As the personnel director for the New Cruise Line Company, you want to create a form that will display each employee's ID number, first name, and last name. You also want to display with this form salary information that is contained in another table. Use Access's Help system to find more information on creating subforms. Write a short essay that explains how you would proceed in setting up the main form and subform for the New Cruise Line Company.

LESSON 4

ANALYZING DATA

OBJECTIVES

Upon completion of this lesson, you should be able to:

- Calculate data using the Expression Builder.
- Build summary queries.
- Concatenate field values using a query.
- Create AND and OR queries.
- Apply filters.

Estimated time: 1.5 hours

Introduction

Queries are database objects that you use to search tables for records that meet certain criteria. You can design queries so that they display only selected fields and so that the results are sorted according to a certain field or fields. You can then generate reports that attractively present the query results.

In this lesson, you'll learn how to use queries to calculate and analyze records. Although databases are designed primarily to store and organize data, the query provides analytical capabilities that make database applications all the more powerful.

Using Queries to Calculate Data

Suppose you have a table of customer orders that contains fields for the quantity of a product purchased and the price per unit of the product. You'd like to be able to generate an invoice for the customer using the information in the table, but you realize that the invoice has to contain a total amount due. You can create a query that multiplies the quantity by the price per unit and then generates a total in a calculated field. This field is displayed in the query results, just like any other field in the table. You can rename the field as you desire, format it, and then include it on a form or report.

Using the Expression Builder

For many calculations, you'll want to use the *Expression Builder* to help you build the calculation or formula to be performed. The Expression Builder lets you select the type of operation or *function* you want to perform on selected fields. The commonly used types of operations are listed in Table 4-1.

TABLE 4-1
Types of operations

OPERATOR	WHAT IT DOES
+	Adds
–	Subtracts
*	Multiplies
/	Divides
=	Finds equal values or enters an equals sign
>	Finds values that are greater than the value entered
<	Finds values that are less than the value entered
<>	Finds values that are not equal to the value entered

A function, as you may know from working with spreadsheets, is a preset formula that comes with Access. For example, the SUM function lets you total the values in selected fields. Based on the selections you make, the Expression Builder "builds" the formula or expression for you.

To open the Expression Builder, click the Build button in the query Design window. The Expression Builder dialog box displays, as shown in Figure 4-1.

You build your formula or expression in the top portion of the dialog box. The list in the bottom-left pane of the Expression Builder includes the objects within the database file, as well as other elements you might want to use to build your expression. Double-click a folder icon to display a hierarchy

FIGURE 4-1
Expression Builder dialog box

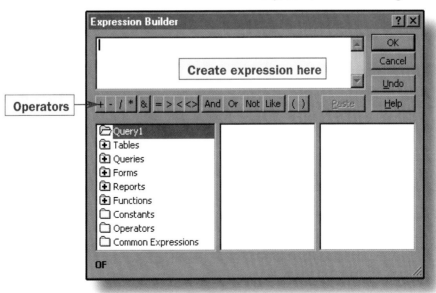

of subfolders that represent each of the objects or elements within the folder. Click the subfolder to display the object's fields (or expression's elements) in the middle pane. From the middle pane, you select the element that you want to add to the top portion of the dialog box by double-clicking the element. You can click an operator button or you can select the operator from the Operators folder in the lower left pane.

Figure 4-2 shows how a formula was built in the Expression Builder.

FIGURE 4-2
Building a formula

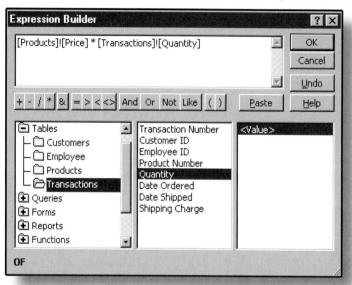

STEP-BY-STEP 4.1

1. Open the **AA Step4-1** database from the student data files.

2. Click **Queries** on the Objects bar.

3. Double-click **Create query in Design view**.

4. In the Show Table dialog box, double-click the **Products** table and then double-click the **Transactions** table to add them to the query. Click **Close**. Notice there is a one-to-many relationship between the two tables.

5. Double-click the **Transaction Number** and **Quantity** fields in the **Transactions** table to add them to the query grid. Double-click the **Price** field in the **Products** table to place it in the query grid.

6. Click in the **Field** cell of the fourth column in the grid and then click the **Build** button.

7. Double-click the **Tables** folder in the lower-left pane and then click the **Products** folder that displays beneath it. The fields in the Products table display in the middle pane.

8. Double-click the **Price** field to place it in the top box.

Concept Builder

If you place an incorrect field or element in the top Expression Builder box, simply highlight it and press **Delete**.

9. Click the * (asterisk) operator to add it to the expression.

10. Click the **Transactions** table folder to display its fields in the middle pane.

11. Double-click the **Quantity** field to place it in the top box. Your Expression Builder should look like Figure 4-2.

12. Click **OK** to close the Expression Builder.

13. Press **Enter** to enter this expression in the Field cell in the query grid.

14. Notice that Access has added *Expr1:* in front of the expression. This is the name that Access will automatically assign to the field in the query results. You can replace the heading with something more appropriate. Place your mouse pointer over **Expr1:** and double-click. Key **Order Total** and press **Enter**. Your screen should look similar to Figure 4-3.

Hot Tip

To increase the size of a column in the query grid, place the mouse pointer over the right border of the thin gray bar above the Field cell. When your mouse pointer turns into a two-headed arrow, simply double-click. The column width is automatically adjusted so you can see the full name entered in the Field cell.

15. Click the **Run** button to run the query. Notice how Order Total appears at the top of the calculated field. Next you will probably want to add a currency format to the data is this column.

16. Save the query as **Qry-Order Totals**. Remain in this screen for the next Step-by-Step.

FIGURE 4-3
Changing the name of the calculation field

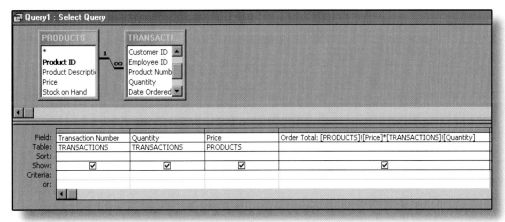

Modifying Query Properties

In the preceding Step-by-Step, you probably noticed that the values in the Order Total field were not formatted as currency. You can apply formats such as this to a field by changing the field's properties.

In the Design view, click the field name in the query grid and then click the Properties button. A Field Properties dialog box opens, like that shown in Figure 4-4.

To change the format to currency, click in the Format box, click the down arrow that appears, and choose Currency from the list.

FIGURE 4-4
Field Properties dialog box

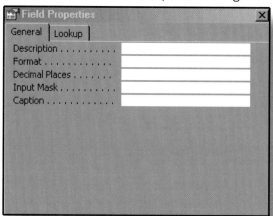

STEP-BY-STEP ▷ 4.2

1. Switch to Design view. Click the **Order Total** Field cell in the query grid and the click the **Properties** button.

2. In the Field Properties dialog box, click the **Format** box, click the down arrow, and then select **Currency**.

3. Click the **Close** button to close the Field Properties dialog box.

4. In the query grid, click in the **Sort** cell for the **Transaction Number** field, and choose

Ascending. Switch to Datasheet view to run the query. You now have the fields you need in order to create a form or report that shows purchase totals.

5. Adjust the column widths, if necessary, and then print the query results.

6. Close the query and then close the database file.

Building Summary Queries

You can summarize values in a field by creating a summary query. Summary queries utilize functions, such as Sum, Avg, Min, and Max, to total or summarize values in a selected field. A list of some of Access's predefined functions is shown in Table 4-2.

In many instances, you'll want to group records for the summary. For example, you might want to know the total number of sales completed by each salesperson. You would group the records by the salesperson and then generate a summary of sales for each salesperson.

You create a summary query in Design view. In the query grid, you select the field by which you want to group the records (if there is one) and the field whose values you want to summarize. To do this, you must display the Total row in the query grid. Simply click the Totals button in the query design window. When you click in the Total cell for a field in the query grid, a drop-down arrow appears. Click the arrow to display the *Group By* option and the summary functions from which you can choose.

TABLE 4-2

Commonly used functions

FUNCTION	HOW IT IS USED
Sum	Totals the values in a field
Avg	Calculates the average of values in a field
Min	Finds the lowest value in the field
Max	Finds the highest value in the field
Count	Counts the number of items in a field
StDev	Finds the standard deviation of values within a field
Var	Finds the variance of values within a field
First	Locates the first value within a field
Last	Locates the last value within a field

STEP-BY-STEP ▷ 4.3

1. Open the **AA Step4-3** database from the student data files.

2. Click **Queries** on the Objects bar and then double-click **Create query in Design view**.

3. Double-click the **Sales Department** table and then double-click the **March Orders** table to add them to the query. Click **Close** to close the Show Table dialog box.

4. Double-click the **Last Name** field in the **Sales Department** table to place it in the query grid. Double-click the **Quantity** field in the **March Orders** table to add it to the query grid.

5. Click the **Totals** button. A Total row now appears in the query grid. Notice that the *Group By* option appears in the **Total** boxes for both fields.

6. You want the query to summarize orders for each salesperson, so leave the **Group By** designation in the **Last Name** column.

7. Click in the **Total** box of the **Quantity** column, click the down arrow, and then click **Sum**. This will apply the SUM function to the orders for each salesperson. Your screen should look similar to Figure 4-5.

8. Click the **Run** button to run the query. Notice how the total quantity sold by each salesperson is displayed. Also note that the column heading, *SumOfQuantity*, is automatically created for the field.

9. Save the query as **Qry-Quantity Sold**.

10. Adjust the column widths, if necessary. Print the query results and then close the query.

(continued on next page)

FIGURE 4-5
Summarizing sales

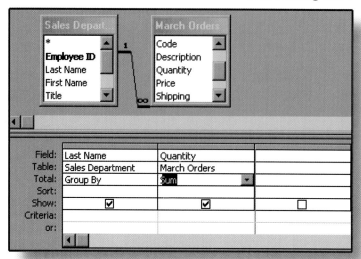

Using Concatenation

FIGURE 4-6
Concatenating field values

When a person's name is part of a record, it is best to put first names and last names in separate fields. But there may be times when you want the first name and last name combined as one value in a field. To join the values of fields, you can use the concatenation feature. *Concatenation* is defined as combining the text from two or more fields into one.

To concatenate fields you must be in the query Design view. In a Field cell of the query grid, first key the name you want to assign to the field followed by a colon (:). Then key in square brackets the complete name of the first field followed by an ampersand (&), opening quotation marks, followed by any other characters that you want to appear between the values, including spaces, the closing quotation marks, another ampersand, and the complete name of the second field in square brackets. So to concatenate a First Name and Last Name field and include a space between these names, you would enter:

```
Full Name: [First Name]&" "&[Last Name]
```

Figure 4-6 shows an example of the query criteria used to concatenate two fields.

When entering text in the Field cell, you might find it easier to view and edit the text by pressing Shift+F2. This opens a Zoom dialog box, shown in Figure 4-7, in which you can key the text. Click OK to close the box.

 **Hot Tip**

You can also use a + (plus sign) to concatenate text values.

FIGURE 4-7
Zoom dialog box

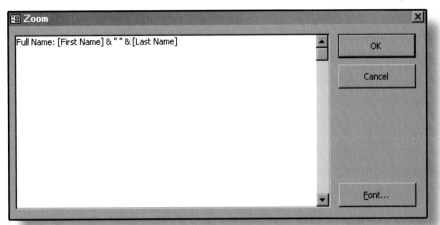

STEP-BY-STEP 4.4

1. Click **Queries** on the Objects bar and then double-click **Create query in Design view**.

2. Double-click the **Sales Department** table and then close the Show Table dialog box.

3. Click the first Field box of the query grid.

4. Key **Full Name: [First Name]&" "&[Last Name]**. Press **Enter** when you finish typing the concatenation.

5. In the second column of the query grid, choose the **Extension** field to include in the query.

6. In the third column, select the **Last Name** field. Click in the **Sort** box and select the **Ascending** option. Click the **Show** box to remove the check mark so that this column does not display in the query results.

7. Run the query. Save the query as **Qry-Telephone List**.

8. Adjust the column widths and then print the query results. Close the query and the database.

Creating an AND Query

You can query a table or form for records that meet more than one set of criteria. This is referred to as an *And query*. For example, you might want to find records in an inventory database that have a cost of $.99 *and* a selling price of $1.99. To create an And query, you enter the search criteria for the appropriate fields in the same Criteria row in the query Design view.

STEP-BY-STEP ▷ 4.5

1. Open the **AA Step4-5** database from the student data files.

2. Open the **Transactions** table and view the records to familiarize yourself with them. Then close the table.

3. Click **Queries** on the Objects bar. Then double-click **Create query in Design view**.

4. Double-click the **Transactions** table in the Show Table dialog box. Then close the Show Table dialog box.

5. Double-click the **Transaction Number**, **Customer ID**, **Employee ID**, and **Quantity** fields to add them to the design grid.

6. Click the **Criteria** cell of the **Customer ID** field and key **5**. (This represents customer number 5.)

7. Click the Criteria cell of the **Employee ID** field and key **1**. (This represents employee number 1.)

8. Click the **View** button to run the query and view the results. You should see four records. Adjust the column widths so the complete field names display.

9. Save the query as **Qry-Cust#5 and Emp#1**.

10. Print the query results. Then, close the query and remain in this screen for the next Step-by-Step.

Creating an OR Query

You can query a table or form for records that meet one criteria or another. This is referred to as an *Or query*. For example, you may want to find records for customers who live in *either* Ohio *or* California. To create an Or query, you enter the first set of criteria in the first Criteria row in the Design view, and the second set of criteria in the or row. You can search for additional criteria by clicking in subsequent rows below the or row.

STEP-BY-STEP ▷ 4.6

1. If necessary, click **Queries** on the Objects bar. Then double-click **Create query in Design view**.

2. Double-click the **Transactions** table in the Show Table dialog box, and then close the dialog box.

3. Double-click the **Transaction Number**, **Customer ID**, **Employee ID**, and **Quantity** fields to add them to the grid.

4. Click the **Criteria** cell of the **Customer ID** field and enter **5**.

5. Click the **or** cell of the **Customer ID** field and enter **3**.

6. Sort the **Customer ID** field in **Ascending Order**.

7. Click the **View** button to run the query and view the results. You should see 26 records. Adjust

the column widths so the complete field names display.

8. Save the query as **Qry-Cust#5,#3**.

9. Print the query results. Then, close the query and remain in this screen for the next Step-by-Step.

Applying Filters to a Query

You can further define your query results by applying filters to them. A filter lets you temporarily "filter out" the records you don't want to see. You cannot save a filter like you do a query. And, once you close the filtered data, the original records redisplay when you open the table, form, or query.

You filter data in Datasheet view. Click in the field you want to filter on, open the Records menu, select Filter, and then select the type of filter you want to run from the submenu. Select Filter by Form to display a form containing only the field names. A drop-down arrow appears by the name of the field you've selected to run the filter on. When you click the arrow, a list displays showing the individual values entered in that field. Select one of the values, and Access filters out all records that do not contain that value in the field. You can also run a Filter by Form by clicking the Filter By Form button on the toolbar, clicking in the appropriate field and selecting the value you want to search for, and then clicking the Apply Filter button.

Filter By Form

Apply Filter

Filter By Selection

The Filter by Selection form works in a similar fashion. Select an existing value in the field you want to filter on, and then open the Records menu, select Filter, and then select Filter by Selection on the submenu. Or, you can click the Filter By Selection button on the toolbar.

To remove a filter, click the Remove Filter button on the toolbar, or select Remove Filter/Sort on the Records menu.

STEP-BY-STEP ▷ 4.7

1. If necessary, click **Queries** on the Objects bar. Then double-click **Qry-Cust#5,#3**.

2. Click in the first record's **Customer ID** field. It should be Customer ID number 3.

3. Click the **Filter By Selection** button. You should see 15 records.

4. Click the **Remove Filter** button.

5. Click the **Filter By Form** button. A form appears that lets you click in the field or fields that you want to filter.

6. Click in the **Customer ID** field, click the down arrow, and choose **5**.

7. Click the **Apply Filter** button. You should see 11 records that have a Customer ID number of 5.

8. Click the **Remove Filter** button. Close the query and close the database file.

Summary

In this lesson, you learned:

■ The Expression Builder assists you in creating a formula to calculate values in a field.

■ You can format fields by changing the field's properties.

■ You can summarize field values by creating a summary query. A summary query lets you summarize groups of records or all the records in a table.

■ You can concatenate text values in two or more fields by entering the concatenation expression in the query Design view.

■ An And query lets you search for records that meet more than one criteria. An Or query lets you search for records that meet one criteria or another.

■ You can further refine query results by applying filters.

LESSON 4 REVIEW QUESTIONS

TRUE/FALSE

Circle T if the statement is true or F if the statement is false.

T F 1. You use the Expression Builder to modify the properties of a field.

T F 2. A concatenated expression can be created by using a plus sign or an ampersand.

T F 3. You click the Query Type button to add the Total row to the query grid.

T F 4. The MAX function will find the first value in a field.

T F 5. You normally use concatenation to combine text values.

WRITTEN QUESTIONS

Write a brief answer to the following questions.

1. What is the purpose of the Expression Builder?

2.   How do you display the Total row in the query grid?

3.   List three of Access's predefined functions and give an example of how one of them might be used.

4.   When would you use the Properties button in a query?

5.   What is the purpose of the text and colon displayed before an expression?

LESSON 4 PROJECTS

PROJECT 4-1

1.   Open the **AA Project4-1** database from the student data files.

2.   Create a query based on the **Customers**, **Transactions**, and **Products** tables.

3.   If necessary, join the **Customer ID** fields in the **Customers** and **Transaction** tables, and join the **Product Number** and **Product ID** fields in the **Transactions** and **Products** tables.

A A - 5 3

4. In the query grid, add the **Customer ID** and **Company Name** fields from the **Customers** table, the **Price** field from the **Products** table, and the **Quantity** field from the **Transactions** table.

5. Create an expression that calculates price (from the **Products** table) times quantity (from the **Transactions** table). Rename the field **Total Price**.

6. Format the **Total Price** field as currency.

7. Save the query as **Qry-Sales Totals**.

8. Adjust column widths, if necessary. Print the results of the query. Then close the database file.

PROJECT 4-2

1. Open the **AA Project4-2** database from the student data files.

2. Create a query that groups the records by class and averages the grade point average of the class. Include only the Class and Grade Point Average fields in the query grid.

3. Format the summary field to display two decimal places. Adjust the column widths in the query results, if necessary. (*Hint*: You may need to set the number format to Standard.)

4. Save the query as **Qry-Class Averages**.

5. Print the results of your query. Then close the database file.

CRITICAL THINKING

ACTIVITY 4-1

SCANS

The pet supply company you work for has just been purchased by a larger supplier. The new owners want you to provide them with some information from the company database. They want to know the total cost of each transaction for the month of August and they also want to know the total transactions for the month. You decide to create queries to generate the information. Open the **AA Activity4-1** database from the student data files. Save your queries as **Qry-August Transactions** and **Qry-Total August Transactions**. Print the results of both queries.

ACTIVITY 4-2

SCANS

You maintain the corporate database for One Star Gas Company. You need to create a number of queries to generate information requested by other officers of the company. You want to present the data in the most attractive way possible. Use Access's Help system to find information on query format properties. Write a brief essay on the Help information you find and explain how you could apply these properties as you create your queries.

ADVANCED QUERIES

OBJECTIVES

Upon completion of this lesson, you should be able to:

- Remove or change a field in a query.

- Create a parameter query.

- Understand action queries.

- Create a delete query.

- Create an update query.

- Create a make-table query.

> ⏱ **Estimated Time: 1.5 hours**

In this lesson, you will explore further the different types of queries you can create in a database. You will learn how to set up a parameter query that lets you set parameters each time a query is run. You will also learn how to build action queries. These types of queries perform an action that changes what records appear in a table or form. The lesson will also review how to modify the design of a query.

Modifying a Query's Design

You can change a query's design by opening it in Design view. You can add or remove fields, change the order of fields, select a different field to sort by, or modify the search criteria.

To replace a field with another, click the Field name in the query grid, click the drop-down arrow at the end of the box, and select the new field you want included in the query. To delete a field, click on the thin gray bar above the field name in the query grid. This will select the entire column. Then press Delete to remove the field from the query grid.

To insert a field, select the field in the field list box and drag it to the Field name box in the query grid where you want it to appear. The existing field and all remaining fields will shift one column to the right. To move a field to a different spot in the query, click the gray bar above the field in the query grid to select the entire column. Then position the mouse pointer on the gray bar and drag the column to the new location. A dark vertical bar indicates where the field is going to be positioned when you release the mouse button.

1. Open the **AA Step5-1** database from the student data files.

2. Click **Queries** in the Object bar.

3. Double-click **Create query in Design view**.

4. Double-click the **Customers** table to add it to the query. Click **Close** to close the Show Table dialog box.

5. Double-click the **Last Name**, **First Name**, and **State** fields to enter them into the grid.

6. Click the **State** field in the query grid. Notice that a down arrow appears on the right side of this cell.

7. Click the down arrow and then click **Postal Code**. This changes the field from State to Postal Code.

8. Place your mouse pointer in the thin gray bar above the **First Name** field. You will see your mouse pointer turn into an arrow pointing downward. Click in this bar to select the field.

9. Press **Delete**. This removes the field from the query grid.

10. Place your mouse pointer over the **Phone Number** field in the field list.

11. Drag the **Phone Number** field to the first cell in the second column where **Postal Code** is currently located. Release the mouse button. Notice how the **Phone Number** field is now inserted in the second column, as shown in Figure 5-1.

12. Close the query without saving any changes. Remain in this screen for the next Step-by-Step.

FIGURE 5-1
Modifying a query's design

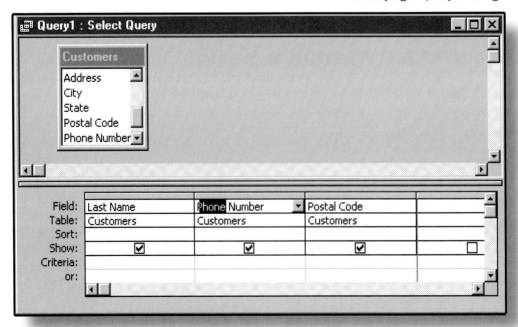

Creating a Parameter Query

Although you've just learned how easy it is to modify a query's design, there are instances when the search criteria changes frequently enough that it's easier and more efficient to create a *parameter query*. For example, suppose you have a large table of customer names and addresses. You want to provide your sales force with the information on customers in their individual sales territories only. Instead of creating half a dozen queries that find customers in each territory, you could create one query that asks you to enter the territory criteria each time it is run.

A parameter query lets you enter different criteria each time you use the query. To create a parameter query, you must enter a "prompt" in the field's Criteria cell in the query grid. A prompt tells the person running the query what criterion needs to be entered. It must be enclosed in brackets, as shown in Figure 5-2.

FIGURE 5-2
Entering a prompt for parameter query

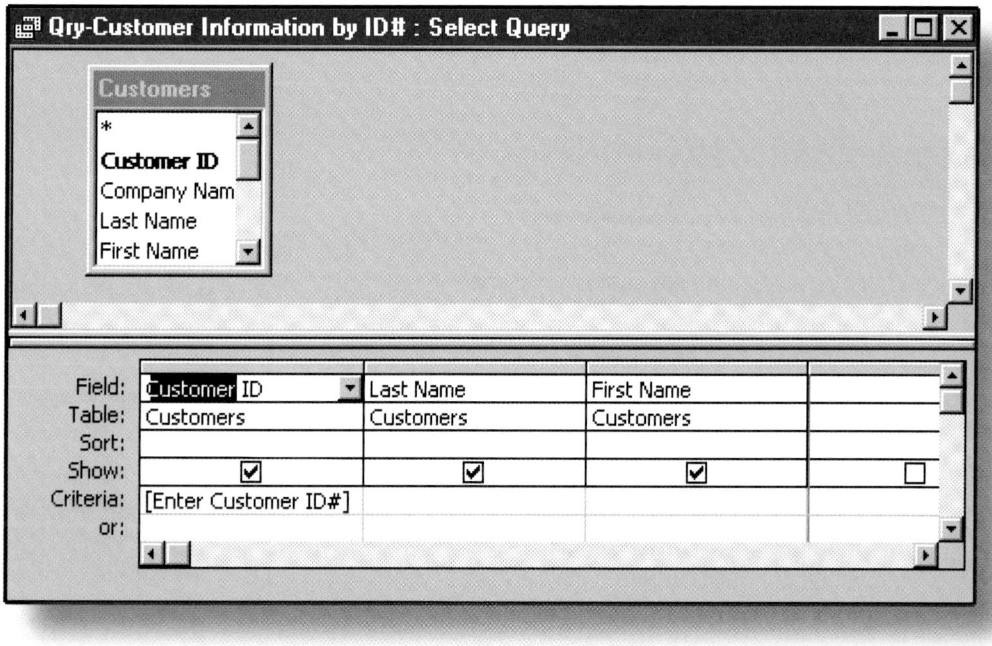

When you run the query, the Enter Parameter Value dialog box opens first, as shown in Figure 5-3. The prompt instructs you to enter the criterion or value for which you are searching. Click OK or press Enter to continue running the query.

Hot Tip

You can run a query by clicking the Run button in the Design view or by simply switching to Datasheet view.

FIGURE 5-3
Enter Parameter Value dialog box

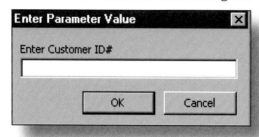

STEP-BY-STEP 5.2

1. Click **Queries** in the Object bar, if necessary.

2. Double-click **Create query in Design view**.

3. Double-click the **Customers** table in the Show Table dialog box and then close the dialog box.

4. Double-click the **Customer ID**, **Last Name**, and **First Name** fields to add them to the grid.

5. Click in the **Criteria** cell of the **Customer ID#** field and key [**Enter Customer ID#**]. Press **Enter**.

6. Save the query as **Qry-Customer Information by ID#**.

7. Click the **Run** button to run the query.

8. In the Enter Parameter Value dialog box, key **9**. Click **OK** or press **Enter**. Your screen should look like Figure 5-4.

9. Close the query and remain in this screen for the next Step-by-Step.

FIGURE 5-4
Parameter query results

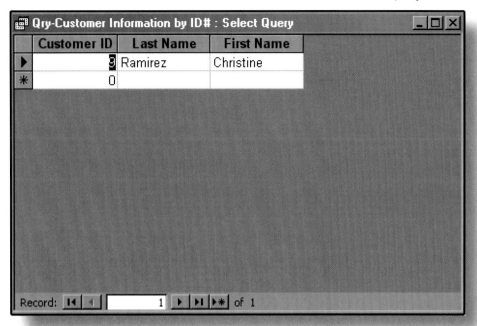

Understanding Action Queries

A query is considered an action query if it makes changes to a table. There are four types of action queries: append, delete, update, and make-table. An **append query** adds records from one table to another table. A **delete query** deletes records within a table. An **update query** changes the values in a field within a specified group of records. For example, if you wanted to give sales personnel a 6% raise, you could use an update query to find sales personnel within the table and increase their salary by 6%. The **make-table query** creates a new table using the records found from one or more other tables.

You design an action query in the Design window. Click the arrow next to the Query Type button and select the query you want to create. Action queries are identified in the Database window by an exclamation mark.

Concept Builder

You can speed up a query's run time by setting the Indexed property on the field by which you are searching. The primary key in a table is automatically indexed. To set the Indexed property on a field other than the primary key, open the table from which you will create the query in Design view, open the Properties dialog box for the field, click in the **Indexed** text box, and select **Yes** on the Indexed property's drop-down list.

Creating a Delete Query

Access lets you delete records that meet specific criteria. However, be very careful when creating a delete query—once you delete records in this manner, they cannot be recovered. It is recommended that you make a copy of the table and run the query on the copied table. If you get the results you want, then you can perform the same query on the original table.

To create a delete query, open the query Design window. Click the Query Type arrow and select Delete Query. In the query grid, enter the criteria for the records you want to delete. For example, you might want to delete the records for all customers who haven't placed an order in two years. An example of a delete query is shown in Figure 5-5.

FIGURE 5-5
Designing a delete query

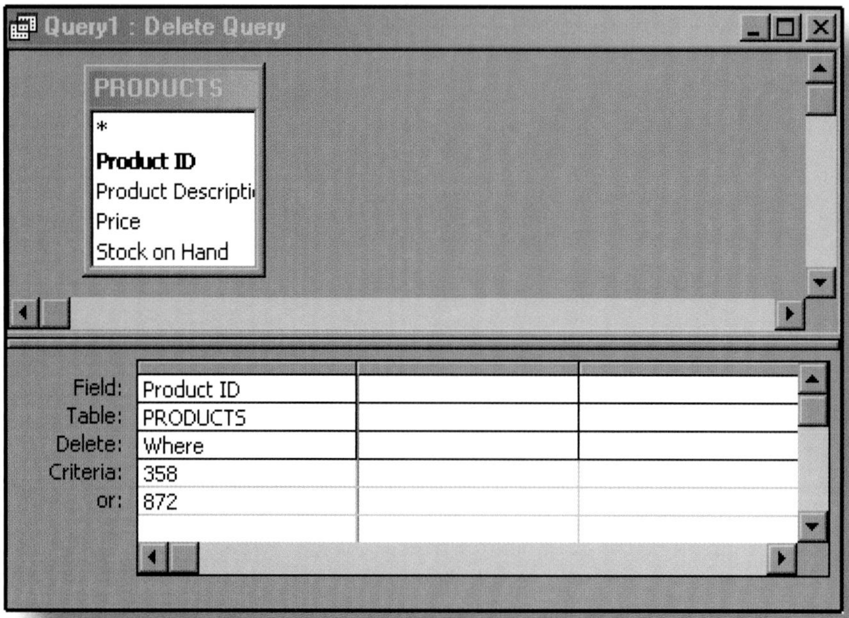

Click the Run button. A message box like that shown in Figure 5-6 appears, asking you to confirm that you want to delete the records that meet the criteria.

FIGURE 5-6
Delete query message box

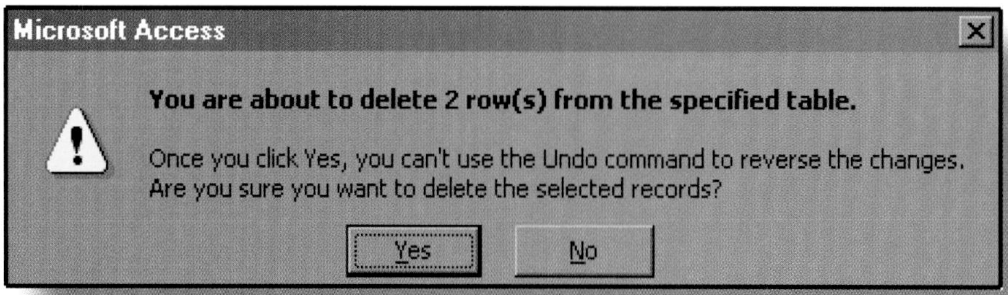

STEP-BY-STEP ▷ 5.3

1. Click **Queries** in the Object bar, if necessary.

2. Double-click **Create query in Design view**.

3. Double-click the **Products** table in the Show Table dialog box and then close the dialog box.

4. Double-click the **Product ID** field to add it to the grid.

5. Click the arrow on the **Query Type** button and select **Delete Query**.

6. Click in the **Criteria** cell of the **Product ID** field and enter **358**. Then press the down arrow key to move to a second Criteria cell and enter **872**.

7. Click the **Run** button.

8. The message box opens, telling you that two records will be deleted. Click **Yes** to confirm the deletion.

9. Close the query without saving the changes.

10. Open the **Products** table and check to be sure the records you deleted are no longer in this table. Sort the records in ascending order by the **Product ID** field and then print the table.

11. Close the table and the database file.

Creating an Update Query

Update queries let you change field values in a table. Table records are permanently changed when the query is run. As with the Delete query, it is recommended that you make a copy of the table and run the query on the copied table. If you get the desired results, you can then run the query on the original table. To create an update query, click the Query Type button arrow in the Design view and select Update Query. Enter the criteria for the field in which you want to change the values. Then enter the value, or expression, that you want to update to. An example of an update query is shown in Figure 5-7.

Click the Run button. A message box like that shown in Figure 5-8 appears, asking you to confirm the update.

FIGURE 5-7
Designing an update query

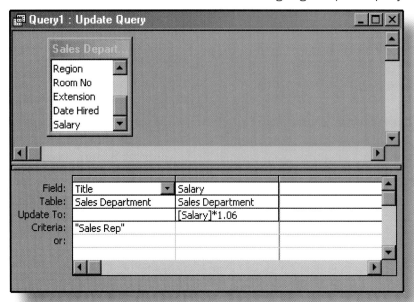

FIGURE 5-8
Update query message box

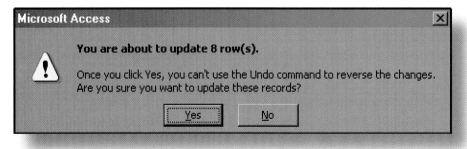

In the following Step-by-Step, you will create an update query in which you find the records for all sales reps and then update their salaries to reflect a 6% raise. Before you create the query, you might want to look at the Sales Department table and make a note of how many records will be changed. In this table, you have eight sales reps. The first sales rep listed is Rosa Navarro and she makes $42,440.00. After her raise, she should be making $44,986.40.

S TEP-BY-STEP ▷ 5.4

1. Open the **AA Step5-4** database file.

2. Click **Queries** in the Objects bar, if necessary.

3. Double-click **Create query in Design view**.

4. Double-click the **Sales Department** table in the Show Table dialog box and then close the dialog box.

5. Double-click the **Title** and **Salary** fields to add them to the query grid.

6. Click the arrow on the **Query Type** button and then select **Update Query**.

7. Click in the **Criteria** cell of the **Title** field and enter **Sales Rep**.

8. Click in the **Update To** cell of the **Salary** field and enter **[Salary]*1.06**. This expression will calculate a 6% raise for each sales rep.

9. Click the **Run** button. You should see a message box showing that eight rows will be updated. Click **Yes** to confirm the update.

10. Close the query without saving.

11. Open the **Sales Department** table and check the salary amount for Rosa Navarro. Adjust the column widths if necessary. Print the table in landscape orientation and then close it. Remain in this screen for the next Step-by-Step.

Hot Tip

Be careful to click the **Run** button only one time. Each time you run the query, it will calculate another 6% raise for the sales reps.

Creating a Make-Table Query

The make-table query is ideal for creating a new table that uses certain fields from one or more other tables. It's also commonly used to duplicate an existing table, minus a specified field or fields. For example, you might want to create a copy of a table containing employee records that does not include the field on 401(k) contributions.

When you select the Make-Table option from the Query Type list, you are asked to enter a name for the new table in the Make Table dialog box, as shown in Figure 5-9. You can also choose to create the table in another database file. Run the query and the new table is created automatically. The table is not linked to the existing table or tables. Therefore, if information in the original table changes, you will need to run the query again if you want to update this information in the new table. You can use the same table name as the previous table you made; simply choose Replace when asked to do so.

FIGURE 5-9
Make Table dialog box

STEP-BY-STEP ▷ 5.5

1. Click **Queries** in the Objects bar, if necessary.

2. Double-click **Create query in Design view**.

3. Double-click the **Sales Department** table in the Show Table dialog box and then close the dialog box.

4. Double-click the **Last Name**, **First Name**, **Title**, and **Extension** fields to add them to the query grid. Sort the **Last Name** field in **Ascending** order.

5. Click the **Query Type** button and then select **Make-Table Query**.

6. The Make Table dialog box appears. Enter **Telephone List** for the new table name and click **OK**.

7. Click the **Run** button. A message box similar to that shown in Figure 5-10 opens.

8. Click **Yes** to confirm that you want to create a new table.

FIGURE 5-10
Make-Table query message box

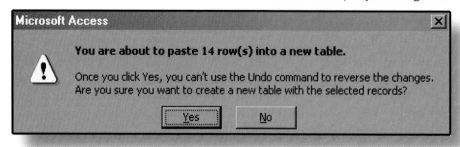

9. Save the query as **Qry-Make Telephone List Table**.

10. Close the query.

11. Open the **Telephone List** table and view the results. Print the table and then close it and the database.

Summary

In this lesson, you learned:

■ You make modifications to a query's design in the Design view. You can add or delete fields, change the order of fields, change the sort order, and modify the search criteria.

■ When the search criteria changes frequently enough, it's usually easier and more efficient to create a parameter query. A parameter query lets you enter different criteria each time you use the query. To create a parameter query, you must enter a "prompt" in the field's Criteria cell in the query grid.

■ The four types of action queries are: append, delete, update, and make-table. An append query adds records from one table to another table. A delete query deletes records within a table. An update query changes field values for a specified group of records. The make-table query creates a new table using the records from one or more tables.

LESSON 5 REVIEW QUESTIONS

TRUE/FALSE

Circle T if the statement is true or F if the statement is false.

T F   1. You can add fields and change the order of fields in a query, but you cannot delete fields in the query Design window.

T F   2. With a parameter query, you add records from one table to another table.

T F   3. The results of a delete action query are irreversible.

T F   4. Action queries are identified by an asterisk in the Database window.

T F   5. A make-table query can only create a new table in the database that contains the original table(s).

Write a brief answer to the following questions.

1. What is the purpose of a parameter query?

2. When would you use an update query?

3. What is the difference between an update query and a delete query?

4. Do you want to save update or delete queries? Why or why not?

5. Can you undelete records after they have been deleted in a delete query?

LESSON 5 PROJECTS

PROJECT 5-1

1. Open the **AA Project5-1** database from the student data files.

2. Create an update query that finds the records in the **Inventory** table whose **Part Number** field begins with **44-**. Update the **On Order** field to **0**. (*Hint*: Use the criteria of **44-*** in the **Part Number** field.)

3. Save the query as **Qry-Discontinued Items**.

4. Sort the updated **Inventory** table by the **Part Number** field. Print the table.

5. Close the table and then close the database file.

PROJECT 5-2

1. Open the **AA Project5-2** database from the student data files.

2. Create a parameter query on the **Customers** table. In the Design window, add the **Company Name**, **Last Name**, **First Name**, **City**, **State**, and **Phone Number** fields to the query grid.

3. Key the following prompt in the **State** field: **Enter TX, OR, or CA**.

4. Sort the query in ascending order by the **Last Name** field.

5. Save the query as **Qry-Customers by State.**

6. Run the query using the **TX** parameter. Adjust the column widths, if necessary. Print the query results.

7. Run the query using the **OR** and **CA** parameters. Print the results of each query.

8. Close the query and the database file.

ACTIVITY 5-1

You know that Access provides you with two tools for searching database tables: the filter and the query. But you're not clear about the differences between the two, and you've scheduled a training workshop with new employees that covers Access's search features. Use the Access Help system to find information on the types of filters and queries you can run on a database. Use one of the databases in the student data files provided with this lesson to experiment with the different filters and queries. Write a brief essay that lists the types of filters and queries, outlines the differences between filters and queries, and provides an example of when you would use each.

ADVANCED REPORT FEATURES

OBJECTIVES

Upon completion of this lesson, you should be able to:

■ Understand bound, unbound, and calculated controls.

■ Create a separate report header page.

■ Customize footers in a report.

■ Add a chart to a report.

■ Create a report in the Design view. **⏱ Estimated time: 1.5 hours**

A report is a database object that is used primarily for summarizing and printing data from tables and queries. You should already understand how to create a report using the Report Wizard. In this lesson, you will build on your knowledge of reports. You will learn how to add an unbound control to a report and how to create a cover page for a report. You will also learn how to modify the design of a report and add graphics, including charts, to a report.

Understanding Bound, Unbound, and Calculated Controls

A report's design is characterized by bound, unbound, and calculated controls. A ***bound control*** is linked to a field in a table or query. It will display information from this field in the report.

An ***unbound control*** displays information that is not found in a table or query. An example of an unbound control would be the report's title. The report title typically describes what information is found in a report. However, the report title does not represent a record or field data in the table or query.

A *calculated control* contains the result of a mathematical calculation. You learned in Lesson 4 how to use queries to calculate field data. You can calculate data in reports, too, by adding a calculated control to the report's design.

Adding Controls to a Report's Design

You use the Toolbox to add controls and modify the design of a report. You display the Toolbox in the report's Design view by clicking the Toolbox button. The Toolbox is shown in Figure 6-1. Your Toolbox may be displayed on the left side of your screen or with the other toolbars.

You can modify the format of the control in Design view. Use the Form/Report Formatting toolbar to change the font, font size, font style, alignment, and color of controls. To change other formats, select the control and then click the Properties button on the toolbar. A dialog box opens, listing all the properties associated with that control.

Hot Tip

You can also open a Properties dialog box by *right*-clicking the control and selecting **Properties** on the shortcut menu.

FIGURE 6-1
Toolbox

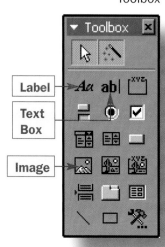

Label
Text Box
Image

STEP-BY-STEP ▷ 6.1

1. Open the database **AA Step6-1** from the student data files.

2. Click **Reports** on the Objects bar.

3. Open the report **Wholesale versus Retail**.

4. Maximize the report.

5. Click the **View** button to switch to Design view.

6. If the Toolbox is not displayed, click the **Toolbox** button on the toolbar.

7. Click the **Text Box** button in the Toolbox.

8. Place your cursor in the **Detail** section of the report at about the 5" marker on the horizontal ruler and click. A text box should appear.

9. Click the label box of the control and press **Delete**. We only want to show the result of the calculation on the report. There's no need to assign a name to it.

10. Click the **Unbound** box to select it and then click in the box again to place the insertion point in the box.

11. Type **=[In-Stock Value]*1.25**. Press **Enter**. (Be sure to use the square brackets.)

12. *Right*-click the *Unbound* box and choose **Properties** on the shortcut menu.

13. Click the **All** tab and then click in the **Format** box. Click the drop-down arrow and choose **Currency**.

14. Close the Properties dialog box.

15. Click the **View** button to switch to Print Preview. Notice how the calculated control has multiplied the In-Stock Value by 1.25. Remain in this screen for the next Step-by-Step.

Adding a Label to a Report

A label is an unbound control in which you can enter text, such as report titles, new names for fields, or other information that is not related to the table or query on which the report is based. Simply click the Label button in the Toolbox and then click in the report where you want to place the label.

S TEP-BY-STEP ▷ 6.2

1. Switch to Design view and click the **Label** button in the Toolbox.

2. Position the crosshair in the **Page Header** section of the report at the 5" marker on the horizontal ruler and click.

3. Type **Retail Value** and press **Enter**. Your screen should look similar to Figure 6-2.

4. If needed, reposition the label to align properly with the other labels in the Page Header section of your report. Change the alignment of the

FIGURE 6-2
Adding a label

(continued on next page)

label to right-aligned. Reposition the calculated control you added to the Detail section to align with the other controls in the section.

5. Click the **Print Preview** button. Your report shows the added control.

6. Click the **Two Pages** button to see both pages. Your screen should look similar to Figure 6-3.

7. Click the **View** button to switch back to Design view. Remain in this screen for the next Step-by-Step.

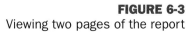

FIGURE 6-3
Viewing two pages of the report

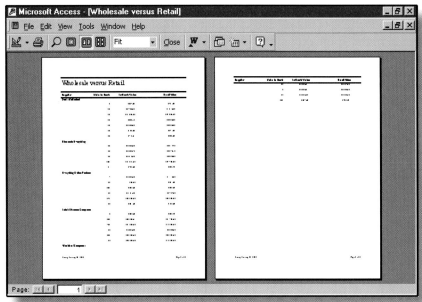

Creating a Title Page

As you are aware, there are several sections to a report. Anything that appears in the Report Header section will print only on the first page of the report and the Report Footer section will only print on the last page of the report. Anything that appears in the Page Header or Page Footer sections will print on every page.

You can place the Report Header section on a page of its own to create a title or cover page for the report. In the Design view, select the Report Header section and then click the Properties button. In the Properties dialog box, click in the *Force New Page* text box, click the down arrow, and select *After Section*. Access will place a page break between the Report Header and the Page Header sections of the report.

You can enhance a title page by using the various text formatting tools on the Formatting toolbar or by placing graphics or other images on it.

STEP-BY-STEP ▷ 6.3

1. Click the gray bar for the **Report Header** section to select it and then click the **Properties** button.

2. In the Properties dialog box, click the **All** tab if necessary and then click in the **Force New Page** text box.

3. Click the arrow and choose **After Section**. Close the **Properties** dialog box.

4. Click **Print Preview** to view your report.

5. Click the **Multiple Pages** button and then select the **1X3 Pages** option.

6. Click **View** to return to Design view.

7. Delete the line above the report title. Click on the solid black horizontal line above the report title to select it. Press **Delete**.

8. Place the mouse pointer on the top border of the Page Header bar. When it turns into a double-headed vertical arrow, drag the Page Header section down approximately 4".

9. Click the **Wholesale versus Retail** label, click the arrow on the **Font/Fore Color** button, and select **Red**.

10. If necessary, display the Toolbox. Click the **Unbound Object Frame** button in the Toolbox.

11. Position the mouse pointer below the report title and click.

12. In the Insert Object dialog box, make sure the **Create New** option is selected. Double-click **Microsoft Clip Gallery** in the Object Type list box, click the **Pictures** tab, and select the **Business** category of pictures. Click a piece of art of your choosing and then click the **Insert clip** button.

13. Center and resize the report title and clip art on the page.

14. Preview your report and remain in this screen for the next Step-by-Step.

Customizing Report Footers

Footers in a report can be used to identify a number of things: the date the report was produced, the name of the report and the name of the person who created it, and the page number. To review, a report footer appears once on the last page of the report. A page footer appears on every page of the report.

But suppose your report has a title page on which you don't want a page footer to appear. You can remove a footer from the title page by changing the report's properties. Click the Select All button in the upper left corner of the report design window to select the entire report. See Figure 6-4. Click the Properties button to display the report's Properties dialog box, as shown in Figure 6-5.

In the Properties dialog box, click in the *Page Footer* box, click the down arrow, and choose *Not with Rpt Hdr*.

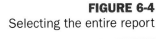

FIGURE 6-4
Selecting the entire report

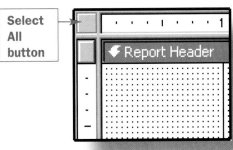

Select All button

FIGURE 6-5

Report's Properties dialog box

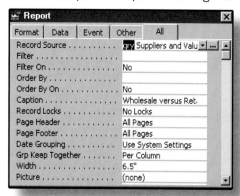

STEP-BY-STEP ▷ 6.4

1. Click the **View** button to switch to Design view. Display the Toolbox, if necessary.

2. Place the mouse pointer on the top border of the Report Footer section. When it turns into a double-headed arrow, drag down approximately $1/2$" to increase the size of the Page Footer section.

3. Click the **Label** button. Click in the **Page Footer** section below the field **=Now()**. The fields that are already in the Page Footer section are default footers assigned to the report by Access. You can delete them by selecting the controls and pressing Delete. Leave them intact for this Step-by-Step.

4. Type your first name and last name. Press **Enter**.

5. *Right*-click on the **Select All** button (located to the left of the horizontal ruler) and select **Properties** on the shortcut menu.

6. Click in the **Page Footer** text box, click the drop-down arrow, and select **Not with Rpt Hdr**. Close the Properties dialog box.

7. Preview the report. Notice how the footer is not displayed on the first page with the report header.

8. Notice how a little of the data in the report spills over to the last page. Switch back to Design view and adjust the size of the Supplier Header and Detail sections so that all the data fits on one page.

9. When you are happy with the appearance of the report, print it and then close it. Remain in this screen for the next Step-by-Step.

Adding a Chart to a Report

In many instances, a chart can help illustrate the data you present in a report. Access's Chart Wizard walks you through the steps for creating a chart. Once you place it in the report's Design view, you can format and customize it as you would any other object or control.

STEP-BY-STEP ▷ 6.5

1. Click **Reports** on the Objects bar and then double-click **Create report by using wizard**.

2. In the first Wizard dialog box, select **Query: qry Supplier Totals** from the Tables/Queries drop-down list. This is the query the report will be based on.

3. Add both the available fields to the Selected Fields list box. Click **Next**.

4. You will not add any grouping levels. Click **Next**.

5. In this Wizard dialog box, choose to sort by the **Supplier** field and click **Next**.

6. In this Wizard dialog box, choose the **Tabular** layout and click **Next**.

7. In this Wizard dialog box, select the **Corporate** style and click **Next**.

8. In the final dialog box, enter **Supplier Totals** for the report title. Click **Finish**. The report opens in the Preview window.

9. Switch to Design view. Enlarge the **Detail** section so it is about 3" deep.

10. To add a chart to the report open the **Insert** menu and select **Chart**. Place the mouse pointer in the **Detail** section beneath the Supplier label. Press and hold the mouse button down and draw a box about $3^1/_2$ inches wide and $2^1/_2$ inches tall. When you release the mouse button, the Chart Wizard opens, as shown in Figure 6-6.

11. Click the **Queries** button in the *View* options and then select **qry Supplier Totals**. Click **Next**.

FIGURE 6-6
Starting the Chart Wizard

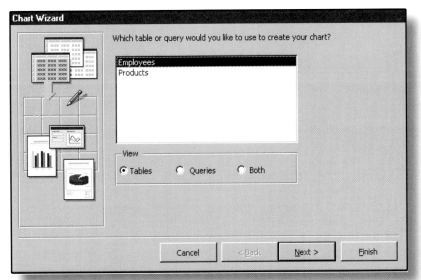

(continued on next page)

12. In this dialog box, the Chart Wizard asks you to select the fields containing the data you want to chart. See Figure 6-7. Add both available fields to the *Fields for Chart* list box. Click **Next**.

13. In this dialog box, the Chart Wizard asks you to determine the type of chart. See Figure 6-8. Select the **3-D Column Chart** (the second chart option in the first row). Click **Next**.

14. In this dialog box, the Chart Wizard asks you to place the fields on the appropriate parts of the chart. See Figure 6-9. Click **Next** to accept the layout proposed by the Chart Wizard.

15. In this dialog box, shown in Figure 6-10, accept the selections made by the wizard and click **Next**.

16. The final dialog box displays, as shown in Figure 6-11. Enter **Supplier Totals** as the

title of the chart. Make sure the **Yes, display a legend** option is selected and click **Finish**.

17. Preview the report. Then print the report, close it, and close the database.

 Concept Builder

You can modify the appearance of the chart just as you would any other object or control in the report's Design view. First, double-click the chart to make it active. A Chart menu appears on the Menu bar and a toolbar with buttons for formatting the chart displays. To format a specific part of the chart, such as its title or legend, right-click the part and then select the Format command on the shortcut menu. A dialog box containing formatting options specific to that part appears.

FIGURE 6-7
Selecting the fields to chart

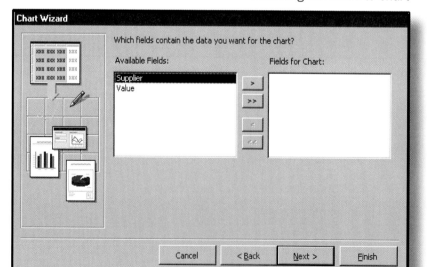

FIGURE 6-8
Selecting the chart type

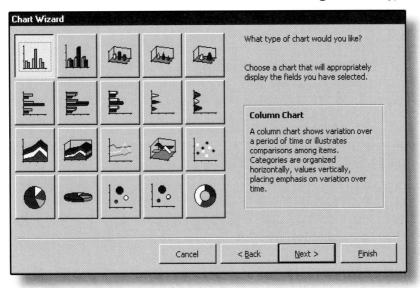

FIGURE 6-9
Determining the layout of the chart

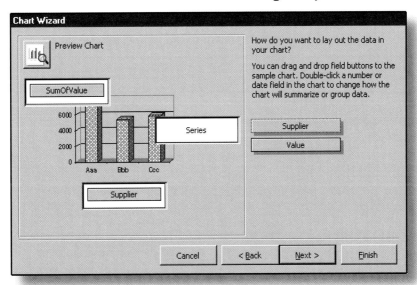

(continued on next page)

A A - 7 7

FIGURE 6-10

Linking chart data to field data

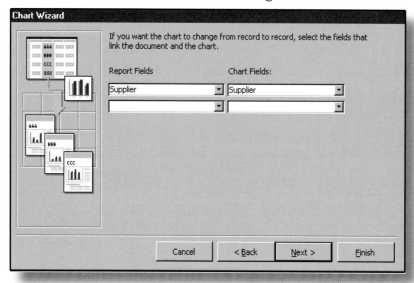

FIGURE 6-11

Entering a title for the chart

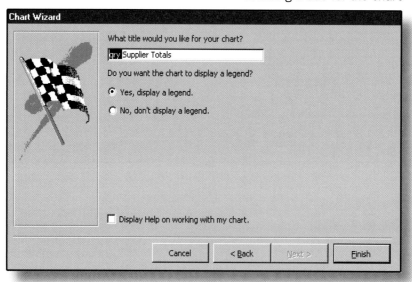

Creating and Modifying a Report in Design View

Instead of using the Report Wizard to create a report, you can design it from scratch in the Design view. Access provides you with a number of tools and options for designing reports that are attractive and easy to read and interpret. You can rearrange the order of fields, change field names, add and delete fields, insert graphics and text, and add title pages, headers, and footers.

You can also add a subreport to a main report. You learned in Lesson 3 how to insert a subform in a main form so that you could display related records from another table. The concept works the same in reports. When the main report and subreport are synchronized, selecting a record in the main report displays the corresponding record(s) in the subreport.

STEP-BY-STEP ▷ 6.6

1. Open the **AA Step6-6** database from the student data files.

2. Click **Reports** on the Objects bar, and then double-click **Create report in Design view**.

3. Place your mouse pointer in a blank area outside the Detail section of the report but within the Report window, and *right*-click. Choose **Properties** on the shortcut menu.

4. In the dialog box, select the **All** tab, if necessary. Click in the **Record Source** text box, click the down arrow, and select **Orders**. You will use the Orders table to create the report.

5. Close the Report Properties dialog box. A window containing the fields in the Orders table should be displayed.

6. Place your mouse pointer over the **Order Number** field and drag it to the intersection of the 1-inch marks on the horizontal and vertical rulers. Then, drag the **Customer Name** field and position it beneath the Order Number field.

Finally, position the **Employee Number** field below the Customer Name field.

7. Now, customize the report's header section. Open the **View** menu and select **Report Header/Footer**. You should now see these sections in the Design view.

8. Click the **Label** button in the Toolbox and then click in the **Report Header** section.

9. Key **Orders** and press **Enter**. You should see selection handles around this box. If not, click on the label box to select it.

10. Click the **Bold** button on the Formatting toolbar. Then, click the down arrow on the **Font Size** button and choose **16**. To automatically increase the size of the label box, double-click the middle right selection handle.

11. To insert a graphic, click the **Unbound Object Frame** button in the Toolbox and draw a box in the upper left corner of the Detail section that's about 1 inch tall and 2

(continued on next page)

inches wide. The Insert Object dialog box should open.

12. Click **Microsoft Clip Gallery** in the Object Type list box and click **OK**.

13. Choose any piece of clip art you like and click **OK**.

14. To modify the graphic so it fits in the box you drew, *right*-click on the box and choose **Properties** on the shortcut menu.

15. With the **All** tab selected, click in the **Size Mode** text box, click the down arrow, and choose **Zoom**. Close the Properties dialog box and view the results.

16. Save the report as **Orders**.

17. Place your mouse pointer on the top edge of the **Page Footer** band. When it becomes a two-headed arrow, drag the band down about 2 inches to increase the size of the Detail section.

18. Click the **Subform/Subreport** button in the Toolbox and draw a box below the field names in the Detail section that's about 2 inches tall and 3 inches wide. When you release the mouse button, the SubReport Wizard opens with step-by-step instructions for creating a subreport.

19. The **Use existing Tables and Queries** option should be selected. Click **Next**.

20. If necessary, click the down arrow on the **Tables/Queries** box and select **Order Details**.

21. Click the double arrow to add all the fields in the Available Fields list box to the Selected Fields box. Click **Next**.

22. Now you will *synchronize* your report. Click **Choose from a list** if necessary, and **Show Order Details for each record in Orders using Order Number**. This will display the corresponding record in the subreport when an order number is selected in the main report. Click **Next**.

23. The name **Order Details subreport** should appear as the name for the subreport. Click **Finish**.

24. Click on the **Order Details subreport** label box that appears above the subreport and then press the **Delete** key to delete this text box.

25. Click the **View** button to preview the report.

26. Save the report and then print it.

27. Close the report and the database file.

Summary

In this lesson, you learned:

- Reports are characterized by bound, unbound, and calculated controls. Bound controls are tied to a field in the table or query on which the report is based. Unbound controls are not tied to a field. For example, a graphic inserted on a report is an example of an unbound field. A calculated control is an unbound control that contains the result of an expression or formula.

- A report header appears once on the first page of the report. You can create a title page for a report by inserting a page break after the Report Header section of the report.

- A report footer appears once on the last page of a report, and a page footer appears at the bottom of each page in a report. Footers typically contain information such as the name of the report, the author of the report, page numbers, and the date the report was created.

- You can add a chart to a report to graphically illustrate data. You can modify a chart in the Design view. First double-click the chart to make it active. Then *right*-click the part you want to modify and select the Format command on the shortcut menu.

- Creating a report from scratch in Design view gives you optimum flexibility in the design and appearance of the report.

LESSON 6 REVIEW QUESTIONS

TRUE/FALSE

Circle T if the statement is true or F if the statement is false.

T F   1.   An unbound control displays information that is not tied to a table or query.

T F   2.   You click the Label button in the Toolbox to add a field from an underlying table or query to a report.

T F   3.   A calculated control is an example of an unbound control.

T F   4.   You cannot change the properties of a bound control.

T F   5.   A report footer appears at the bottom of every page in a report.

WRITTEN QUESTIONS

Write a brief answer to the following questions.

1. What is an unbound calculated control? What could it be used for?

2. Where do you add the expression in an unbound calculated control?

3. In a report, where will the page footer print?

4. In what view must you be to change the properties of a report? Explain two ways for displaying the properties of a control.

5. How would you select an entire report?

LESSON 6 PROJECT

PROJECT 6-1

1. Open the **AA Project6-1** database from the student data files.

2. Create a report with the Report Wizard using **qry Customers by State**.

3. Include all four fields and group the data by state. Use the **Outline 1** layout with the **Formal** style.

4. Title the report **Customers by State**.

5. Create an unbound calculated control that multiplies the price by the stock on hand. (You may need to make room for the new control on your report.)

6. Format the new control for currency.

7. Label the unbound calculated control **Inventory Value**.

8. Delete the lines in the **State Header** section. Make any other modifications to the report's design that you think will enhance its appearance.

9. Print the report. Then close the database.

SCANS

ACTIVITY 6-1

You are the manager for a pet supply company that is undergoing a merger. The owners of the company want you to give them some information about sales and product prices in a report. They ask you to create a report that shows the total transactions for the entire month. Use the **AA Activity6-1** database in the student data files. You will need to create a query that groups and sums the products sales. Then create the report from this query.

SCANS

ACTIVITY 6-2

Your company, the Make-It-Yourself Pizza Parlor, is experiencing an increase in sales due to the popularity of the make-it-yourself concept. You've kept track of the information for your company in an Access database. You decide that you would like to illustrate your sales data in a report that includes a chart. Use Access's Help system to find information on the different types of charts you can create in a report. Write a brief essay outlining how you would proceed in creating a sales report that included a chart.

IMPORTING AND EXPORTING DATA

OBJECTIVES

Upon completion of this lesson, you should be able to:

■ Explain importing and exporting.

■ Import data from other applications.

■ Export data to other applications.

Estimated Time: 1 hour

As part of the Microsoft Office suite of applications, Access is designed so that you can easily exchange data with other programs. In this lesson, you will learn how to import data from and export it to other applications. ***Importing*** refers to bringing information from another program into Access. You can also bring information from one Access database into another. Once this data is imported, you can treat it as any other Access data. ***Exporting*** refers to placing Access data into another program or another Access database file.

Importing Data

Access can import and read files created in other programs and saved in different formats. Table 7-1 lists the types of files Access can read.

You can import a file into a table that already exists in Access, or you can import a file and let Access create the table for you. If you have Access create the table, the file will need to be in a database table format with columns, or fields, of data. If the data you're importing is already set up with column names or titles, Access will automatically transfer these to the new table as field names. Otherwise Access will assign numbers for the field names; you simply modify the names in the table's Design view.

TABLE 7-1
Types of files Access can read

PROGRAM	TYPES OF FILES
Microsoft Access database	2.0, 7.0/95, 97, 2000
Microsoft Access project	2000
dBASE	III, III+, IV, and 5 7 (Linking [read/write] requires Borland Database Engine 4.x or later)
Paradox, Paradox for Windows	3.x, 4.x, and 5.0 8.0 (Linking [read/write] requires Borland Database Engine 4.x or later)
Microsoft Excel spreadsheets	3.0, 4.0, 5.0, 7.0/95, 97, and 2000
Lotus 1-2-3 spreadsheets (link is read-only)	.wks, .wk1, .wk3, and .wk4

Microsoft Exchange
   Delimited text files
   Fixed-width text files
	
	All character sets
	All character sets

HTML	1.0 (if a list); 2.0, 3.x (if a table or list)
SQL tables, Microsoft Visual FoxPro, and data from other programs and databases that support the ODBC protocol	Visual FoxPro 2.x, 3.0, 5.0, and 6.x (import only)

To import data into a database file, open the database file and select the Get External Data command on the File menu. From the submenu, choose Import. Access will take you step-by-step through importing a file.

STEP-BY-STEP ▷ 7.1

1. Open the **AA Step7-1** database from the student data files.

2. Click the **File** menu, choose **Get External Data**, and then select **Import**.

3. In the Import dialog box, click the **Files of type** drop-down arrow and select **Microsoft Excel**.

4. Select the **Sales Personnel** file and click the **Import** button. The Import Spreadsheet Wizard appears, as shown in Figure 7-1. Notice you have the option to import a specific worksheet or a range of data on a worksheet.

FIGURE 7-1
Starting the Import Spreadsheet Wizard

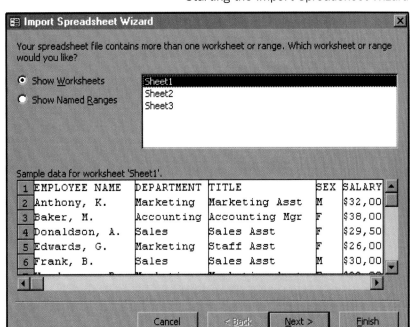

5. Click **Next**. The second dialog box of the Import Spreadsheet Wizard appears, as shown in Figure 7-2. Notice that the first row of the spreadsheet contains column headings (field names).

6. Select **First Row Contains Column Headings** and click **Next**.

7. The next dialog box of the Import Spreadsheet Wizard appears, as shown in Figure 7-3. If necessary, select the **In a New Table** option and click **Next**.

(continued on next page)

FIGURE 7-2
Specifying field names

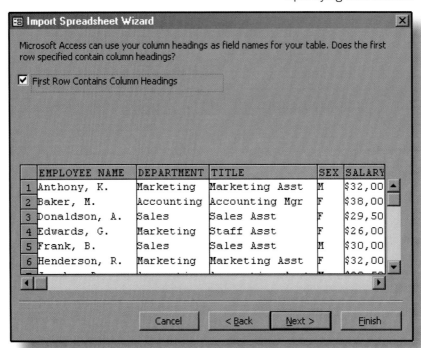

FIGURE 7-3
Placing data

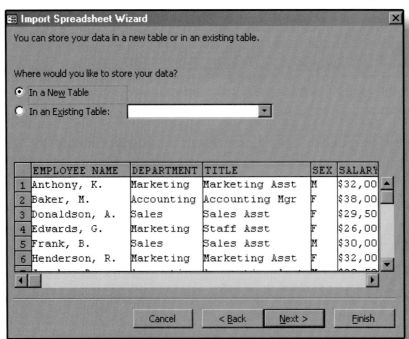

8. In this dialog box (see Figure 7-4), you can specify information about each field, such as its name and the data type. Typically, Access can determine the data type for each field. Click **Next**.

9. The fifth wizard dialog box appears, as shown in Figure 7-5. In this dialog box, you select whether you want Access to assign a primary key field. Choose **Let Access add primary key** and click **Next**.

10. The last dialog box appears, as shown in Figure 7-6. Key **New Sales Department** in the *Import to Table* box.

11. Click **Finish**.

12. You will see a message box letting you know that the import is complete. Click **OK**.

13. Open the **New Sales Department** table and view the results. Your screen should look similar to Figure 7-7.

14. Adjust the column widths in the table, if necessary, and then print it.

15. Close the table and then close the database.

FIGURE 7-4
Setting field names and options

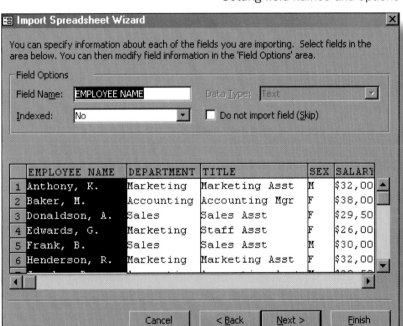

(continued on next page)

FIGURE 7-5
Setting a primary key

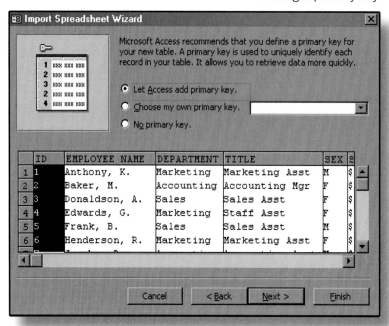

FIGURE 7-6
Identifying the table to contain the imported data

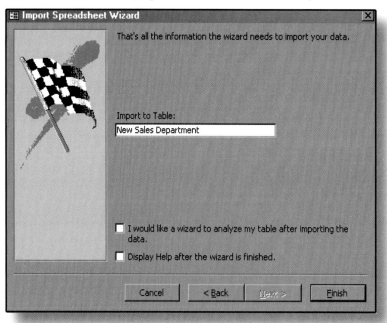

FIGURE 7-7
Excel data imported to a table

ID	EMPLOYEE NA	DEPARTMENT	TITLE	SEX	SALARY	DATE HIRED
1	Anthony, K.	Marketing	Marketing Asst	M	$32,000.00	2/1/89
2	Baker, M.	Accounting	Accounting Mgr	F	$38,000.00	5/26/84
3	Donaldson, A.	Sales	Sales Asst	F	$29,500.00	3/15/91
4	Edwards, G.	Marketing	Staff Asst	F	$26,000.00	8/17/90
5	Frank, B.	Sales	Sales Asst	M	$30,000.00	4/10/88
6	Henderson, R.	Marketing	Marketing Asst	F	$32,000.00	10/24/89
7	Jacobs, D.	Accounting	Accounting Ass	M	$28,500.00	1/20/91
8	Kilpatrick, S.	Legal	Attorney	M	$50,000.00	6/11/87
9	Matthew, H.	Marketing	Marketing Mgr	M	$35,000.00	5/5/90
10	Nicholson, P.	Sales	Staff Asst	F	$25,000.00	12/9/91
11	O'Hara, J.	Sales	Sales Mgr	M	$38,000.00	7/1/84
12	Rose, V.	Legal	Attorney	F	$45,000.00	9/16/88
13	Sanders, N.	Marketing	Marketing Asst	M	$31,500.00	2/10/90
14	Willis, E.	Accounting	Accounting Ass	M	$29,000.00	11/28/89
* (AutoNumber)						

New Sales Department : Table

Exporting Data to Other Programs

You can also export Access data to other programs. For example, with the compatibility features in Office 2000, you can export an Access table, query, form, or report to Word or Excel.

S TEP-BY-STEP ▷ 7.2

1. Open the **AA Step7-2** database from the student data files.

2. If necessary, click **Tables** on the Objects bar, and then select the **Employee Information** table.

3. Click the down arrow on the **Office Links** button and then select **Analyze It with MS Excel**. The Excel program opens and the records from the Employee Information table are automatically inserted in a new worksheet. The Excel file is automatically named **Employee Information.xls**.

Hot Tip

You can also use the OfficeLinks button to quickly export Access data to a Word document.

4. Close the **Employee Information.xls** file.

5. Click the **AA Step7-2** button on the taskbar to return to Access. Remain in this screen for the next Step-by-Step.

Linking to Existing Data

You can link data that's shared between Access and Excel, so that changes made to the records in the original application are reflected in the records in the destination application. In other words, if you import data from Excel into an Access table, and then make changes to the data in the Excel worksheet, these changes will automatically be reflected in the Access table.

To link data, select Get External Data on Access's File menu, and then choose **Link Tables** on the submenu. Select the file you want to link and click OK. The Link Spreadsheet Wizard will take you through the process of creating a link to existing data. Once the link is created, a special link icon precedes the table's name in the Access Database window.

Using Drag-and-Drop to Integrate Data

Y ou can also insert records from Access into Excel by using the drag-and-drop method. Make sure both applications are open with the appropriate files opened between which you will share the records. Size and position the application windows so you can see both files on the screen. To do this, simply right-click an empty area on the taskbar, and choose Tile Windows Vertically on the shortcut menu. Select the data you want to move and drag it to the new location. If you want to copy the data rather than move it, make sure you hold down the Ctrl key as you drag and drop.

S TEP-BY-STEP ▷ 7.3

1. Start the **Microsoft Excel** program.

2. Switch back to Access and open the **Employee Information** table in the AA Step7-2 database.

3. *Right*-click an empty area on the taskbar and choose **Tile Windows Vertically** on the shortcut menu.

4. Select all the records in the Access table by clicking the **Select All** button located to the left of the *Employee Number* field name.

5. Place your mouse pointer on the border of the selected records. When it turns into the standard arrow pointer shape, press the mouse button, hold down the **Ctrl** key, and drag to cell **A1** in the Excel worksheet. Release the mouse button and then release the **Ctrl** key.

6. Change the column widths in Excel to accommodate the data by placing your mouse pointer over the right border of the column heading (gray area with column letters) and

double-clicking when your mouse pointer turns into a two-headed arrow. You can also adjust row heights by double-clicking the border lines between the row numbers.

7. Save the Excel workbook as **Emp** followed by your initials. Then, click the **Print** button on the toolbar to print the worksheet.

8. Close the Excel workbook file. Then, click the **New** button to open a blank workbook.

9. Now you will use the drag-and-drop method to copy query result records. Switch to Access, close the **Employee Information** table, and then click **Queries** on the **Objects** bar.

10. Open the **Qry-Employee Data and Benefits** query.

11. Select all the records in the query by clicking the **Select All** button located to the left of the *Employee Number* field name.

12. Place your mouse pointer on the border of the selected records. When it turns into the standard arrow pointer shape, press the mouse button, hold down the **Ctrl** key, and drag to cell **A1** in the Excel worksheet. Release the mouse button and then release the **Ctrl** key.

13. Change the column widths in Excel to accommodate the data by placing your mouse pointer over the right border of the column heading (gray area with column letters) and double-clicking when your mouse pointer turns into a two-headed arrow. You can also adjust row heights by double-clicking the border lines between the row numbers.

14. Save the Excel workbook as **EmpDandB** followed by your initials. Click the **Print** button on the toolbar to print the worksheet.

15. Close the Excel workbook and exit Excel. Switch back to Access and maximize the window, close the query, and then close the database.

Summary

In this lesson, you learned:

■ Importing refers to bringing data from other Access databases or applications into Access. The Import Wizard takes you step-by-step through the process of importing data.

■ You can easily export Access data to another application, such as Microsoft Word or Excel, using the OfficeLinks button, or the drag-and-drop method.

LESSON 7 REVIEW QUESTIONS

TRUE/FALSE

Circle T if the statement is true or F if the statement is false.

T F 1. You can import Lotus files into Access.

T F 2. Importing refers to moving or copying Access information to another application, such as Microsoft Word.

T F 3. You can import files that Access does not recognize, but you cannot use the Import Wizard to bring them into Access.

T F 4. When you export a file, the file is placed in Windows Explorer until the export is complete.

T F 5. When you import data into an Access table, the data being imported must already have column names.

WRITTEN QUESTIONS

Write a brief answer to the following questions.

1. When importing data into an Access table, what must you know about the first row of information in the imported data?

2. When importing spreadsheet information, such as from Excel, can you specify which information you want to import, or do you have to import the entire spreadsheet?

3. List two types of file formats that can be imported into Access.

4. Can you export Access data into a form letter in Word?

5. What applications does the OfficeLinks button allow you to quickly export Access data to?

LESSON 7 PROJECT

PROJECT 7-1

1. Open the **AA Project7-1** database file.

2. Import the **Accounting Department** file into Access as a table. The Accounting Department file is a spreadsheet in Excel.

3. Let Access set the primary key field for you and name the table **Accounting Department**.

4. Adjust column widths in the table, if necessary. Then print the table.

5. Close the database file.

CRITICAL THINKING

SCANS

ACTIVITY 7-1

You are the database administrator for the Last Resort Sales Company. You want to import a file from Excel into Access. Once this spreadsheet is imported into Access, you will create a report from the new table. Open the **AA Activity7-1** database from the student data files. Import the **Addresses** workbook. Let Access set the primary key field for you and name the table **Addresses**. Name the report you create appropriately. Modify the design of the report as you think is necessary. Then print the report.

ACTIVITY 7-2

Use the Access Help system to find out what types of graphics files you can import into Access. Write a brief essay explaining how the procedure works and give a couple of examples of when you would want to import a graphics file.

CREATING MACROS AND SWITCHBOARDS

OBJECTIVES

Upon completion of this lesson, you should be able to:

- Discuss the purpose of macros.
- Create and run a macro.
- Edit a macro.
- Add macro buttons to a form.
- Create a switchboard.
- Create a conditional macro.
- Add macro actions to a single condition.
- Use the Macro Builder.

⏱ Estimated Time: 1.5 hours

A macro is a handy tool you use to automate tasks you perform in Access. You may have used macros in other computer programs, and you'll find that they work in basically the same way: You record a set of commands in a macro; then to complete the task, you simply run the macro instead of executing the individual commands. In this lesson, you will learn how to create macros using the predesigned macros available in Access. You will also learn how to set up a switchboard. A switchboard utilizes macros to make moving around and working in a database a simple operation, even for the novice user.

Creating a Basic Macro

A *macro* is a set of actions necessary to complete a certain task. For example, you may use a form frequently, and every time you open this form, you need to go to a new record to begin entering record information. It can be time consuming to do these same steps over and over each time you need to enter new records. With a macro, these steps are recorded as a single operation. All you have to do is run the macro to automatically open the form and go to a new record.

You create a macro in the Macro Design window. See Figure 8-1. In the Action column, you determine the "actions" that you want the macro to perform. If you want to make a note as to why you selected a certain action or what you intend for this action to do, you can enter this information in the Comment column. In the Action Arguments section, you can apply more specific directions for each action.

After you create and save the macro, you run it by clicking the Run button in the Design window. You can also run a macro directly from the Database window by selecting it and then clicking the Run button. Or you can simply double-click the macro's name in the Database window. Let's review how to create and run a macro.

FIGURE 8-1
Macro Design window

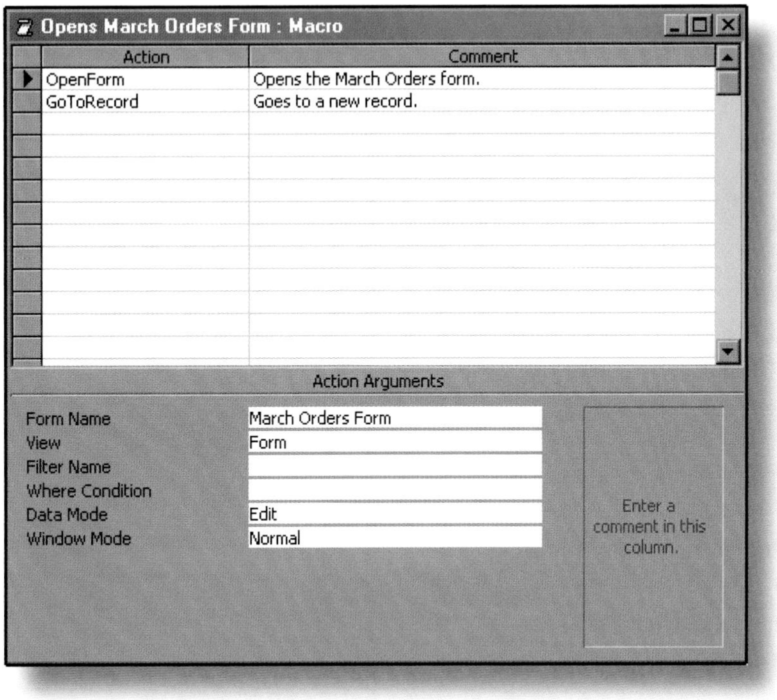

STEP-BY-STEP ▷ 8.1

1. Open the **AA Step8-1** database from the student data files.

2. Click **Macros** in the Objects bar.

3. Click the **New** button.

4. If necessary, click in the first row of the **Action** column, click the down arrow, and then select **OpenForm** from the *Action* list.

5. Click in the **Comment** box for this action and key **Opens the March Orders form**.

6. Click in the **Form Name** box in the *Action Arguments* section, click the down arrow, and then select **March Orders Form** from the list.

7. Click in the **Data Mode** box, click the down arrow, and then select **Edit**. This allows you to edit or add new records to the form after it is opened. You will not change the other Action Arguments.

8. In the second row of the *Action* column, click the down arrow and select **GoToRecord** from the *Action* list.

(continued on next page)

9. For the comment, key **Goes to a new record**.

10. Click the **Object Type** box in the *Action Arguments* section and click the down arrow.

11. Select **Form** from the list.

12. For the **Object Name** action argument, click the down arrow, and select **March Orders Form** from the list.

13. For the **Record** action argument, click the down arrow and select **New** from the list.

14. Click the **Save** button, enter **Open March Orders Form** for the macro name, and click **OK**. You have just created a macro that will open the March Orders Form and go to a new record. Your screen should look similar to Figure 8-1.

15. Click the **Run** button. The form should open automatically and a new record data should be displayed, as shown in Figure 8-2.

16. Close the form.

17. The next two macros you create will be used in the switchboard you create at the end of this lesson. Do not try to run these macros at this time. First create a macro that will close **March Orders Form**. Click **Macros** in the Objects bar, and then click the **New** button.

18. If necessary, click in the first row of the **Action** column, click the down arrow, and then select **Close** from the *Action* list.

19. Click in the **Comment** box for this action and key **Closes an object**.

20. Click the **Save** button and enter **Close** for the macro name. Close the Macro Design window.

21. Select **Macros** in the Objects bar, if necessary, and click the **New** button.

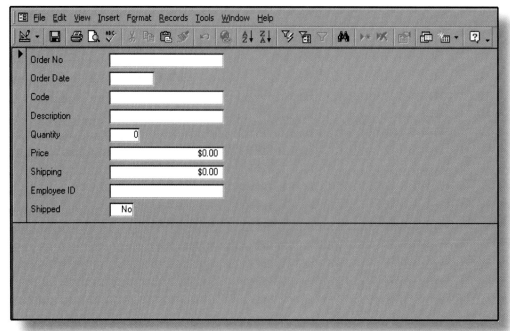

FIGURE 8-2
Opening the March Orders Form with a macro

22. If necessary, click in the first row of the **Action** column, click the down arrow, and then select **Quit** from the Action list.

23. Click in the **Comment** box for this action and key **Closes the Access program**.

24. Click the **Save** button and enter **Exit Access** for the macro name. Close the Macro Design window and remain in this screen for the next Step-by-Step.

Editing a Macro

You can easily modify a macro in the Macro Design window. Simply add or delete actions and change the Action Arguments as necessary. Then make sure you save the changes to the macro.

S TEP-BY-STEP ▷ 8.2

1. Display the **Open March Orders Form** macro in the Macro Design window. Let's add a third action.

2. Click in the third Action row, click the down arrow, and choose **Maximize**. This action will maximize the form when you open it. Your macro design should look similar to Figure 8-3.

3. Click **Save** and close the Macro Design window.

4. Run the macro from the Database window.

5. Close **March Orders Form** and remain in this screen for the next Step-by-Step. If necessary, click the **Restore** button in the Database window.

FIGURE 8-3
Modifying a macro

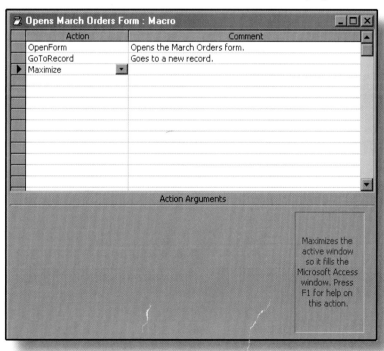

Creating a Macro Button in a Form

You can represent a macro as a button in a database form or report. For example, you might create a macro that prints and closes a report. You could insert a button for this macro directly in the report's Design view. All you have to do is click the button and the report will print and then close.

To create a button, simply drag the macro from the Database window to the object in which you want to place it. The button is named according to the macro name.

Hot Tip

If you cannot see the full name of the macro in the button, simply place your mouse pointer over the right-middle selection handle until it turns into a double-headed arrow. Then double-click.

STEP-BY-STEP ▷ 8.3

1. You will now add a macro button for the **Close** macro in March Orders Form. Open **March Orders Form** in Design view. If necessary, widen the **Details** section by about an inch.

2. Redisplay the Database window and make sure **Macros** is selected in the Objects bar. Resize the March Orders Form window and the Database window so they are side by side, as shown in Figure 8-4.

FIGURE 8-4
Creating a macro button

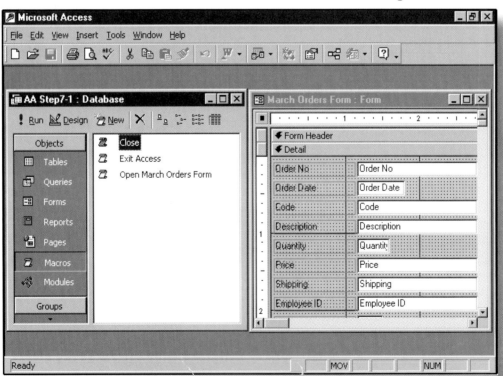

3. In the Database window, press and hold down your mouse button and drag the **Close** macro to the right of the field names in the **Detail** section of March Orders Form. See Figure 8-5.

4. Maximize the **March Orders Form** window and then switch to **Form** view. Navigate through various forms. The Close button should appear on each form.

5. Go to record **4** and print it. Then click the **Close** button to close the form. If you are asked if you want to save changes to the design of the form, click **Yes**. Remain in this screen for the next Step-by-Step.

FIGURE 8-5
Form with macro button

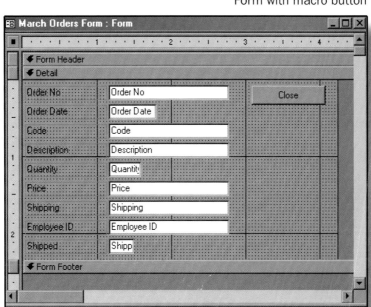

Creating a Switchboard

A switchboard is a powerful feature in Access in that it serves as the "command center" for working with your database objects. It's different from the Database window in that it generally contains macro buttons that let you open, close, and perform various other actions on database objects simply by clicking a single button.

You set up a switchboard on a form. Create a new form in Design view and move macros from the Database window to the switchboard, just as you did in the previous Step-by-Step. As you can imagine, a switchboard is a useful tool for novice users of a database who aren't familiar with the various database objects or how to work with them.

STEP-BY-STEP 8.4

1. Open a new form in Design view.

2. Select **Macros** in the Objects bar in the Database window and then adjust the Form window and the Database window until they are side-by-side as shown in Figure 8-6.

3. Drag the **Open March Orders Form** macro to the form's **Detail** section.

4. Drag the **Exit Access** macro to the form's **Detail** section.

5. Maximize the Form window. Then adjust the size of the macro buttons on the form so you can see the full name of each.

6. Save the form as **Switchboard**. Your screen should look similar to Figure 8-7.

7. Switch to Form view and click the **Open March Orders Form** macro button.

8. Close **March Orders Form** and the **Switchboard** form. Remain in this screen for the next Step-by-Step.

FIGURE 8-6
Creating a switchboard

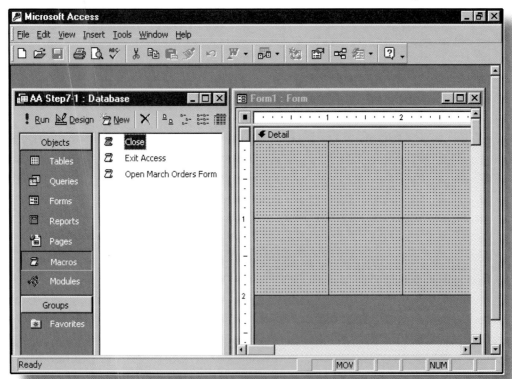

FIGURE 8-7
Switchboard form

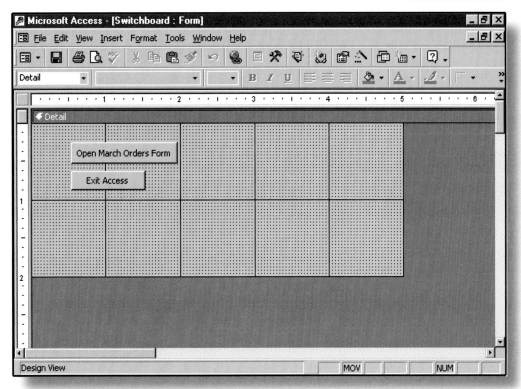

Creating an Autoexec Macro

You can create a macro that automatically opens the switchboard form when you open the database. To create such a macro, you select the object you want to open in the macro Design window, and you save it using the name "autoexec."

Hot Tip

Each database file can have only one autoexec macro.

STEP-BY-STEP ▷ 8.5

1. In the Objects bar, click **Macros** and then click **New**.

2. Click in the first Action cell and select **OpenForm**.

3. In the argument section, select **Switchboard** from the *Form Name* drop-down list.

4. Click in the second Action cell, click the down arrow, and choose **Maximize**.

5. Save the macro as **autoexec**.

6. Close the macro and then close the database file.

7. Open the database file. The Switchboard form should open automatically.

8. Click the **Exit Access** button to exit Access.

Creating Conditional Macros

You can design a macro that will run only if a condition is true. If the condition tests false, the action will not take place. This is called a *conditional macro*. For example, you could create a macro in which a message box displays if a certain value is entered in a specified field. Suppose you want to remind employees to mail out a new products brochure to any customer placing an order for a new product.

To create a conditional macro, you need to display the Condition column in the macro Design window. Click the Conditions button in the Design view. A Condition column now appears to the left of the Action column in the upper pane. Enter an expression that you want Access to test as either true or false in the Condition column. Select the action you want the macro to execute if the condition is true, and enter a comment describing the action, if desired. An example of a conditional macro is shown in Figure 8-8.

FIGURE 8-8
Conditional macro

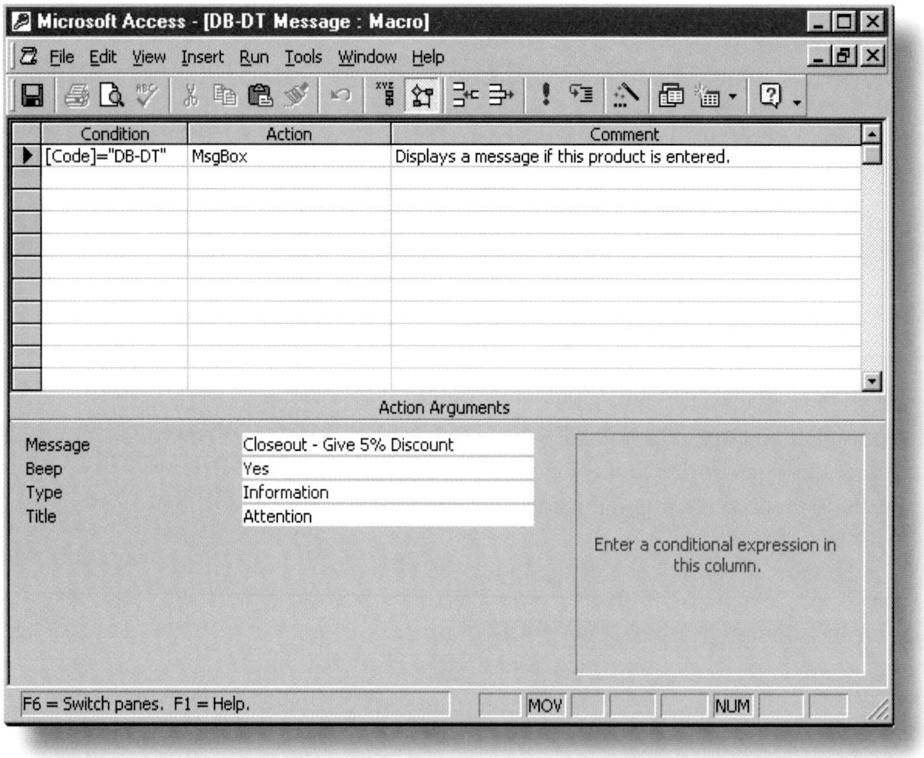

In this example, if the data entered in the field named "Code" is *DB-DT*, then a message box will be displayed to indicate that this is a closeout product and the customer is entitled to a discount.

Once you've created a conditional macro, you attach it to a field in a form by entering it in one of the field's *event properties*. Every time an action occurs, such as selecting the field, entering data into the field, or exiting the field, Access will look to see if there is a conditional macro action associated with the field. For example, if you want the macro to run after you have entered data into the field and before you exit the field, you would select the On Exit event. The macro would run as you leave this field if the condition of the macro is met. Event properties are described in Table 8-1.

TABLE 8-1
Event properties

EVENT	DESCRIPTION OF EVENT
Before Update	Occurs after information in a record is changed but before saving it
After Update	Occurs after information in a record is changed and saved
On Change	Occurs when a value is changed
On Enter	Occurs as you select a field
On Exit	Occurs before leaving a field
On Got Focus	Occurs when a field is selected
On Lost Focus	Occurs when a field is exited or another field is selected
On Click	Occurs when a mouse button is clicked over the object
On Dbl Click	Occurs when a mouse button is clicked twice over the object
On Mouse Down	Occurs when a mouse button is pressed
On Mouse Move	Occurs whenever a mouse is moved over the object
On Mouse Up	Occurs when a mouse button is released
On Key Down	Occurs when a key is pressed in a field
On Key Press	Occurs when a key is pressed and released in a field

S TEP-BY-STEP ▷ 8.6

1. Open the **AA Step8-6** database from the student data files.

2. Click **Macros** in the Objects bar, if necessary, and then click the **New** button.

3. Click the **Conditions** button to add the Condition column.

4. Click the first **Condition** cell and key **[Code]= "DB-DT"**.

5. Click the first **Action** cell, click the down arrow, and select **MsgBox**.

6. Click the first **Comment** cell and enter **Displays a message if this product is entered**.

7. Click in the **Message** argument box and key **Closeout - Give 5% Discount**.

(continued on next page)

8. In the **Beep** argument box, click the down arrow and select **Yes**. This means a beep will sound if the condition is met.

9. In the **Type** argument box, click the down arrow and select **Information**. This indicates the type of message box that will display when the condition is met.

10. In the **Title** argument box, key **Attention**. This will display in the title bar of the message box.

11. Save the macro as **DB-DT Message**. Your screen should look similar to Figure 8-8. Close the macro Design window.

12. To attach this macro to a form, click **Forms** in the Object bar.

13. Click the **February Orders Entry Form** and click the **Design** button.

14. *Right*-click the text box (this is the box on the right of the control) for the **Code** field to display the shortcut menu. Select **Properties**.

15. Click the **Event** tab, click the **On Exit** box, and click the down arrow.

16. Click the **DB-DT Message** macro. This attaches the conditional macro to the **Code** field. Now, if the conditions of the macro are met as a person leaves the **Code** field, the macro action will be performed. Your screen should look similar to Figure 8-9.

17. Close the Properties dialog box. Click the **Save** button.

18. To test the macro, switch to Form view.

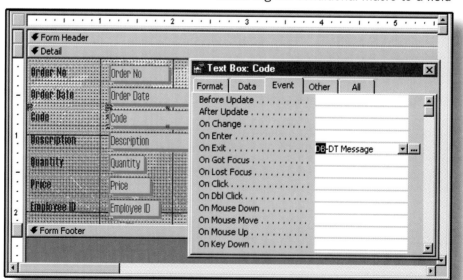

FIGURE 8-9
Attaching the conditional macro to a field

19. Enter the following record. The message box shown in Figure 8-10 will be displayed when you attempt to exit the Code field. Click **OK** to close the message box.

Order No.: 3090
Order Date: 3/14/2000
Code: DB-DT
Description: Introduction to Databases
Quantity: 200
Price: $15.95
Employee ID: N175

20. Print the form for the new record. Close the form. Remain in this screen for the next Step-by-Step.

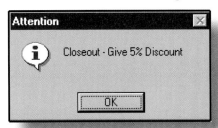

Extra Challenge

For the preceding Step-by-Step, create a calculated field in the **February Orders Entry Form** that calculates a 5% discount on the **Price** field. This way, when the message box appears, the data entry person will know to invoice the customer for the discounted price rather than the regular price.

Adding Actions to a Condition

You can design a conditional macro so that more than one action takes place if the condition tests true. For example, using the example you have been working with in this section, you might want the message box to display for items to be discounted *and* you might want the price automatically adjusted for the discount. You can easily link a series of actions to a single condition in the macro Design window. In the row directly beneath the existing condition, type an ellipsis (...) in the *Condition* column. Then specify the subsequent action in the *Action* column. Enter a comment for the action, if desired, and specify its arguments. Figure 8-11 shows an example of two actions applied to a single condition. You can add as many actions as you want to a condition.

In this example, if the item code entered is *DB-DT*, then the first message box will be displayed, explaining that this item is discontinued. When you click on OK in this message box, another message box then will be displayed, indicating that the item code for the replacement item is *BP-RR*.

FIGURE 8-11
Two actions for a condition

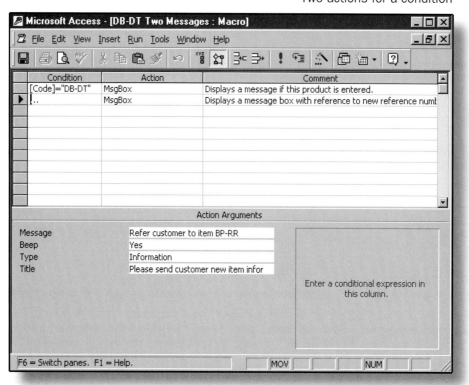

STEP-BY-STEP ▷ **8.7**

1. Click **Macros** on the Object bar, if necessary.

2. Click the **DB-DT Message** macro and then click the **Design** button.

3. In the second **Condition** cell, key **...** (an ellipsis).

4. In its **Action** cell, click the down arrow and select **MsgBox**.

5. For its comment, key **Displays a message box with reference to new reference number**.

6. Click the **Message** argument box and key **Refer customer to item BP-RR**.

7. In the **Beep** argument box, click the down arrow and select **Yes**.

8. In the **Type** argument box, click the down arrow and select **Information**.

9. In the **Title** argument box, key **Please send customer new item information**.

10. Save the macro as **DB-DT Two Messages**. Then close the macro.

11. Open **January Orders Entry Form** and attach the **DB-DT Two Messages** macro to the **On Exit** event property for the **Code** field just as you did in the preceding Step-by-Step in *February Orders Entry Form.*

12. Switch to Form view and enter the following new record. When you press Enter after entering the code, the first message box is displayed. When you click **OK**, the second message box will display. Click **OK**.

Order No.: 3091
Order Date: 1/15/2000
Code: DB-DT
Description: Introduction to Databases
Quantity: 19
Price: $15.95
Employee ID: N175

13. Print the form for the new record. Then close the form and the database.

Using the Macro Builder

Access has a helpful feature called the Macro Builder that lets you create a macro as you work with a form or other object. In the object's Design view, open the Properties dialog box for the field to which you want to apply the macro. Select the Event tab in the dialog box, and then click the Build button at the end of the event text box. Once you open the Macro Builder, you will notice that it looks identical to the macro design window. When you have "built" the macro, you are returned to the object's Design view.

STEP-BY-STEP 8.8

1. Open the **AA Step8-8** database from the student data files. Then, open the **Order Details** form in Design view.

2. *Right*-click the **Product ID** text box, and select **Properties** on the shortcut menu.

3. Click the **Event** tab and then click in the **On Exit** box. Click the **Build** button (...), select **Macro Builder**, and click **OK**.

4. Save the macro as **New Product** and click **OK**.

5. Click the **Conditions** button to add the Condition column.

6. Click in the first cell of the **Condition** column and type **[Product ID]="32"**

7. Click in the first **Action** cell and choose **MsgBox**.

8. Click in the **Message** text box in the Action Arguments pane, and key **Please send new product information!**

(continued on next page)

9. Click in the **Type** Action Arguments box, click the down arrow, and choose **Information**.

10. Click in the **Title** Action Arguments box and key **New Product**.

11. Click the **Save** button, and then close the macro design window. You are returned to the form Design view. Close the Text Box Properties dialog box.

12. To see how this macro works, click the **Save** button and then click the **View** button.

13. Click the **New Record** button and enter the following data:

Order Number   2005
Product ID   32 (The message box should display when you attempt to exit the field. Click **OK**.)
Selling Price $17.95

14. Close the form and then close the database.

Summary

In this lesson, you learned:

■ A macro lets you automate frequently performed tasks. To create a macro, simply select the actions you want the macro to perform and then save the macro.

■ You can modify the actions in a macro by opening it in the Design window. Make sure you save the macro after you've modified it.

■ Macros can be displayed as a button placed on a form or report. Simply drag the macro from the Database window to the Design view of the object in which you want the button to appear.

■ A switchboard serves as the "command center" for a database. It is typically set up as a form that contains macro buttons allowing the user of the database to execute certain actions at the click of a button.

■ A conditional macro will run only if a condition tests true. You can apply a number of actions to a single condition.

LESSON 8 REVIEW QUESTIONS

TRUE/FALSE

Circle T if the statement is true or F if the statement is false.

T   F   1. You can only create macros to perform actions on database forms and reports.

T   F   2. You would use the OpenForm macro action to automatically open any database object.

T   F   3. You can run a macro directly from the Database window.

T   F   4. You can represent a macro with a button in forms and reports.

T   F   5. A database file can have only one macro named "autoexec."

WRITTEN QUESTIONS

Write a brief answer to the following questions.

1.   What is a macro?

2.   Why would you want to enter comments for an action in the macro Design window?

3.   List the steps for creating a macro.

4. Describe two methods for running a macro.

5. After a macro is created and saved, can changes be made to the macro? Explain.

LESSON 8 PROJECTS

PROJECT 8-1

1. Open the **AA Project8-1** database from the student data files.

2. View the **Dairy and Grains** form and the **Discontinued Items** form.

3. Create a macro that opens each form in Form view and maximizes the form window.

4. Save the macros as **Open Dairy Form and Maximize** and **Open Discontinued Form and Maximize**.

5. Run the macros.

6. Close the forms. Remain in this screen for Project 8-2.

PROJECT 8-2

1. In the **AA Project8-1** database file, create a **Close** macro and place it as a button on both the **Dairy and Grains** form and the **Discontinued Items** form.

2. Create another new macro using the GoToRecord action and save it as **New Record**. Place the macro as a button on both the **Dairy and Grains** form and the **Discontinued Items** form.

3. Print the **Dairy and Grains** form. Then close it.

4. Create a switchboard that contains buttons for the **Open Dairy Form and Maximize** macro and the **Open Discontinued Form and Maximize** macro. Save the form as **Switchboard**.

5. Create a macro to exit the Access program. Save it as **Exit Access** and place it as a button on the Switchboard form.

6. Make any modifications you feel are necessary to the **Switchboard** form's design.

7. Create an **autoexec** macro that displays the Switchboard form and maximizes it when the database is opened.

8. Close the database.

PROJECT 8-3

1. Open the **AA Project8-3** database from the student data files.

2. Create a conditional macro that displays an **information** box when the state of **CA** is entered into the **State** field. Enter an appropriate title and message informing the person entering data that a promotional gift should be sent to California customers.

3. Save the macro as **California Promotion.**

4. Attach this macro to the **State** field in the **Promotion List** form and have the macro run as the field is exited.

5. Save the form.

6. Enter a record in the form to test the macro. Make sure you key **CA** in the State field.

7. Print the form. Then close the form and the database file.

SCANS

ACTIVITY 8-1

As the database administrator for a pet store, you want to provide quick and easy access to the product and transaction information stored in the **AA Activity8-1** database in the student data files. You want people in the company to be able to find a price of a product and to be able to view transactions. Your first task will be to create a form using the **Products** table. Design the form in any manner you feel appropriate. Then create a switchboard in the database file. Be creative in the types of macros you create and the design of the switchboard form.

SCANS

ACTIVITY 8-2

You've been designated to create a database switchboard for your company, One Star Gas Company. Use what you've learned in this lesson and the Access Help system to write a brief essay that explains to novice users of the database how a switchboard works.

WORKING WITH WEB FEATURES

OBJECTIVES

Upon completion of this lesson, you should be able to:

■ Create a hyperlink in a database object.

■ Build data access pages
for use on the Internet.

⏱ Estimated Time: 1 hour

Like other Microsoft Office 2000 applications, Access is designed with a number of Web-related features that make it easy for you and other users to work with database information. This lesson focuses on hyperlinks and data access pages.

Creating a Hyperlink

A *hyperlink* represents a direct link between one file and another stored on the same computer, on another computer in a network, or on the Internet. If you've spent any time browsing the Web, you've clicked hyperlinks to jump to different Web sites or pages. The hyperlink actually contains the address of the Web page to which you are jumping. Hyperlinks are easily identified because they normally appear in a different color and are underlined, or the mouse pointer takes on a different shape, like a pointing finger, when you place it on the hyperlink.

You can insert hyperlinks in database objects that link the object to another file. The concept works the same as it does on Web pages. The address contained in the hyperlink might be the URL (Uniform Resource Locator) for a Web page or it might be the path name for another computer file.

1. Open the **AA Step9-1** database from the student data files.

2. Click **Forms** in the Objects bar and then open **March Orders Form** in Design view.

3. Click the **Insert Hyperlink** button on the toolbar. The Insert Hyperlink dialog box opens, as shown in Figure 9-1. (Your screen may alredy contain links depending on the setup options and the computer you are using.)

4. Click the **File** button to "browse" for the file you want the hyperlink to jump to.

5. Double-click the file **New Products** in the student data files. This is an Excel file that you will jump to when you click the hyperlink.

6. Click **OK**. The hyperlink should be selected in your form.

7. Move the hyperlink to the Form Header section.

8. If necessary, edit the text of the hyperlink so it reads **New Products**. Change the font size of the hyperlink to **18** and change the font color to white. Your screen should look similar to Figure 9-2.

9. Switch to Form view.

10. Place the mouse pointer on the hyperlink in the form. Your cursor should turn into the shape of a pointing hand. Then click. This will open the Microsoft Excel program if it's not already open, and the New Products work-

FIGURE 9-1
Insert Hyperlink dialog box

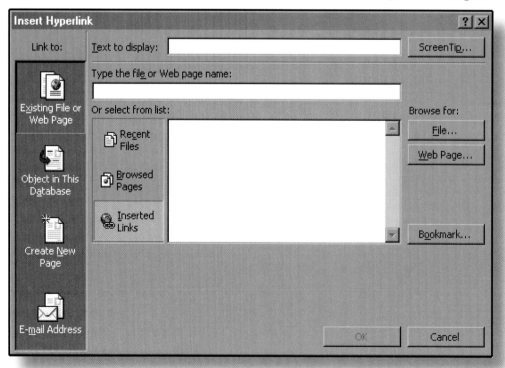

FIGURE 9-2

Formatting the hyperlink

FIGURE 9-3

Web toolbar

sheet will be displayed. The Web toolbar, shown in Figure 9-3, also displays.

11. Click the **Back** button on the Web toolbar to return to your form.

12. If necessary, display the **Web** toolbar in Access. Click the **Forward** button on the Web toolbar to return to Excel spreadsheet.

13. Close the New Products file and exit Excel.

14. Maximize **March Orders Form** if necessary. Close the **Web** toolbar. Print the first record in **March Orders Form** and then close the database.

To modify a hyperlink, *right*-click the hyperlink and select **Hyperlink**, **Edit Hyperlink** on the shortcut menu.

Understanding Data Access Pages

Data access pages are a new feature in Access 2000. A ***data access page*** is an object in the database that lets you set up other objects, such as tables, forms, and reports, so that they can be published to the Web. Then Web users can view and work with the data.

Creating Pages

You create a data access page in much the same manner as you create a form or report. You work in the page's Design view to add and manipulate fields and other controls. You can also group and sort the information that appears in a data access page.

There are three methods for creating a data access page:

- You can use the AutoPage feature. With AutoPage, all you have to do is select a record source, such as a table or query, and then AutoPage automatically creates a data access page using all the fields from this record source.

- You can use the Page Wizard to design a data access page. The wizard asks you questions about the record source, fields, layout, styles, and formats you want to use and then creates a page based on your selections.

- You can also convert an existing Web page into a data access page.

Once you've created a page, you can select Web Page Preview on the File menu to start your browser and view the page. In the following Step-by-Step, you'll create a data access page using AutoPage.

STEP-BY-STEP ▷ 9.2

1. Open the **AA Step9-2** database from the student files.

2. Click **Pages** on the Objects bar and then click **New**.

3. Click the down arrow in the *Choose the table or query* box. Choose the **Book Sales** table.

4. Click **AutoPage: Columnar**. Your screen should look similar to Figure 9-4.

5. Click **OK**. Your screen should look similar to Figure 9-5. Notice the toolbar that displays.

In addition to navigation buttons, the toolbar contains other Access buttons for sorting and filtering data. AutoPage automatically names the page using the table name from which it was created.

6. Close the page. If a message box appears asking if you want to save changes to the page, click **Yes**. Remain in this screen for the next Step-by-Step.

FIGURE 9-4

New Data Access Page dialog box

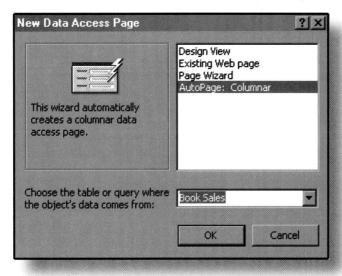

FIGURE 9-5

Data access page

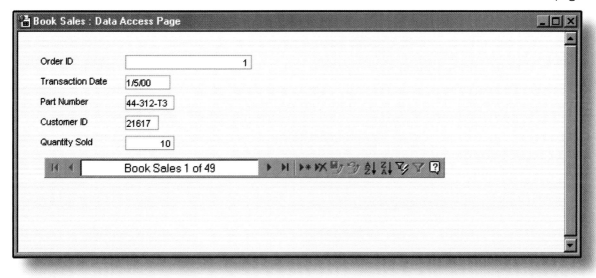

CREATING PAGES WITH THE WIZARD

AutoPage is a suitable tool for quickly creating a data access page using all the fields in the record source. However, you may want a little more flexibility in choosing the fields you want on the page, and you might want to group or sort the page data. The Page Wizard lets you choose the desired fields, the field you would like the page to be grouped by, and how you want the records sorted.

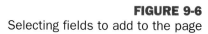

1. If necessary, click **Pages** on the Objects bar.

2. Double-click **Create data access page by using wizard**. The Page Wizard opens.

3. Click the down arrow in the *Table/Queries* box and select the **Inventory** table.

4. Click the right-pointing double-arrow button to place all the fields in the table in the *Select Fields* box. Your screen should look similar to Figure 9-6.

5. Click **Next**. The Page Wizard asks if you want grouping levels applied. Click the **Part Number** field and click the single right-pointing arrow to group the records by part number. Your screen should look similar to Figure 9-7.

6. Click **Next**. The Page Wizard asks if you want to sort the records. Click the arrow in the first text box and choose **In Stock**. Your screen should look like Figure 9-8.

FIGURE 9-6
Selecting fields to add to the page

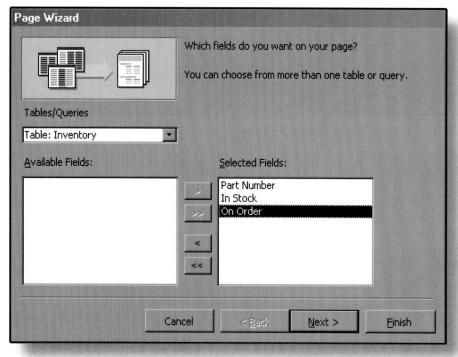

FIGURE 9-7
Choosing a field to group by

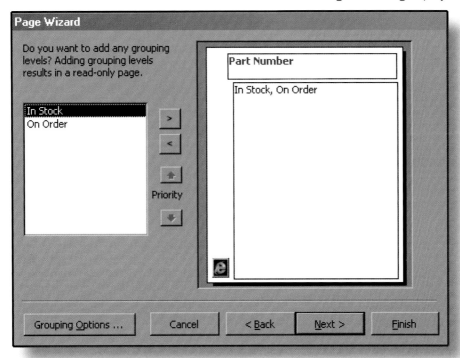

FIGURE 9-8
Choosing a field to sort by

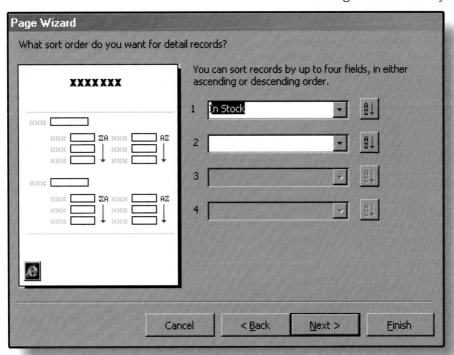

(continued on next page)

A A - 1 2 1

7. Click **Next**. The Page Wizard asks you to name the page. Key **In Stock Inventory** in the title box and select the **Open the page** option, if necessary. Your screen should look similar to Figure 9-9.

8. Click **Finish**. Click the **+** button next to *GroupOfInventory-Part Number* to display the field information on the part. Your screen should look similar to Figure 9-10.

9. Use the record movement buttons to move to other records. You can click the **+** button in each record to display the In Stock and On Order information.

10. Close the page. Click **Yes** if you are asked if you want to save design changes and remain in this screen for the next Step-by-Step.

FIGURE 9-9
Naming the data access page

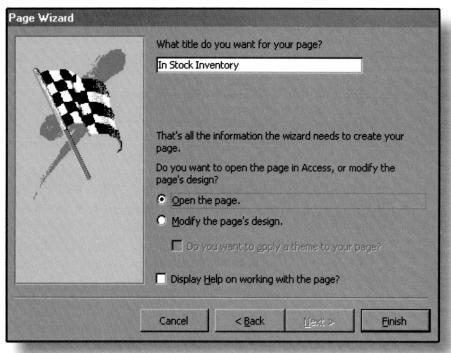

FIGURE 9-10
Completed page

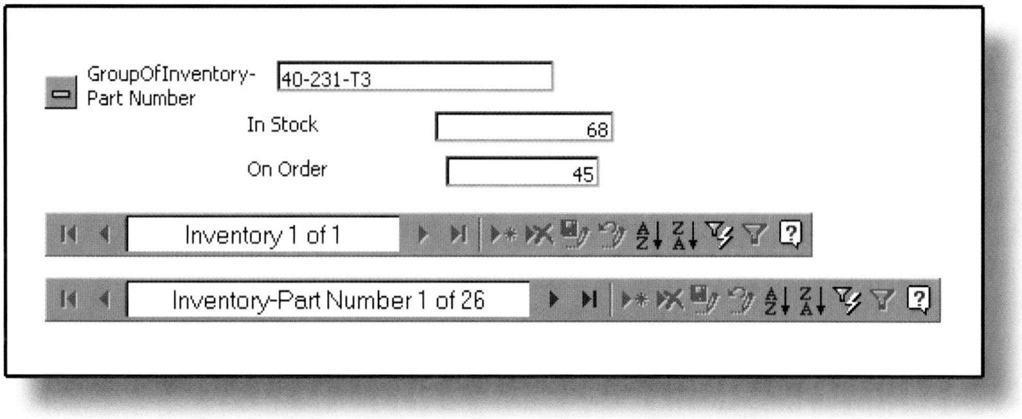

Making Changes to Page Design

You can change a page's design much like you modify the design of a form or report. You can add or remove fields. Fields and controls can be sized and moved and data can be formatted in the same manner. When you place the mouse pointer over a field in the Page Design view, your mouse pointer turns into a four-headed arrow, instead of the two-headed arrow you saw in forms and reports.

STEP-BY-STEP ▷ 9.4

1. If necessary, click **Pages** on the Objects bar, select the **In Stock Inventory**, and then click the **Design** button.

2. Click the **Click here and type title text** and key **Inventory**. Click outside the text area to deselect it.

3. Place your mouse pointer over the right side of the In Stock field and click. Notice how your mouse pointer turns into a four-headed arrow as you move it over the selection handles.

4. Place your mouse pointer over the middle right selection handle. When you see the four-headed arrow, press and hold the mouse button down and drag to the right about $1/2$ inch. The In Stock field should be about $1/2$ inch wider than it was before you resized it.

5. You will now move the On Order field. Place your mouse pointer over the right side of the **On Order** field. Press and hold the mouse button down and drag to the right. Notice how both sides of the field control move. Position

(continued on next page)

the right box of the control so it is centered under the right box of the In Stock field.

6. Now let's move the left side of the On Order field. Place your mouse pointer over the left side of the **On Order** field, press and hold the mouse button down, and drag until the left side of the On Order box is aligned with the left side of *In Stock*.

7. Click the **View** button to see how your modifications look. If necessary, click the **+** sign. Your screen should look similar to Figure 9-11.

8. Click the **Save** button to save the page. Then select **Web Page Preview** on the **File** menu. This will start Internet Explorer and display the page as it will appear to other users on the Web.

9. Close Internet Explorer. In Access, close the **In Stock Inventory** page and then close the database.

FIGURE 9-11
Moving and resizing controls

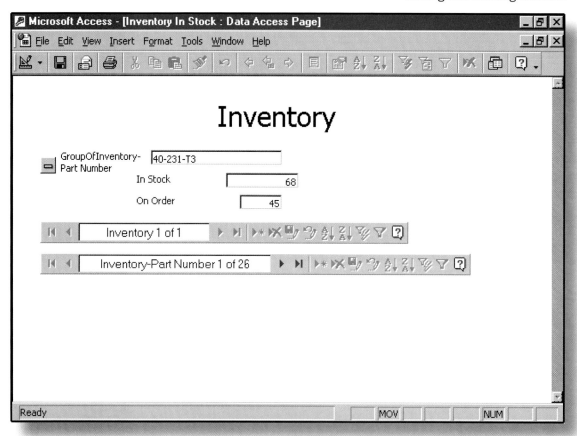

Summary

In this lesson, you learned:

■ You can insert hyperlinks in database objects that link the object to another file. The concept works the same as it does on Web pages. The address contained in the hyperlink might be the URL (Uniform Resource Locator) for a Web page or it might be the path name for another computer file.

■ A data access page is an object in the database that lets you set up other objects, such as tables, forms, and reports, so that they can be published to the Web. Other Web users can then view and work with the data. You design and modify data access pages in much the same manner as you would a form or report.

LESSON 9 REVIEW QUESTIONS

TRUE/FALSE

Circle T if the statement is true or F if the statement is false.

T F   1.   A hyperlink in a database object can only link the object to another file on the same computer.

T F   2.   To insert a hyperlink, you click the Insert Hyperlink button on the Web toolbar.

T F   3.   You can edit and format a hyperlink once it has been inserted in the object's Design view.

T F   4.   You can modify and format the design of a data access page just as you would a form or report.

T F   5.   You cannot add fields to a page after it has been created using the Page Wizard.

WRITTEN QUESTIONS

Write a brief answer to the following questions.

1. What is a hyperlink? Why might you want to create one?

2. How do you create a hyperlink?

3. How can you identify a hyperlink in a file?

4. What is the purpose of a page?

5. What are the three methods for creating a page?

LESSON 9 PROJECTS

PROJECT 9-1

1. Open the **AA Project9-1** database from the student data files.

2. Open the **Products Purchased by Customer** form in Design view.

3. Insert a hyperlink in the Form Header section that jumps to the **Product List** Excel file in the student data files. Edit the label for the hyperlink, if desired.

4. Change the name of the hyperlink label, if desired. Test the hyperlink by moving forward and back between programs.

5. Close the **Product List** file and Excel.

6. Print the first page of the form. Then close the form and the database.

PROJECT 9-2

1. Open the **AA Project9-2** database from the student data files.

2. Create a data access page for the **Products** table. Use the **Product ID**, **Product Name**, **English Name**, and **Units in Stock** fields. Sort by the **English Name** field.

3. Save the page as **Available Products**. View the page on the Web, if desired.

4. Key a title in the page's Design view of **Available Products**.

5. Close the database.

CRITICAL THINKING

ACTIVITY 9-1

You want to create a data access page for your company's intranet that your sales force can access to review transactions. You also want a page that alphabetically lists employees by their last names (and then first names) and their telephone numbers. Use the **AA Activity9-1** database in the student data files to create the pages.

ACTIVITY 9-2

Several months ago, you inserted a hyperlink in a database report that jumps to the Web site for one of your company's distributors. Today, you click the hyperlink and you get a message telling you the Web site cannot be found. Write a brief essay that explains what the problem might be.

USING ADVANCED ACCESS TOOLS

OBJECTIVES

Upon completion of this lesson, you should be able to:

■ Compact a database.

■ Distinguish between encrypting and decrypting a database.

■ Secure a database.

■ Set a password for a database.

■ Set startup options.

■ Understand the use of add-ins.

⏱ Estimated Time: 1 hour

Access offers a variety of features that can assist you in managing your database files. In this lesson, you will learn how to compact a fragmented database so that it is stored most efficiently on disk. You will also learn about the various security features you can apply to the information contained in a database. Databases often contain sensitive information, such as employee salaries, so it is important for you to understand how to protect them. Access also comes with a number of "add-in" applications that are designed to give you more control over the objects in the database. These applications are called add-ins because they typically are not included in the standard installation of Access.

Compacting a Database

When you use a database over time or if you delete database objects, your database can become fragmented. *Fragmentation* occurs when parts of the database file become scattered over an area of the disk where the file is stored. This can cause the database to run slower and less efficiently.

Compacting or *defragmenting* a database removes the unused or wasted space within the database file. A database should be compacted on a regular basis. Compacting is also a great method for making a copy of your database. For example, if your database is saved to a shared location, you may want to make a copy of it and store it on your computer's hard drive. This procedure will create a backup of the database on your hard drive.

 Concept Builder

You can convert a database file to a previous version of Access. To convert an opened database file, open the **Tools** menu, choose **Database Utilities**, choose **Convert Database**, and then select **To Prior Access Database Version**. A dialog box opens that asks you to enter a filename for the converted file. Click **Save**.

1. Open the **AA Step10-1** database from the student files.

2. Open the **Tools** menu and select **Database Utilities**.

3. Click **Compact and Repair Database**. Your database is now compacted. Close the database.

Hot Tip

To compact a database that isn't open, open the Tools menu in Microsoft Access select Database Utilities. Click Compact Database and Repair Database. In the Database To Compact From dialog box, select the database you want to compact. Click Compact. In the Compact Database Into dialog box, enter a file name for the new compacted file.

Encrypting and Decrypting a Database

Encrypting means to take meaningful information and turn in into scrambled code of some sort. When you encrypt a database, Access compacts the database file and then makes it indecipherable.

Decrypting refers to removing the encryption. The decryption process unscrambles the encryption code so that your database file once again displays meaningful information.

To encrypt or decrypt a database file, open the Tools menu, select Security, and then select Encrypt/Decrypt Database. Then simply follow the directions provided for using this feature.

Hot Tip

Do not encrypt or decrypt a database when it is open. In a multiuser environment, everyone must close the database file before either of these procedures will work.

Securing a Database

Microsoft Access gives you two methods of securing a database. You can set a password for the database or you can limit what parts of a database can be viewed or changed by setting user-level protection.

Setting a Password

The easiest way to secure a database is to assign a password to the database file. Then when someone tries to open the database file, he or she will need to know the password before it can be opened. You can remove and change a password as well. Open the database using the *Open Exclusive* option in the Open dialog box. Open the Tools menu, select Security, and then select Unset Database Password.

Hot Tip

A password is case sensitive. For example, if you entered **Cat** as your password, you will need to enter **Cat** for the password every time. You could not use **cat**, **CAT**, **cAT**, or any other uppercase/lowercase combination.

C

1. Open the **File** menu, select **Open**, and select the **AA Step10-2** database in the student data files. Click the down arrow on the **Open** button in the lower-right corner and select **Open Exclusive** from the list box.

2. Open the **Tools** menu, select **Security**, and then click **Set Database Password**.

3. In the **Password** box, type **CAT**.

4. In the **Verify** box, type **CAT** again. Your screen should look similar to Figure 10-1.

FIGURE 10-1
Password dialog box

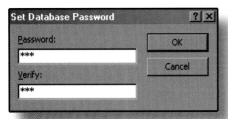

5. Click **OK**. The password is now set. The next time you or anyone else tries to open the database, a password will be required before it will open. Let's try closing and opening this database file.

6. Close the database file.

7. Open the **AA Step 10-2** database file using the **Open Exclusive** option in the Open dialog box. You should see a message box like that shown in Figure 10-2. Key the password and press **OK**.

FIGURE 10-2
Password Required message box

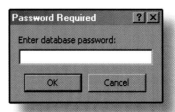

8. Change the database password: Open the **Tools** menu, select **Security**, and then select **Unset Database Password**.

9. Key **CAT** in the Unset Database Password dialog box, and then click **OK**.

10. Close the database and then reopen it. You do not need to enter a password now. Close the data base again.

 **Hot Tip**

If you lose or forget your password, it can't be recovered. You will not be able to open the database file again.

Applying User-Level Security

Another method for securing a database is to set user-level security. Then any individual who wants to use the database is required to enter his or her name and a password when the Access program is started. You typically designate security levels for "users" and "admins." Users are restricted to the information that they can view or change, whereas admins have permission to use all the database objects.

The easiest method for applying user-level security is with the Security Wizard. Open the Tools menu, select Security, and then select User-Level Security Wizard. The first dialog box of the Security Wizard is shown in Figure 10-3. Simply follow the directions in the wizard dialog boxes to set the security options on the file.

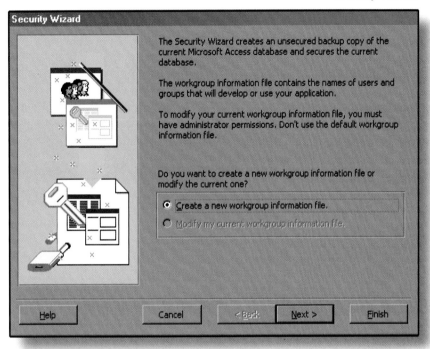

FIGURE 10-3
Security Wizard

Setting Startup Options

As you've worked through this course, you've probably become used to seeing certain screens each time you start Access and a database file. For example, you always see the Menu bar and the Database window when you first start Access and select a database file to open. You can control what you see when you start the program by modifying the program's startup options. The startup options determine how your screen will look when Access is started. These options also let you control which add-ins need to be loaded (you'll learn about these later in this lesson) and various other features, such as whether shortcut menus will be available. To view or change the startup options, select Startup on the Tools menu. The Startup dialog box opens, as shown in Figure 10-4.

Clicking the Advanced button in the Startup dialog box displays the options shown in Figure 10-5. Any changes you make to the startup options will take effect the next time you start Access.

 Did You Know?

Replication of a database enables users at different locations to work with the database and make modifications to it. For example, if you're a salesperson, you can maintain a replica of your company's database on your laptop computer. When you connect to the company's network, you can incorporate the changes you made into the company's existing file. The Replication feature can be found on the Tools menu. This feature is typically not included in the standard Access installation.

FIGURE 10-4
Startup dialog box

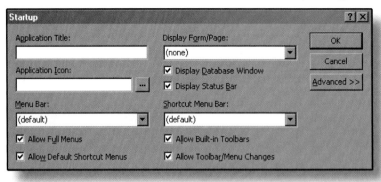

FIGURE 10-5
Advanced startup options

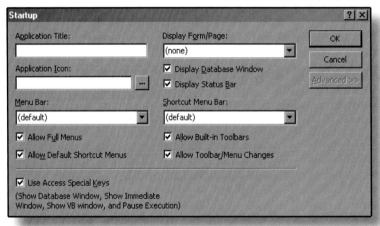

S TEP-BY-STEP ▷ 10.3

1. Open the **AA Step10-3** database from the student data files.

2. Open the **Tools** menu and select **Startup**.

3. Deselect the **Allow Default Shortcut Menus** option, and click **OK**.

4. Close the database file. Then, reopen it.

5. Place your mouse pointer on a table name in the Database window and *right*-click. Notice that a shortcut menu does not appear.

6. Close the database file.

Using Add-Ins

Add-ins are programs, procedures, or objects that can be added to increase the available features in Access. To add an add-in, you can use the Add-in feature. Open the Tools menu, choose Add-Ins, and then select Add-In Manager.

Some of the add-ins that are available in Access are the Database Splitter, Analyzer, and the Link Table Manager. The Database Splitter splits a database file into two files. One file contains the tables and the other file contains the queries, forms, reports, data access pages, macros, and modules. By splitting the database into two files, users can access the data but create their own queries, forms, reports, and so on. This allows for a single source of data on a network. The Database Splitter can be found under Database Utilities on the Tools menu. The first screen of the Database Splitter Wizard is shown in Figure 10-6.

FIGURE 10-6
Database Splitter Wizard

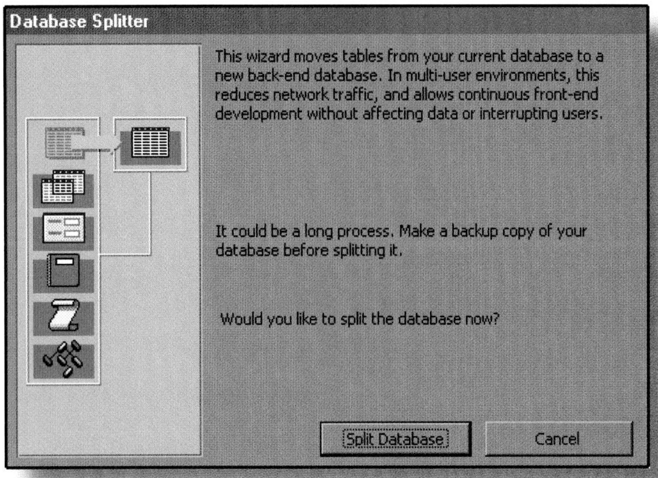

The Table Analyzer Wizard can be used to find a table that contains duplicate information in one or more fields. The Analyzer will locate this data and store it in a related table. This stores your data more efficiently. The Analyzer process is called *normalization*. The first dialog box of the Table Analyzer Wizard is shown in Figure 10-7. This dialog box explains the problems that the Table Analyzer will be looking for. Figure 10-8 shows the second dialog box of the Table Analyzer Wizard. In this dialog box, Access explains how it will take care of the problems it finds. You can find the Table Analyzer under Analyze on the Tools menu. The Linked Table Manager assists you with the process of linking tables located outside the current database.

FIGURE 10-7
Table Analyzer Wizard explains problems it will be looking for

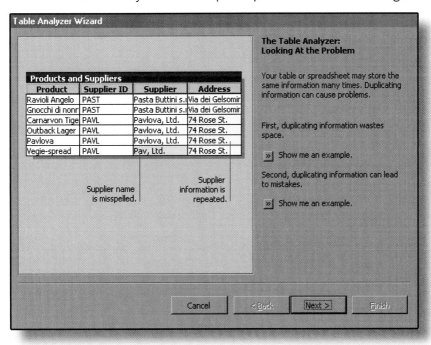

FIGURE 10-8
Table Analyzer Wizard explains how it will solve the problems

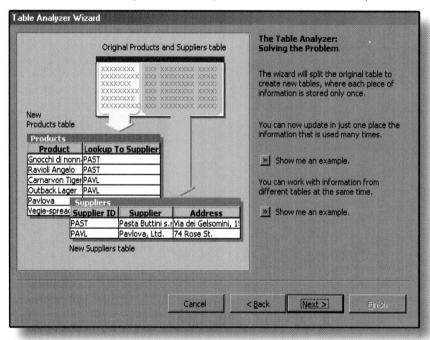

In the following Step-by-Step, you will use the Table Analyzer feature to look for problems in a database table within a database. If Table Analyzer Wizard does not find any problems, Access will display a message to let you know.

S TEP-BY-STEP ▷ 10.4

1. Open the **AA Step10-4** database from the student data files.

2. Click once on the **Transactions** table to highlight the table name in the Database window.

3. Open the **Tools** menu, choose **Analyze**, and then select **Table**.

4. Read the information in the first dialog box of the Table Analyzer Wizard. Then, click **Next**.

5. Read the information in the second dialog box of the Table Analyzer Wizard and click **Next**.

6. Read the information in the next dialog box and then click **Next**.

7. If necessary, click the **Yes, let the wizard decide** option and then click **Next**.

8. A message should appear stating that the wizard does not recommend splitting your table. To close the Table Analyzer Wizard, click **Cancel**.

9. Close the database file.

Summary

In this lesson, you learned:

■ Compacting a database compresses the database and removes any wasted space within the file. This will increase the efficiency of the database.

■ Encrypting scrambles database information so that it cannot be read; decrypting unscrambles the encryption.

■ A database can be secured by creating a password for it or by applying user-level security. If a password is set for a database file, it cannot be opened unless the user enters the password. Database security can be set on an individual basis by giving each user specific permission to view or change data in tables, forms, reports, and so on.

■ You can control the way your screen looks when you start Access by modifying the startup options.

■ Add-ins are additional programs, procedures, and objects that expand the capabilities of Access. Some of the add-ins that are available are the Database Splitter, Analyzer, and the Link Table Manager.

LESSON 10 REVIEW QUESTIONS

WRITTEN QUESTIONS

Write a brief answer to the following questions.

1. Describe what happens to a database file once you encrypt the file.

2. If you wanted to prevent unauthorized personnel from opening a database file, which feature could you use?

3. Which feature would you use to give certain persons access to specific information within a database file?

4. Give a brief description of the Table Analyzer feature.

5. List two two startup options you can modify.

6. Over time, a database becomes fragmented. Describe what you could do to fix this problem.

7. Define fragmentation.

8. What is meant by defragmentation?

9. If you wanted to prevent an individual from having any access to database information, would you set password protection or user-level security? Why?

10. Describe how the Database Splitter works.

LESSON 10 PROJECT

PROJECT 10-1

1. Assign a password of DOG to the **AA Project10-1** database in the student data files.

2. Close the file and reopen it to test the password.

CRITICAL THINKING

ACTIVITY 10-1

As the new systems manager for a small business, you want to know how to secure the information contained in the company's database. Specifically, you need to know how to apply user-level security to a new workgroup. Use Access's Help system and resources on the Internet to find information. Write a brief essay that describes how you would go about adding a new workgroup and securing the database file.

A A - 1 3 9

COMMAND SUMMARY

FEATURE	MENU COMMAND	TOOLBAR BUTTON	LESSON
Build expression			4
Condition, add to macro action			8
Datasheet View	View, Datasheet View		
Deletes selected record	Edit, Delete Record		
Field List	View, Field List		
Find Record	Edit, Find		
Form View	View, Form View		
Hyperlink	Insert, Hyperlink		9
Macro, run		Run	8
Merge table with Word or Excel			7
Moves to the first record	Edit, Go To, First		
Moves to the last record	Edit, Go To, Last		
Moves to the next record	Edit, Go To, Next		
Moves to the previous record	Edit, Go To, Previous		
New Record	Insert, New Record		
Properties	View, Properties		3
Query, create			4
Query, run		Run	2
Relationship, create			2
Toolbox	View, Toolbox		6
Totals			4
Undo	Edit, Undo		

TRUE/FALSE

Circle T if the statement is true or F if the statement is false.

T F   1. Before you can add a subform to a form, both the main form and subform must already be created.

T F   2. You must use the Expression Builder to calculate values in fields.

T F   3. You do not have to enforce referential integrity in a table.

T F   4. A data access page allows Web users to interact with selected database objects.

T F   5. A lookup field is created automatically by the Input Mask Wizard.

MULTIPLE CHOICE

Select the best response for the following statements.

1. To create a subform you must open the main form and switch to
    A. Form view
    B. Print Preview
    C. Form Design view
    D. Table Design view
    E. None of the above

2. A hyperlink allows you to
    A. jump from one document to another
    B. jump from a subform to Web sites
    C. jump to an intranet site
    D. all of the above
    E. none of the above

3. In the Query Design screen, the primary field is
    A. indicated on the status bar
    B. bolded
    C. the field that is linked
    D. all of the above
    E. none of the above

4. On the relationship line connecting two tables, a *1* indicates
   A. the primary table
   B. the related table
   C. the related field
   D. the primary key of the related table
   E. none of the above

5. Setting required properties in a table field to *Yes*
   A. forces data to be entered into the field
   B. prohibits you from moving to the next record until data is entered into the field
   C. forces you to use an input mask for the field
   D. both A and B are correct
   E. both B and C are correct

APPLICATIONS

APPLICATION 1

SCANS

1. Open the **AA App1** database from the student data files.

2. Create a query using the **Employees** table that displays only those employees who work in the Sales Department. Show all the fields in the query and name the query **Sales Department**. Print the query results in landscape orientation.

3. Create a query using both the **Employees** and **Personnel Information** tables that displays the last name, first name, department, and telephone number for each employee and name the query **Telephone List**. Print the query results.

4. Create a report from the **Telephone List** query with the employee information grouped by **Department** and sorted by **Last Name** and then **First Name** within the department. Use a layout and style of your choice. Name the report **Telephone List**. Make any modifications to the design of the report that you feel are necessary. Print the report.

APPLICATION 2

SCANS

1. Open the **AA App2** database from the student data files.

2. Create a query from the **Products** table that displays Dairy products (Category ID 4) and Grains/Cereals products (Category ID 5) only. Display all the fields. Name the query **Dairy and Grains/Cereals**. Print the query results in landscape orientation.

3. Create a query from the **Products** table that displays Discontinued items only. Display all the fields. Name the query **Discontinued Products**. Print the query results in landscape orientation.

4. Create a form for each of the above queries. The forms should be in a tabular format using a style of your choice. Name the forms using the same names as the queries from which you created them. Modify the design of each form as you feel necessary. Then print each form.

5. Create a switchboard form that automatically appears maximized when the database file is opened. The switchboard form should include macro buttons that open and maximize the **Discontinued Products** form and the **Dairy and Grains/Cereals** form.

6. Test the macros and then close the database file.

ON-THE-JOB SIMULATION

JOB 1

SCANS

You are the new administrative assistant for the Registrar's Office at WUC University. The employees in the Registrar's Office are challenged by the current database and they want you to make it easier for them to use. Open the **AA Job1** database from the student data files. In reviewing the objects in the database, you realize that in order to make it more user friendly, you need to create the following information.

1. Forms that display each level of student Class status. (*Hint*: Create the forms from queries that display students from each class.) Name each form according to the class.

2. A form that displays students who are at risk for scholastic probation with grade point averages lower than 2.25. (*Hint*: Create the form from a query that finds students with the lower GPAs.) Name the form **Probation Possibles**.

3. A form that displays students who will appear on the Dean's List with grade point averages of 3.5 or higher. (*Hint*: Create the form from a query that finds students with the higher GPAs.) Name the form **Dean's List**.

4. To make these forms user-friendly, you decide to include a Close macro button in each form. After you have added the macro button, print the forms.

5. Finally, you decide that you would like a switchboard form to appear when a user opens the database file. The form will contain macro buttons to display the forms. Name the form **Switchboard**.

JOB 2

You are the owner of the Best Bet Products Distribution Center. You've created an Access database that contains the names and addresses of your customers, the products your company sells, and the costs of the products. Sales are excellent this year and you want to show appreciation to your customers for their loyalty. Therefore, you create a query that calculates total sales by customer using the **Customers**, **Products**, and **Transactions** tables. Then you need to create mailing labels for the customers whose sales were greater than $100. These mailing labels will be used to send out discount coupons to each customer. Use the **AA Job2** database in the student data files for this job.

APPROVED COURSEWARE
EXPERT

THE MICROSOFT OFFICE USER SPECIALIST PROGRAM

What Is Certification?

The logos on the cover of this book indicate that the book is officially certified by Microsoft Corporation at the **Core** and **Expert** user skill level for Access 2000 in Word. This certification is part of the **Microsoft Office User Specialist (MOUS)** program that validates your skills as knowledgeable of Microsoft Access.

The following grids outline the various Core and Expert skills and where they are covered in this book.

MICROSOFT ACCESS 2000 CORE
TOTAL OBJECTIVES: 48

Standardized Coding Number	Activity	ICV Performance based?	Lesson #	Pages	Exercise #
AC2000.1	**Planning and designing databases**				
AC2000.1.1	Determine appropriate data inputs for your database	No	1	4	
AC2000.1.2	Determine appropriate data outputs for your database	No	1	4-5	
AC2000.1.3	Create table structure	**Yes**	**1**	**11**	**SBS1.6**
AC2000.1.4	Establish table relationships	**Yes**	**4**	**73**	**SBS4.9**
AC2000.2	**Working with Access**				
AC2000.2.1	Use the Office Assistant	No	IN-1	10	
AC2000.2.2	Select an object using the Objects Bar	**Yes**	**1**	**6**	**SBS1.3**
AC2000.2.3	Print database objects (tables, forms, reports, queries)	**Yes**	**1, 3, 4, 5**	**18, 50, 65, 92**	**SBS1.10, 3.6, 4.3, 5.6**
AC2000.2.4	Navigate through records in a table, query, or form	**Yes**	**1, 3**	**16, 48**	**SBS1.9, 3.5**
AC2000.2.5	Create a database (using a Wizard or in Design View)	**Yes**	**1**	**8**	**SBS1.4**
AC2000.3	**Building and modifying tables**				
AC2000.3.1	Create tables by using the Table Wizard	**Yes**	**1**	**24**	**ACT1-1**
AC2000.3.2	Set primary keys	**Yes**	**4**	**72**	**SBS4.8**
AC2000.3.3	Modify field properties	No	2	35	SBS2.9
AC2000.3.4	Use multiple data types	**Yes**	**1**	**11**	**SBS1.6**
AC2000.3.5	Modify tables using Design View	**Yes**	**2**	**35**	**SBS2.9**
AC2000.3.6	Use the Lookup Wizard	No	1	11	
AC2000.3.7	Use the input mask wizard	No	2	35	
AC2000.4	**Building and modifying forms**				
AC2000.4.1	Create a form with the Form Wizard	**Yes**	**3**	**43**	**SBS3.1**

Standardized Coding Number	Activity	ICV Performance based?	Lesson #	Pages	Exercise #
AC2000.4.2	Use the Control Toolbox to add controls	Yes	3	50	SBS3.6
AC2000.4.3	Modify Format Properties (font, style, font size, color, caption, etc.) of controls	Yes	3	50	SBS3.6
AC2000.4.4	Use form sections (headers, footers, detail)	Yes	3	50	SBS3.6
AC2000.4.5	Use a Calculated Control on a form	Yes	3	54	SBS3.7
AC2000.5	**Viewing and organizing information**				
AC2000.5.1	Use the Office Clipboard	No	2	41	ACT2-2
AC2000.5.2	Switch between object Views	Yes	1	16	SBS1.9
AC2000.5.3	Enter records using a datasheet	No	1	15-16	
AC2000.5.4	Enter records using a form	Yes	3	48	SBS3.5
AC2000.5.5	Delete records from a table	Yes	2	29	SBS2.3
AC2000.5.6	Find a record	Yes	4	61	SBS4.1
AC2000.5.7	Sort records	Yes	4	69	SBS4.5
AC2000.5.8	Apply and remove filters (filter by form and filter by selection)	Yes	4	67	SBS4.4
AC2000.5.9	Specify criteria in a query	Yes	4	65	SBS4.3
AC2000.5.10	Display related records in a subdatasheet	No	4	76	SBS4.11
AC2000.5.11	Create a calculated field	Yes	4	65	SBS4.3
AC2000.5.12	Create and modify a multi-table select query	Yes	4	78	SBS4.12
AC2000.6	**Defining relationships**				
AC2000.6.1	Establish relationships	Yes	4	73	SBS4.9
AC2000.6.2	Enforce referential integrity	Yes	4	73	SBS4.9
AC2000.7	**Producing reports**				
AC2000.7.1	Create a report with the Report Wizard	Yes	5	85	SBS5.1
AC2000.7.2	Preview and print a report	Yes	5	92	SBS5.6
AC2000.7.3	Move and resize a control	No	5	94	SBS5.7
AC2000.7.4	Modify format properties (font, style, font size, color, caption, etc.)	Yes	5	94	SBS5.7
AC2000.7.5	Use the Control Toolbox to add controls	Yes	5	94	SBS5.7
AC2000.7.6	Use report sections (headers, footers, detail)	Yes	5	94	SBS5.7
AC2000.7.7	Use a Calculated Control in a report	Yes	5	94	SBS5.7
AC2000.8	**Integrating with other application**				
AC2000.8.1	Import data to a new table	Yes	6	106	SBS6.1
AC2000.8.2	Save a table, query, form as a Web page	No	4	65-Did You Know?	
AC2000.8.3	Add Hyperlinks	No	3, 6	55, 118	ACT6-2
AC2000.9	**Using Access Tools**				
AC2000.9.1	Print Database Relationships	Yes	4	75	SBS4.10
AC2000.9.2	Backup and Restore a database	No	6	106-HOT TIP	
AC2000.9.3	Compact and Repair a database	No	3	55	

MICROSOFT ACCESS 2000 EXPERT
TOTAL OBJECTIVES: 44

Standardized Coding Number	Activity	ICV Performance based?	Lesson #	Pages	Exercise #
AC2000E.1.	**Building and modifying tables**				
AC2000E.1.1	Set validation text	Yes	1	8	SBS1.3
AC2000E.1.2	Define data validation criteria	Yes	1	8	SBS1.3
AC2000E.1.3	Modify an input mask	No	1	2	SBS1.1
AC2000E.1.4	Create and modify Lookup Fields	Yes	1	10	SBS1.5
AC2000E.1.5	Optimize data type usage (double, long, int, byte, etc.)	No	1	15	ACT1-2
AC2000E.2	**Building and modifying forms**				
AC2000E.2.1	Create a form in Design View	Yes	3	37	SBS3.4
AC2000E.2.2	Insert a graphic on a form	No	3	37	SBS3.4
AC2000E.2.3	Modify control properties	Yes	3	37	SBS3.4
AC2000E.2.4	Customize form sections (headers, footers, detail)	Yes	3	37	SBS3.4
AC2000E.2.5	Modify form properties	No	3	36	SBS3.3
AC2000E.2.6	Use the Subform Control and synchronize forms	Yes	3	30	SBS3.1
AC2000E.2.7	Create a Switchboard	Yes	8	101	SBS8.4
AC2000E.3	**Refining queries**				
AC2000E.3.1	Apply filters (filter by form and filter by selection) in a query's recordset	Yes	4	51	SBS4.7
AC2000E.3.2	Create a totals query	Yes	4	46	SBS4.3
AC2000E.3.3	Create a parameter query	Yes	5	57	SBS5.2
AC2000E.3.4	Specify criteria in multiple fields (AND vs. OR)	Yes	4	49, 50	SBS4.5, 4.6
AC2000E.3.5	Modify query properties (field formats, caption, input masks, etc.)	Yes	4	46	SBS4.2
AC2000E.3.6	Create an action query (update, delete, insert)	Yes	5	59-64	SBS5.3, 5.4, 5.5
AC2000E.3.7	Optimize queries using indexes	No	5	59-Concept Builder	
AC2000E.3.8	Specify join properties for relationships	Yes	2	23	SBS2.7
AC2000E.4	**Producing reports**				
AC2000E.4.1	Insert a graphic on a report	No	6	72	SBS6.3
AC2000E.4.2	Modify report properties	Yes	6	73	SBS6.4
AC2000E.4.3	Create and modify a report in Design View	Yes	6	79	SBS6.6
AC2000E.4.4	Modify control properties	Yes	6	69-72	SBS6.1, 6.2, 6.3
AC2000E.4.5	Set section properties	No	6	72	SBS6.3
AC2000E.4.6	Use the Subreport Control and synchronize reports	Yes	6	79	SBS6.6
AC2000E.5	**Defining relationships**				
AC2000E.5.1	Establish one-to-one relationships	Yes	2	25	SBS2.8
AC2000E.5.2	Establish many-to-many relationships	Yes	2	25	SBS2.9

Standardized Coding Number	Activity	ICV Performance based?	Lesson #	Pages	Exercise #
AC2000E.5.3	Set Cascade Update and Cascade Delete options	No	2	19	
AC2000E.6	**Utilizing web capabilities**				
AC2000E.6.1	Create hyperlinks	**Yes**	**9**	**115**	**SBS9.1**
AC2000E.6.2	Use the group and sort features of data access pages	**Yes**	**9**	**120**	**SBS9.3**
AC2000E.6.3	Create a data access page	**Yes**	**9**	**118, 120**	**SBS9.2, 9.3**
AC2000E.7	**Using Access tools**				
AC2000E.7.1	Set and modify a database password	**Yes**	**10**	**131**	**SBS10.2**
AC2000E.7.2	Set startup options	**Yes**	**10**	**133**	**SBS10.3**
AC2000E.7.3	Use Add-ins (Database Splitter, Analyzer, Link Table Manager)	**Yes**	**10**	**134**	**SBS10.4**
AC2000E.7.4	Encrypt and Decrypt a database	No	10	131	
AC2000E.7.5	Use simple replication (copy for a mobile user)	No	10	133-Did You Know?	
AC2000E.7.6	Run macros using controls	No	8	100	SBS8.3
AC2000E.7.7	Create a macro using the Macro Builder	**Yes**	**8**	**109**	**SBS8.8**
AC2000E.7.8	Convert database to a previous version	No	10	130-Concept Builder	
AC2000E.8	**Data Integration (New Skill Set)**				
AC2000E.8.1	Export database records to Excel	Yes	7	91	SBS7.2
AC2000E.8.2	Drag and drop tables and queries to Excel	**Yes**	**7**	**92**	**SBS7.3**
AC2000E.8.3	Present information as a chart (MS Graph)	**Yes**	**6**	**74**	**SBS6.5**
AC2000E.8.4	Link to existing data	No	7	92	

Key: SBS: Step-by-Step   P: Project   ACT: Critical Thinking Activity
           AP: Application   SIM: On-the-Job Simulation   UR: Unit Review

APPENDIX B

MICROSOFT WINDOWS 98 BASICS

This appendix is designed to familiarize you with the Windows 98 operating system. It provides you with the basic information you need to move around your desktop and manage the files, folders, and other resources you work with on a daily basics. It also covers the Windows 98 Help system.

Starting Windows 98

If Windows 98 is already installed, it should start automatically when you turn on the computer. If your computer is on a network, you may need some help from your instructor.

STEP-BY-STEP ▷ B.1

1. Turn on the computer.

2. After a few moments, Microsoft Windows 98 appears.

The Desktop

When Windows 98 starts up, the first window you see is the desktop. The *desktop* is the space where you access and work with programs and files. Figure B-1 illustrates a typical desktop screen. Your screen may vary slightly from the figure. For example, your screen may display icons that were installed with Windows 98 or shortcut icons you've created. You can customize and organize your desktop by creating files, folders, and shortcuts.

The main features of the desktop screen are labeled and numbered on the figure and discussed below:

1. The *Start* button brings up menus that give you a variety of options, such as starting a program, opening a document, finding help, or shutting down the computer.

2. The *Quick Launch* toolbar to the right of the Start button contains icons so you can display the desktop or quickly start frequently used programs.

3. The *taskbar,* located at the bottom of the screen, tells you the names of all open programs. Figure B-1 shows that Microsoft Word is open.

4. *My Computer* is a program that allows you to see what files and folders are located on your computer.

5. *Internet Explorer* is a Web browser that allows you to surf the Internet, read e-mail, create a Web page, or download your favorite Web sites right to your desktop.

6. **Network Neighborhood** shows all the folders and printers that are available to you through the network connection, if you have one.

7. The **Recycle Bin** is a place to get rid of files or folders that are no longer needed.

8. Other **icons,** or small pictures, represent programs waiting to be opened.

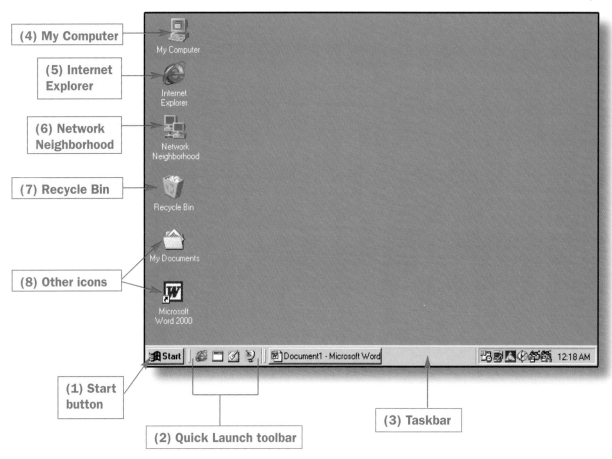

FIGURE B-1
Windows 98 desktop

Windows 98 makes it easy to connect to the Internet. Just click the Launch Internet Explorer Browser button on the Quick Launch toolbar. The Quick Launch toolbar also has buttons so you can launch Outlook Express, view channels, and show the desktop.

With Windows 98 you can incorporate Web content into your work by using the Active Desktop, an interface that lets you put "active items" from the Internet on your desktop. You can use channels to customize the information delivered from the Internet to your computer. By displaying the Channel bar on your desktop you can add, subscribe to, or view channels.

1. Click the **Launch Internet Explorer Browser** button on the Quick Launch toolbar.

2. Click the **Show Desktop** button on the Quick Launch toolbar to display the Windows 98 desktop.

3. Click the **Internet** | about:blank - Microsoft I... | **Explorer** button on the taskbar to return to the browser window. (Your button may look a little different.)

4. Choose **Close** on the **File** menu to close Internet Explorer.

5. Point to the **Start** button.

6. Click the left mouse button. A menu of choices appears above the Start button as shown in Figure B-2.

7. Point to **Settings** without clicking. A submenu appears.

8. Click on **Control Panel**. A new window appears. The title bar at the top tells you that *Control Panel* is the name of the open window.

9. Leave this window on the screen for the next Step-by-Sep.

FIGURE B-2
Clicking the
Start button

Using Windows

Many of the windows you will work with have similar features. You can work more efficiently by familiarizing yourself with some of the common elements, as shown in Figure B-3, and explained below.

1. A *title bar* is at the top of every window and contains the name of the open program, window, document, or folder.

2. The *menu bar* lists available menus from which you can choose a variety of commands.

3. The *standard toolbar,* located directly below the menu bar, contains commands you can use by simply clicking the correct button.

4. The *Address bar* tells you which folder's contents are being displayed. You can also key a Web address in the Address bar without first opening your browser.

5. At the bottom of the window is the *status bar* that gives you directions on how to access menus and summarizes the actions of the commands that you choose.

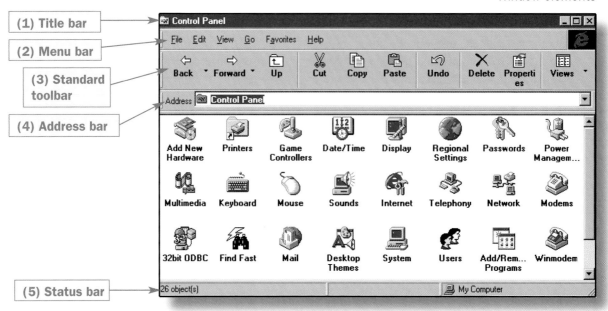

(1) Title bar
(2) Menu bar
(3) Standard toolbar
(4) Address bar
(5) Status bar

Moving and Resizing Windows

Sometimes you will have several windows open on the screen at the same time. To work more effectively, you may need to move or change the size of a window. To move a window, click the title bar and drag the window to another location. You can resize a window by dragging the window borders. When you position the pointer on a horizontal border, it changes to a vertical two-headed arrow. When you position the pointer on a vertical border, it changes to a horizontal two-headed arrow. You can then click and drag the border to change the width or height of the window. It is also possible to resize two sides of a window at the same time. When you move the pointer to a corner of the window's border, it becomes a two-headed arrow pointing diagonally. You can then click and drag to resize the window's height and width at the same time.

STEP-BY-STEP ▷ B.3

1. Move the **Control Panel** window by clicking on the title bar and holding the left mouse button down. Continue to hold the left mouse button down and drag the Control Panel until it appears to be centered on the screen. Release the mouse button.

2. Point anywhere on the border at the bottom of the Control Panel window. The pointer turns into a vertical two-headed arrow.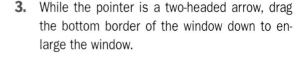

3. While the pointer is a two-headed arrow, drag the bottom border of the window down to enlarge the window.

4. Point to the border on the right side of the Control Panel window. The pointer turns into a horizontal two-headed arrow.

5. While the pointer is a two-headed arrow, drag the border of the window to the right to enlarge the window.

6. Point to the lower right corner of the window border. The pointer becomes a two-headed arrow pointing diagonally.

7. Drag the border upward and to the left to resize both sides at the same time until the window is

about the same size as the one shown in Figure B-4.

8. Leave the window on the screen for the next Step-by-Step.

FIGURE B-4
Scroll bars, arrows, and boxes

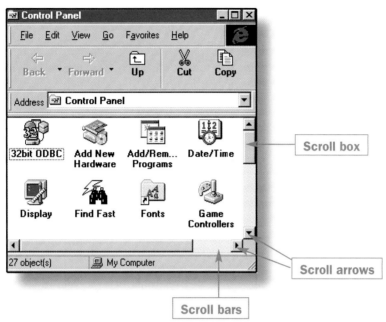

Scroll Bars

A *scroll bar* appears on the edges of windows any time there is more to be displayed than a window can show at its current size. See Figure B-4. A scroll bar can appear along the bottom edge (horizontal) and/or along the right side (vertical) of a window. Scroll bars appeared in the last step of the preceding Step-by-Step because the window was too small to show all the icons at once.

Scroll bars are a convenient way to bring another part of the window's contents into view. On the scroll bar is a sliding box called the *scroll box*. The scroll box indicates your position within the window. When the scroll box reaches the bottom of the scroll bar, you have reached the end of the window's contents. *Scroll arrows* are located at the ends of the scroll bar. Clicking on a scroll arrow moves the window in that direction one line at a time.

S TEP-BY-STEP ▷ B.4

1. On the horizontal scroll bar, click the scroll arrow that points to the right. The contents of the window shifts to the left.

2. Press and hold the mouse button on the same scroll arrow. The contents of the window scroll

(continued on next page)

quickly across the window. Notice that the scroll box moves to the right end of the scroll bar.

3. You can also scroll by dragging the scroll box. Drag the scroll box on the horizontal scroll bar to the left.

4. Drag the scroll box on the vertical scroll bar to the middle of the scroll bar.

5. The final way to scroll is to click on the scroll bar. Click the horizontal scroll bar to the right of the scroll box. The contents scroll left.

6. Click the horizontal scroll bar to the left of the scroll box. The contents scroll right.

7. Resize the Control Panel until the scroll bars disappear.

Other Window Controls

Three other important window controls, located on the right side of the title bar, are the **maximize button,** the **minimize button,** and the **Close button** (see Figure B-5). The maximize button enlarges a window to the full size of the screen. The minimize button shrinks a window to a button on the taskbar. The button on the taskbar is labeled and you can click it any time to redisplay the window. The Close button is used to close a window.

When a window is maximized, the maximize button is replaced by the restore button (see Figure B-6). The **restore button** returns the window to the size it was before the maximize button was clicked.

FIGURE B-5
Maximize, minimize, and Close buttons

FIGURE B-6
Restore button

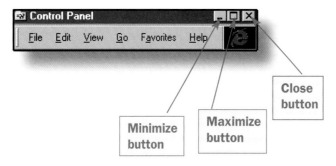

1. Click the **maximize** button. The window enlarges to fill the screen.

2. Click the **restore** button on the Control Panel window (see Figure B-6).

3. Click the **minimize** button on the Control Panel window. The window is reduced to a button on the taskbar.

4. Click the **Control Panel** button on the taskbar to open the window again.

5. Click the **Close** button to close the window.

Menus and Dialog Boxes

To find out what a restaurant has to offer, you look at the menu. You can also look at a *menu* on the computer's screen to find out what a computer program has to offer. Menus in computer programs contain options for executing certain actions or tasks.

When you click the Start button, as you did earlier in this appendix, a menu is displayed with a list of options. If you choose a menu option with an arrow beside it, a submenu opens that lists additional options. A menu item followed by an ellipsis (...) indicates that a dialog box will appear when chosen. A *dialog box,* like the Shut Down Windows dialog box shown in Figure

FIGURE B-7
Dialog box

B-7, appears when more information is required before the command can be performed. You may have to key information, choose from a list of options, or simply confirm that you want the command to be performed. To back out of a dialog box without performing an action, press Esc, click the Close button, or choose Cancel (or No).

STEP-BY-STEP ▷ B.6

1. Click the **Start** button. A menu appears.

2. Click **Shut Down**. The Shut Down Windows dialog box appears, as shown in Figure B-7.

3. Click **Cancel** to back out of the dialog box without shutting down.

In a Windows application, menus are accessed from a menu bar (see Figure B-8). A menu bar appears beneath the title bar in each Windows program and consists of a row of menu names such as File and Edit. Each name in the menu bar represents a separate *pull-down menu*, containing related options. Pull-down menus are convenient to use because the commands are in front of you on the screen, as shown in Figure B-8. Like a menu in a restaurant, you can view a list of choices and pick the one you want.

You can give commands from pull-down menus using either the keyboard or the mouse. Each menu on the menu bar and each option on a menu is characterized by an underlined letter called a *mnemonic*. To open a menu on the menu bar using the keyboard, press Alt plus the mnemonic letter shown on the menu name. To display a menu using the mouse, simply place the pointer on the menu name and click the left button.

Just as with the Start menu, pull-down menus also have items with right-pointing arrows that open submenus, and ellipses that open dialog boxes. Choosing an item without an ellipsis or a right-pointing arrow executes the command. To close a menu without choosing a command, press Esc.

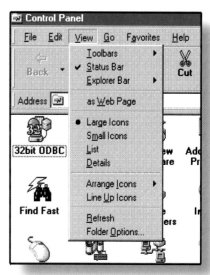

FIGURE B-8
Menu bar

1. Open the Notepad accessory application by clicking **Start**, **Programs**, **Accessories**, and then **Notepad**. (See Figure B-9.)

2. Click **Edit** on the menu bar. The Edit menu appears.

3. Click **Time/Date** to display the current time and date.

4. Click **File** on the menu bar. The File menu appears (see Figure B-10).

5. Click **Exit**. A save prompt box appears.

6. Click **No**. The Notebook window disappears and you return to the desktop.

FIGURE B-9
Opening menus in an application

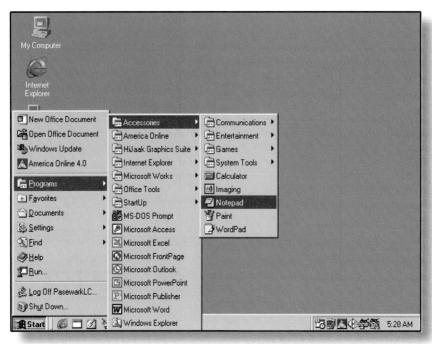

FIGURE B-10
Selecting the Exit command on the File menu

Windows 98 Help

This appendix has covered only a few of the many features of Windows 98. For additional information, Windows 98 has an easy-to-use help system. Use Help as a quick reference when you are unsure about a function. Windows 98 Help is accessed through the Help option on the Start menu. Then, from the Windows Help dialog box, you can choose to see a table of contents displaying general topics and subtopics, as shown in Figure B-11, or to search the help system using the Index or Search options. If you are working in a Windows 98 program, you can get more specific help about topics relating to that program by accessing help from the Help menu on the menu bar.

FIGURE B-11
Windows 98 Help program

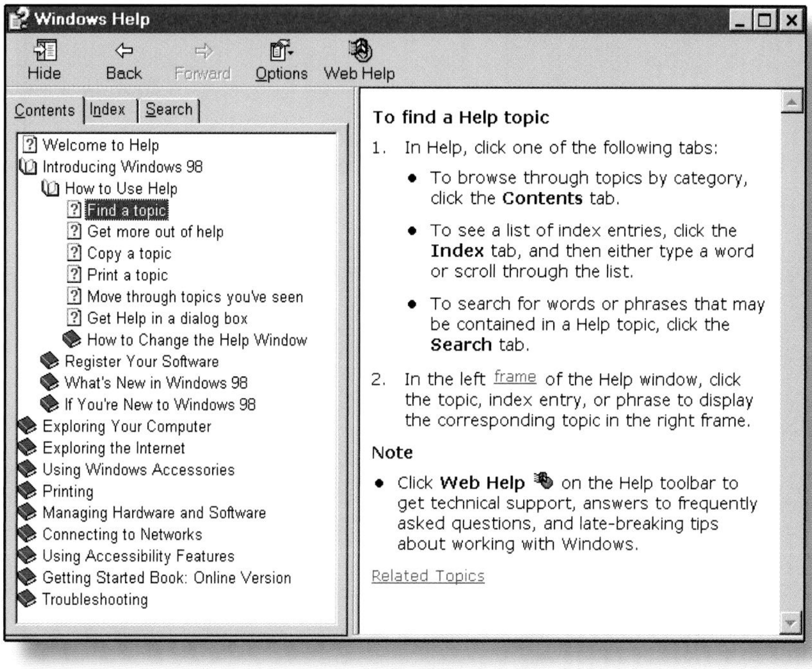

Many topics in the Help program are linked. A *link* is represented by colored, underlined text. By clicking a link, the user "jumps" to a linked document that contains additional information.

Using the buttons on the toolbar controls the display of information. The Hide button removes the left frame of the help window from view. The Show button will restore it. Back and Forward buttons allow you to move back and forth between previously displayed help entries. The Options button offers navigational choices, as well as options to customize, refresh, and print help topics.

The Contents tab is useful if you want to browse through the topics by category. Click a book icon to see additional help topics. Click a question mark to display detailed help information in the right frame of the help window.

STEP-BY-STEP ▷ B.8

1. Open the Windows 98 Help program by clicking the **Start** button, and then **Help**.

2. Click the **Hide** button on the toolbar to remove the left frame, if necessary.

(continued on next page)

3. Click the **Show** button to display it again, if necessary.

4. Click the **Contents** tab if it is not already selected.

5. Click **Introducing Windows 98** and then Click **How to Use Help**. Your screen should appear similar to Figure B-11.

6. Click **Find a topic**.

7. Read the help window and leave it open for the next Step-by-Step.

When you want to search for help on a particular topic, use the Index tab and key in a word. Windows will search alphabetically through the list of help topics to try to find an appropriate match, as shown in Figure B-12. Double-click a topic to see it explained in the right frame of the help window. Sometimes a Topics Found dialog box will appear that displays subtopics related to the item. Double-click the one on which you want more information.

FIGURE B-12
Index tab

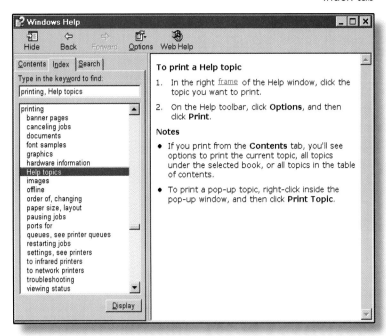

STEP-BY-STEP ▷ B.9

1. Click the **Index** tab.

2. Begin keying **printing** until *printing* is highlighted in the list of index entries.

3. Double-click the **Help topics** subtopic to display information in the right frame as shown in Figure B-12.

4. Read the help window, and then print the infor-mation by following the instructions you read.

5. Click **Back** to return to the previous help entry.

6. Click **Forward** to advance to the next help entry.

7. Close the Help program by clicking the Close button.

The Search tab is similar to the Index tab, but will perform a more thorough search of the words or phrases that you key. By using the Search option, you can display every occurrence of a particular word or phrase throughout the Windows 98 Help system. Double-click on the topic most similar to what you are looking for and information is displayed in the help window.

If you need assistance using the Windows 98 Help program, choose *Introducing Windows 98, How to Use Help* from the Contents tab.

If you are using an Office 2000 application, you can also get help by using the Office Assistant feature. These features are covered in the *Office 2000 Basics and the Internet* lesson.

Other Features

You need to know about several other features of Windows 98 before moving on, including My Computer, Windows Explorer, and the Recycle Bin. When open, these utilities display a standard toolbar like the one shown in Figure B-13.

FIGURE B-13
Standard toolbar

The Back and Forward buttons let you move back and forth between folder contents previously displayed in the window. The Up button moves you up one level in the hierarchy of folders. You can use the Cut, Copy, and Paste buttons to cut or copy an object and then paste it in another location. The Undo button allows you to reverse your most recent action. The Delete button sends the selected object to the Recycle Bin. The Properties button brings up a Properties dialog box with information about the selected object. The View button lists options for displaying the contents of the window.

My Computer

As you learned earlier, there is an icon on your desktop labeled My Computer. Double-clicking this icon opens the My Computer window, which looks similar to the one shown in Figure B-14. The My Computer program is helpful because it allows you to see what is on your computer. First double-click the icon for the drive you want to look at. That drive's name appears in the title bar and the window displays all the folders and files on that drive.

FIGURE B-14
My Computer window

Because computer disks have such a large capacity, it is not unusual for a floppy disk to contain dozens of files or for a hard disk to contain hundreds or thousands of files. To organize files, a disk can be divided into folders. A *folder* is a place where files and other folders are stored. They help keep documents organized on a disk just the way folders would in a file cabinet. Folders group files that have something in common. You can also have folders within a folder. For example, you could create a folder to group all of the files you are working on in computer class. Within that folder, you could have several other folders that group files for each tool or each chapter.

When you double-click on a folder in My Computer, the contents of that folder are displayed—including program files and data files. Double-clicking on a program file icon will open that program. Double-clicking on a data file icon opens that document and the program that created it.

To create a new folder, double-click on a drive or folder in the My Computer window. Choose New on the File menu and then choose Folder on the submenu. A folder titled *New Folder* appears, as shown in Figure B-15. You can rename the folder by keying the name you want. Once you have created a folder, you can save or move files into it.

 **Hot Tip**

You can change how folders and files are displayed by choosing **as Web Page**, **Large Icons**, **Small Icons**, **List**, or **Details** on the **View** menu.

FIGURE B-15
Creating a new folder in My Computer

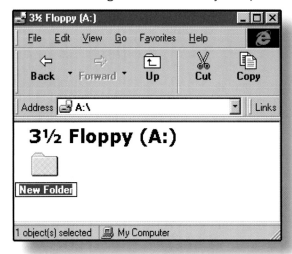

STEP-BY-STEP ▷ B.10

1. Double-click the **My Computer** icon on your desktop.

2. Double-click the drive where you want to create a new folder.

3. Choose **New** on the **File** menu and then choose **Folder** on the submenu. A folder titled *New Folder* appears, similar to Figure B-15.

4. Name the folder by keying **Time Records**. Press **Enter**.

5. Choose **Close** on the **File** menu to close the window.

Windows Explorer

Another way to view the folders and files on a disk is to use the Windows Explorer program. To open it, click Start, Programs, and then Windows Explorer. The Explorer window is split into two panes, as shown in Figure B-16. The left pane shows a hierarchical, or "tree" view of how the folders are organized on a disk; the right side, or Contents pane, shows the files and folders located in the folder that is currently selected in the tree pane.

The Explorer is a useful tool for organizing and managing the contents of a disk because you can create folders and rename them and easily delete, move, and copy files.

FIGURE B-16
Explorer window

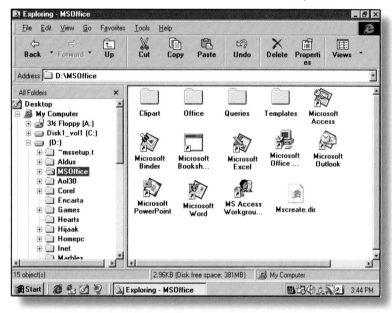

STEP-BY-STEP ▷ B.11

1. Open Windows Explorer by clicking **Start**, **Programs**, and then **Windows Explorer**.

2. In the tree pane, double-click the drive where the *Time Records* folder you just created is located.

3. Select the **Time Records** folder in the Contents pane of the Explorer window.

4. Choose **Rename** on the **File** menu.

5. Key **Finance**. Press **Enter**.

6. Leave Windows Explorer open for the next Step-by-Step.

Recycle Bin

Another icon on the desktop that you learned about earlier is the Recycle Bin. It looks like a wastebasket and is a place to get rid of files and folders that you no longer need. Until you empty the Recycle Bin, items that have been "thrown away" will remain there and can still be retrieved.

Recycle Bin

S TEP-BY-STEP ▷ B.12

1. *Right*-click on the **Finance** folder.

2. Choose **Delete** on the shortcut menu. The Confirm Folder Delete dialog box appears, as shown in Figure B-17.

3. Click **Yes**. The folder is removed.

4. Choose **Close** on the **File** menu to close Windows Explorer.

FIGURE B-17
Confirm Folder Delete dialog box

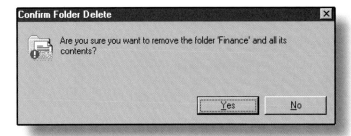

Summary

In this appendix, you learned:

■ The desktop organizes your work. Clicking the Start button displays options for opening programs and documents, and shutting down the computer. You can connect to the Internet using the Explorer browser and you can use the Active Desktop and channels to incorporate Web content into your work.

■ Windows can be moved, resized, opened, and closed. If all the contents of a window cannot be displayed in the window as it is currently sized, scroll bars appear to allow you to move to the part of the window that you want to view. Windows can be maximized to fill the screen or minimized to a button on the taskbar.

■ Menus allow you to choose commands to perform different actions. Menus are accessed from the Start button or from a program's menu bar near the top of the window. When you choose a menu command with an ellipsis (…), a dialog box appears that requires more information before performing the command. Choosing a menu option with an arrow opens a submenu.

- The Windows 98 Help program provides additional information about the many features of Windows 98. You can access the Help program from the Start button and use the Contents, Index, or Search tabs to get information. You can also get help from the Help menu within Windows programs.

- Folders group files that have something in common. To organize a disk, it can be divided into folders where files and other folders are stored. Other useful features of Windows 98 include: My Computer, which lets you see what is on your computer; Windows Explorer, which helps organize and manage your files; and the Recycle Bin for deleting unneeded files or folders.

APPENDIX REVIEW QUESTIONS

TRUE/FALSE

Circle T if the statement is true or F if the statement is false.

T F 1. The Quick Launch toolbar tells you the name of all the open programs.

T F 2. Channels allow you to customize the information delivered from the Internet to your computer.

T F 3. Scroll bars appear when all items in the window are visible.

T F 4. A menu item with an arrow indicates that a dialog box will appear when chosen.

T F 5. The Index tab is useful if you want to browse through help topics by category.

WRITTEN QUESTIONS

Write a brief answer to the following questions.

1. What is the interface that lets you put "active items" from the Internet on the desktop?

2. What button do you click to have the option of starting a program, opening a document, finding help, or shutting down the computer?

3. How do you move a window?

4. Where is the Close button located?

5. What is the purpose of the Recycle Bin?

APPENDIX C

COMPUTER CONCEPTS

What Is a Computer?

A computer is a mechanical device that is used to store, retrieve, and manipulate information (called data) electronically. You enter the data into the computer through a variety of input devices, process it, and output it in a number of ways. Computer software programs run the computer and let you manipulate the data.

Hardware

The physical components, or parts, of the computer are called hardware. The main parts are the central processing unit (CPU), the monitor, the keyboard, and the mouse. Peripherals are additional components like printers and scanners.

Input Devices. You enter information into a computer by typing on a keyboard or by using a mouse, a hand-held device, to move a pointer on the computer screen. Other input devices include a joystick, a device similar to the control stick of an airplane that moves a pointer or character on the screen, and a modem, which receives information via a telephone line. Other input devices include scanners, trackballs, and digital tracking. You can use scanners to "read" text or graphics into a computer from a printed page or to read bar codes (coded labels) to keep track of merchandise in a store or other inventory. Similar to a mouse, a trackball has a roller ball you turn to control a pointer on the screen. Digital tracking devices let you press a finger on a small electronic pad on the keyboard of a laptop to control the pointer on the screen, instead of using a trackball or a mouse.

Processing Devices. The central processing unit (CPU), is a silicon chip that processes data and carries out instructions given to the computer. The data bus includes the wiring and pathways by which the CPU communicates with the peripherals and components of the computer.

Storage Devices. The hard drive, is a device that reads and writes data to and from a round magnetic platter, or disk. The data is encoded on the disk much the same as sounds are encoded on magnetic tape. The hard drive is called hard because the disk is rigid, unlike a floppy disk drive, which reads and writes data to and from a removable non-rigid disk, similar to a round disk of magnetic tape. The floppy disk, is encased in a plastic sleeve to protect its data. The floppy disk's main advantage is portability. You can store data on a floppy disk and transport it to another computer to use the data there.

At one time, the largest hard drive was 10 MB, or 10,000,000 bytes of data. A byte stands for a single character of data. Currently, hard drives can be up to 14 gigabytes (GB). That's 14,000,000,000 bytes of data.

The most recent storage device is the CD, or compact disk, which is a form of optical storage. Information is encoded on the disk by a laser and read by a CD-ROM drive in the computer. These disks have a great advantage over floppies because they can hold vast quantities of information—the entire contents of a small library, for instance. However, most computers cannot write (or save) information to these disks; CD-ROMs are Read-Only Memory (ROM) devices. Drives are now available that write to CDs. Although these drives used to be very expensive and therefore were not used widely, they are becoming more affordable. The great advantage of CDs is their ability to hold graphic information—including moving pictures with the highest quality stereo sound. Similar to a CD, the digital video drive (DVD) can read high-quality cinema-type disks.

Another storage medium is magnetic tape. This medium is most commonly used for backing up, making a copy of files from a hard drive. Although it is relatively rare for a hard drive to crash (that is, to have the data or pointers to the data be partially or totally destroyed), it can and does happen. Therefore, most businesses and some individuals routinely back up files on tape. If you have a small hard drive, you can use floppy disks to back up your system.

Output Devices.   The monitor on which you view your work is an output device. It provides a visual representation of the information stored in or produced by your computer. The monitor for today's typical system is the SVGA (super video graphics array). It provides a very sharp picture because of the large number of tiny dots, called pixels, that make up the display as well as its ability to present the full spectrum of colors. Most laptop computers use a liquid crystal display (LCD) screen that is not as clear a display because it depends on the arrangement of tiny bits of crystal to present an image. However, the latest laptops use new technology that gives quality near or equal to that of a standard monitor.

Printers are another type of output device. They let you produce a paper printout of information contained in the computer. Today, most printers are of the laser type, using light to burn in an image as a copy machine does. Ink-jet printers use a spray of ink to print. Laser printers give the sharpest image. Ink jet printers provide nearly as sharp an image but the wet printouts can smear when they first come out. However, most color printers are ink jet; these printers let you print information in its full array of colors as you see it on your SVGA monitor. Laser color printers, are available but are more costly.

Modems are another output device, as well as an input device. They allow computers to communicate with each other by telephone lines. Modems convert information in bytes to sound media to send data and then convert it back to bytes after receiving data. Modems operate at various rates or speeds; typically today, a computer will have a modem that operates at 33,600 baud (a variable unit of data transmission) per second or better.

Laptops and Docking Stations.   A laptop computer is a small folding computer that literally fits in a person's lap. Within the fold-up case is the CPU, data bus, monitor (built into the lid), hard drive (sometimes removable), a 3.5-inch floppy drive, a CD-ROM drive, and a trackball or digital tracking device. The advantage of the laptop is its portability—you can work anywhere because you can use power either from an outlet or from the computer's internal, rechargeable batteries. The drawbacks are the smaller keyboard, liquid crystal monitor, smaller capacity, and higher price. The newer laptops offer full-sized keyboards and higher quality monitors. As technology allows, storage capacity on smaller devices is making it possible to offer laptops with as much power and storage as a full-sized computer. The docking station is a device into which you slide a closed laptop that becomes the desktop computer. Then you can plug in a full-sized monitor, keyboard, mouse, printer, and so on. Such a setup lets you use the laptop like a desktop computer while at your home or office.

Functioning

All of the input, processing, storage, and output devices function together to make the manipulation, storage, and distribution of data and information possible.

Data and Information Management.   Data is information entered into and manipulated in a computer. Manipulation includes computation, such as adding, subtracting, and dividing; analysis planning, such as sorting data; and reporting, such as presenting data for others in a chart. Data and information management runs software on computer hardware.

Memory.   There are two kinds of memory in a computer—RAM and ROM. RAM, or Random Access Memory, is a number of silicon chips inside a computer that hold information as long as the computer is turned on. RAM is what keeps the software programs up and running and keeps the visuals on your screen. RAM is where you work with data until you "save" it to a hard or floppy disk. Early computers had simple programs and did little with data, so they had very little RAM—possibly 4 or fewer megabytes. Today's computers run very complicated programs that "stay resident" (remain available to the user at the same time as other programs) and run graphics. Both of these tasks take a lot of memory; therefore, today's computers have at least 32 or more megabytes of RAM. ROM, or read-only memory, is the small bit of memory that stays in the computer when it is turned off. It is ROM that lets the computer "boot up," or get started. ROM holds the instructions that tell the computer how to begin to load its operating system software programs.

Speed.   The speed of a computer is measured by how fast the drives turn to reach information to be retrieved or to save data. The measurement is in megahertz (MHz). Early personal computers worked at 4.77 to 10 megahertz; today, machines run at 150 MHz or more. Another factor that affects the speed of a computer is how much RAM is available. Since RAM makes up the work area for all programs and holds all the information that you input until you save, the more RAM available, the quicker the machine will be able to operate.

One other area of speed must be considered, and that is how quickly the modem can send and receive information. As mentioned earlier, modem speed is measured in baud. The usual modem runs at 33,600 OR 56,000 baud per second or more.

Communications.   Computers have opened up the world of communications, first within offices via LANs (local area networks that link computers within a facility via wires) and, later, via the Internet. Using the Internet, people can communicate across the world instantly with e-mail and attach files that were once sent by mailing a floppy disk. Also, anyone with a modem and an access service can download information from or post information to thousands of bulletin boards.

Software

A program is a set of mathematical instructions to the computer. Software is the collection of programs and other data input that tells the computer how to operate its machinery, how to manipulate, store, and output information, and how to accept the input you give it. Software fits into two basic categories: systems software and applications software. A third category, network software, is really a type of application.

Systems Software.   Systems software refers to the operating system (OS) of the computer. The OS is a group of programs that is automatically copied in RAM every couple of seconds from the time the computer is turned on until the computer is turned off. Operating systems serve two functions: they control data flow among computer parts and they provide the platform on which application and network software work—in effect, they allow the "space" for software and translate its commands to the computer. The most popular operating systems in use today are the *Macintosh* operating system, and a version of Microsoft Windows, such as Windows 95 or Windows 98.

Macintosh has its own operating system that has evolved over the years since its introduction. From the beginning, Macintosh has used a graphical user interface (GUI) operating system—quite an innovation at its introduction in the mid-1970s. The OS is designed so users "click" with a mouse on pictures, called icons, or on text to give commands to the system. Data is available to you in WYSIWYG (what-you-see-is-what-you-get) form; that is, you can see on-screen what a document will look like when it is printed. Graphics and other kinds of data, such as spreadsheets, can be placed into text documents. However, GUIs take a great deal of RAM to keep all of the graphics and programs operating.

The OS for IBM and IBM-compatible computers (machines made by other companies that operate similarly) originally was DOS (disk operating system). It did not have a graphical interface. The GUI system, Windows™, was developed to make using the IBM/IBM-compatible computer more "friendly." Users no longer had to memorize written commands to make the computer carry out actions but could use a mouse to point and click on icons or words. Windows 3.1, however, was a translating system that operated on top of DOS—not on its own., and newer versions of Windows are continually being developed.

Windows 3.1 was a GUI system that operated on top of DOS; Windows 3.1 was *not* an operating system by itself. It allowed you to point and click on graphics and words that then translate to DOS commands for the computer. Data was available to you in WYSIWYG (what-you-see-is-what-you-get) form. Graphics and other kinds of data, such as spreadsheets, could be placed into text documents by Object

Linking and Embedding (OLE). However, Windows 3.1, because it was still using DOS as its base, was not really a stay-resident program. In other words, it did not keep more than one operation going at a time; it merely switched between operations quickly. Using several high-level programs at the same time, however, could cause problems, such as memory failure. Therefore, improvements were inevitable.

Windows 95 is its own operating system, unlike the original Windows 3.1, and is the replacement for Windows 3.1. Windows 95 has DOS built-in but does not operate on top of it—if you go to a DOS prompt from Windows 95, you will still be operating inside a Windows 95 system, not in traditional DOS. Windows 95 is the logical evolution of GUI for IBM and IBM-compatible machines. It is a stay-resident, point-and-click system that automatically configures hardware to work together. With all of its ability comes the need for more RAM or this system will operate slowly. Newer versions of Windows continue to be released.

Applications Software.   When you use a computer program to perform a data manipulation or processing task, you are using applications software. Word processors, databases, spreadsheets, desktop publishers, fax systems, and online access systems are all applications software.

Network Software.   Novell™ and Windows are two kinds of network software. A network is a group of computers that are hardwired (hooked together with cables) to communicate and operate together. One computer acts as the server, which controls the flow of data among the other computers, called nodes, on the network. Network software manages this flow of information. Networks have certain advantages over stand-alone computers. They allow communication among the computers; they allow smaller capacity nodes to access the larger capacity of the server; and they allow several computers to share peripherals, such as one printer, and they can make it possible for all computers on the network to have access to the Internet.

History of the Computer

Though various types of calculating machines were developed in the nineteenth century, the history of the modern computer begins about the middle of this century. The strides made in developing today's personal computer have been truly astounding.

Early Development

ENIAC, designed for military use in calculating ballistic trajectories, was the first electronic, digital computer to be developed in the United States. For its day, 1946, it was quite a marvel because it was able to accomplish a task in 20 seconds that took a human three days to do. However, it was an enormous machine that weighed more than 20 tons and contained thousands of vacuum tubes, which often failed. The tasks that it could accomplish were limited, as well.

From this awkward beginning, however, the seeds of an information revolution grew. Significant dates in the history of computer development are the first electronic stored program in 1948, the first junction transistor in 1951, the replacement of tubes with magnetic cores in 1953, the first high-level computer language in 1957, the first integrated circuit in 1961, the first minicomputer in 1965, the invention of the microprocessor (the silicon chip) and floppy disk in 1971, and the first personal computer in 1974 (made possible by the microprocessor). These last two inventions launched the fast-paced information revolution in which we now all live and participate.

The Personal Computer

The PC, or personal computer, was mass marketed by Apple, beginning in 1977, and by IBM, beginning in 1981. It is this desktop device with which people are so familiar and which, today, contains much more power and ability than did the original computer that took up an entire room. The PC is a small computer (desktop size or less) that uses a microprocessor to manipulate data. PCs may stand alone, be linked together in a network, or be attached to a large mainframe computer.

Computer Utilities and System Maintenance

Computer operating systems let you run certain utilities and perform system maintenance. When you add hardware or software, you might need to make changes in the way the system operates. Beginning with the Windows 95 version most configuration changes are done automatically; however, other operating systems might not, or you might want to customize the way the new software or hardware will interface (coordinate) with your system. Additionally, you can make alterations such as the speed at which your mouse clicks, how fast or slow keys repeat on the keyboard, and what color or pattern appears on the desktop or in GUI programs.

You need to perform certain maintenance regularly on computers. You should scan all new disks and any incoming information from online sources for viruses. Some systems do this automatically; others require you to install software to do it. From time to time, you should scan or check the hard drive to see that there are no bad sectors or tracks and to look for corrupted files. Optimizing or defragmenting the hard disk is another way to keep your computer running at its best. You can also check a floppy disk if it is not working properly. Programs for scanning a large hard drive could take up to half an hour to run; checking programs run on a small hard drive or disk might take only seconds or minutes. Scanning and checking programs often offer the option of "fixing" the bad areas or problems, although you should be aware that this could result in data loss.

Society and Computers

With the computer revolution have come many new questions and responsibilities. There are issues of responsibility and ethics, access control, and privacy and security.

Responsibility and Ethics

When you access information—whether online, in the workplace, or via purchased software—you have a responsibility to respect the rights of the creator of that information. You must treat electronic information in a copyrighted form the same way as you would a published book or article or a patented invention. For instance, you must give credit when you access information from a CD-ROM encyclopedia or a download from an online database. Also, information you transmit must be accurate and fair, like that printed in a book. When you use equipment that belongs to your school, a company for which you work, or others, the following ethical guidelines apply:

1. You must not damage computer hardware and must not add or remove equipment without permission.

2. You must not use an access code or equipment without permission.

3. You must not read others' electronic mail.

4. You must not alter data belonging to someone else without permission.

5. You must not use the computer for play during work hours or use it for personal profit.

6. You must not access the Internet for nonbusiness use during work hours.

7. You must not add to or take away from the software programs and must not make unauthorized copies of data or software.

8. You must not copy software programs to use at home or at another site in the company without multisite permission.

9. You must not copy company files or procedures for personal use.

10. You must not borrow computer hardware for personal use without asking permission.

Internet Access and Children

Children's access to the Internet is another matter to consider. Many of the online services allow parents or guardians to control what areas of the service users can access. Because there are some discussion topics and adult information that are inappropriate for younger computer users, it is wise to take advantage of this access-limiting capability. Families using direct Internet access can purchase software for this purpose. If this software is not available, the solution must be very careful monitoring of a child's computer use.

Privacy and Security

Not only are there issues of privacy in accessing work on another's computer, there are also issues that revolve around privacy in communicating on the Internet. Just as you would not open someone else's mail, you must respect the privacy of e-mail sent to others. When interacting with others online, you must keep confidential information confidential—such as the address of a new friend made online. You must think, too, about the information that you are providing. You do not want to endanger your privacy, safety, or financial security by giving out personal information to someone you do not know. A common scam (trick) on some online services is for someone to pretend to work for the service and ask for your access code or password, which controls your service account. *Never* give this out to anyone online because the person can use it and charge a great deal of costly time to your account. Also, just as you would not give a stranger your home address, telephone number, or credit card number if you were talking on the street, you should take those same precautions online.

Career Opportunities

In one way or another, all of our careers involve the computer. Whether you are a grocery checker using a scanner to read the prices, a busy executive writing a report on a laptop on an airplane, or a programmer creating new software—almost everyone uses computers in their jobs. And, everyone in a business processes information in some way. There are also specific careers available if you want to work primarily with computers.

Schools offer computer programming, repair, and design degrees. The most popular jobs are systems analysts, computer operators, and programmers. Analysts figure out ways to make computers work (or work better) for a particular business or type of business. Computer operators use the programs and devices to conduct business with computers. Programmers write the software for applications or new systems.

There are courses of study in using CAD (computer-aided design) and CAM (computer-aided manufacturing). Computer engineering and architectural design degrees are now available. Scientific research is done on computers today, and specialties are available in that area. There are positions available to instruct others in computer software use within companies and schools. Also, technical writers and editors must be available to write manuals on using computers and software. Computer-assisted instruction (CAI) is designing a system of teaching any given subject on the computer. The learner is provided with resources, such as an encyclopedia on CD-ROM, in addition to the specific learning program with which he or she interacts on the computer. Designing video games is another exciting and ever-growing field of computer work.

What Does the Future Hold?

The possibilities for computer development and application are endless. Things that were dreams or science fiction only 10 or 20 years ago are a reality today. New technologies are emerging. Some are replacing old ways of doing things; others are merging with those older devices. We are learning new ways to work and play because of the computer. It is definitely a device that has become part of our offices and our homes.

Emerging Technologies

The various technologies and systems are coming together to operate more efficiently. For instance, since their beginnings, Macintosh and IBM/IBM-compatible systems could not exchange information well. Today, you can install compatibility cards in the Power Macintosh and run Windows, DOS, and Mac OS on the same computer and switch between them. Macs (except for early models) can read from and write to MS-DOS and Windows disks. And you can easily network Macintosh computers with other types of computers running other operating systems. In addition, you can buy software for a PC to run the Mac OS and to read Macintosh disks. New technology in the works will allow you to incorporate both systems and exchange information even more easily.

Telephone communication is also being combined with computer e-mail so users can set a time to meet online and, with the addition of new voice technology, actually speak to each other. The present drawbacks are that users must e-mail and make an appointment to meet online rather than having a way just to call up each other, and speaking is delayed rather than in real-time. Although not perfected, this form of communication will certainly evolve into an often-used device that will broaden the use of both the spoken and written word.

Another emerging technology is the CUCME (see you, see me) visual system that allows computer users to use a small camera and microphone wired into the computer so, when they communicate via modem, the receiver can see and hear them. This technology is in its infancy—the pictures tend to be a bit fuzzy and blur with movement; however, improvements are being made so sharp pictures will result. For the hearing impaired, this form of communication can be more effective than writing alone since sign language and facial expression can be added to the interaction. CUCME is a logical next step from the image transfer files now so commonly used to transfer a static (nonmoving) picture.

A great deal of research and planning has gone into combining television and computers. The combined device has a CPU, television-as-monitor, keyboard, joystick, mouse, modem, and CUCME/quick-cam. Something like the multiple communications device that science fiction used to envision, this combined medium allows banking, work, entertainment, and communication to happen all through one piece of machinery—and all in the comfort of your home. There are already printers that function as a copier, fax machine, and scanner.

Trends

One emerging trend is for larger and faster hard drives. One- and two-gigabyte hard drives have virtually replaced the 540 megabyte drives, and 14.4 gigabyte drives are appearing on the scene. RAM today is increasing exponentially. The trend is to sell RAM in units of 8 or 16 megabytes to accommodate the greater purchases of 32, 64, and larger blocks of RAM. The 32-bit operating system is becoming the norm. All of these size increases are due to the expanding memory requirements of GUIs and new peripherals, such as CUCME devices and interfaces with other devices. Although the capacities are increasing, the actual size of the machines is decreasing. Technology is allowing more powerful components to fit into smaller devices—just as the $3\,^{1}/_{2}$-inch floppy disk is smaller and holds more data than the obsolete $5\,^{1}/_{4}$-inch floppy.

Another trend is the increased use of computers for personal use in homes. This trend is likely to continue in the future.

Home Offices.   More and more frequently, people are working out of their homes—whether they are employees who are linked to a place of business or individuals running their own businesses. Many companies allow certain workers to have a computer at home that is linked by modem to the office. Work is done at home and transferred to the office. Communication is by e-mail and telephone. Such an arrangement saves companies work space and, thus, money. Other employees use laptop computers to work both at home and on the road as they travel. These computers, in combination with a modem, allow an employee to work from virtually anywhere and still keep in constant contact with her or his employer and customers.

With downsizing (the reduction of the workforce by companies), many individuals have found themselves unemployed or underemployed (working less or for less money). These people have, in increasing numbers, begun their own businesses out of their homes. With a computer, modem, fax software, printer, and other peripherals, they can contract with many businesses or sell their own products or services. Many make use of the Internet and World Wide Web to advertise their services.

Home Use.   As the economy has tightened, many people are trying to make their lives more time- and cost-efficient. The computer is one help in that search. Having banking records, managing household accounts, and using electronic banking on a computer saves time. The games and other computer interactions also offer a more reasonable way of spending leisure dollars than some outside entertainment. For instance, it might not be feasible to travel to Paris to see paintings in the Louvre Museum; however, it might be affordable to buy a CD-ROM that lets you take a tour of that famous facility from the comfort of your chair in front of your computer. This can be quite an educational experience for children and a more restful one for those who might tire on the trip but can easily turn off the computer and come back to it later. Young people can benefit enormously from this kind of education as well as using the computer to complete homework, do word processing, create art and graphics, and, of course, play games that sharpen their hand-to-eye coordination and thinking skills.

Purchasing a Computer

Once you decide to take the plunge and purchase a computer, the selection of a new computer system should be a careful and meticulous one to ensure that your needs are fulfilled. This section will help you evaluate what computer is best suited for you and help you select a new computer for purchase.

Choosing a Computer System

This is perhaps the most critical step in your quest for the ultimate computer system. It is generally best to buy a computer with an operating system and format you know. If you learned or are learning computers on a Macintosh, then you will most likely want to purchase a Macintosh system. It is also important to consider what kinds of tasks you wish to perform on your computer. IBM and IBM-compatibles have more available software and are more common in businesses, whereas Macintosh computers excel at desktop publishing and graphics. After you decide which type of computer you will buy, you must decide whether to buy a desktop or laptop. This will probably be decided for you by your pocketbook. Laptops generally cost more than desktop computers. If you need the portability a laptop has to offer and can afford the additional cost, then it might be the choice for you. Otherwise, desktops are very suitable for use in business, home, and school.

Outlining Your Needs

After you decide what kind of computer you will buy, it is time to confirm the details. When purchasing a computer, you should consider several specific components. The recommended *minimum* of a few of these are noted in Table C–1.

TABLE C-1

	IBM AND IBM-COMPATIBLES	MACINTOSH
Processor	Pentium	PowerPC 603e RISC processor
Speed	133 MHz	120 MHz
Memory (RAM)	32 MB	16 MB
Hard Drive	1.0 GB	1.0 GB
CD-ROM	8x (Eight-speed)	8x (Eight-speed)
Fax/Modem	33.6 kbps	28.8 kbps
Expansion Slots	5	3 to 6
Operating System	Windows 98	Mac OS 7.5 or higher

Depending on what you plan to do with your computer, you might need different components. For instance, if you plan to do a large amount of video and graphical analysis and manipulation, you probably want at least 64 MB of RAM, rather than 16 MB. High-powered gaming requires a faster video card with more RAM, as would any emerging technologies such as MPEG and virtual reality. If your office plans to do a large amount of online publishing and commerce via the Internet, a faster modem is a necessity.

Comparative Shopping

Next comes the most challenging task: finding your computer system. Perhaps the most effective way of doing this is to make a spreadsheet similar to the one in Table C–2. This lets you directly compare different systems from different companies while saving time. Using what you have learned in this book, you could even create charts to show how the different computer systems relate to each other graphically.

TABLE C-2

COMPUTER SYSTEM COMPARISON CHART

FEATURES	PREFERRED FEATURES	SYSTEM 1	SYSTEM 2	SYSTEM 3
Manufacturer	not applicable			
Model				
Processor	Pentium			
Speed	133 MHz			
Expansion slots	5			
3.5-inch drive	Yes (included)			
Price				
RAM	32 MB			
Price (if additional)				
Hard Drive	2.5 GB			
Price (if additional)				
Monitor	15" SVGA			
Price (if additional)				
Video Card	2 MB RAM			
Price (if additional)				
Sound Card	16-bit			
Price (if additional)				
CD-ROM	8x			
Price (if additional)				
Fax/Modem	33.6 kbps			
Price (if additional)				
Printer	ink jet			
Price (if additional)				
Software	Windows 98			
Price (if additional)				
Subtotal				
Sales tax				
Shipping and Handling				
TOTAL PRICE				

Before you begin comparison shopping, it is important to be aware of hidden costs. For instance, many large chain stores offer computer packages that might not include a monitor. If a system does not include a monitor, you must add this cost. In addition to your system, you might need a printer or extra software. If your system will be mailed to you, then you must also consider shipping and handling costs. Sales tax, when applicable, is another hidden cost. On large purchases such as a computer, tax can rapidly add up, so it is important to figure this in before making the final decision.

Making the Final Decision

After you complete the chart, it is time to purchase your computer. Resist the temptation to buy the cheapest or most powerful system. The cheapest computer might be of lesser quality and might not have the features you desire. It is important to get a system powerful enough to last you at least three years but still be within your budget. The most powerful system might contain more features than you need, and could be too expensive. Also, remember that the most expensive does not necessarily guarantee superior quality. Sometimes the most expensive system contains "free" software or other extras that you do not need. It is good to consider the manufacturer's reputation when deciding where to purchase your system. Some good unbiased sources for this information include the Internet, where customers who have purchased computers often voice their opinions, and consumer magazines. Other points to consider include financing, warranty, available training, and technical support and service.

GLOSSARY

A

And operator Used to find records that meet more than one criteria.

Append query Query that adds records from one table to another table.

Argument A variable that supplies additional information, such as a file name. Arguments are enclosed in parentheses after the procedure name. You do not always need to use arguments but the parentheses will be added whether you add arguments or not.

Ascending sort Sort that arranges records from A to Z or smallest to largest.

AutoForm A format that displays an entire record on the screen.

AutoReport A format that displays records specifically for printing.

B

Bound Control Connected or bound to a field in a table.

C

Calculated control A control that displays the results of the mathematical calculation that has been entered into it.

Close Removing a document or window from the screen.

Close button "X" on the right side of the title bar that closes a window

Concatenation Combining text from two or more fields into one.

Control This is an object that can be inserted into a form or report. There are three type of controls: bound, unbound, and calculated controls.

D

Data access page Object in the database that lets you set up other objects, such as tables, forms, and reports, so that they can be published to the Web.

Database A list of related information arranged in a useful manner.

Database management system Any system for managing data.

Database report A report that allows you to organize, summarize, and print all or a portion of the data in a database.

Database Wizard A step-by-step process of creating a database file.

Datasheet view A form similar to a spreadsheet that allows records to be entered directly into a table.

Data source Contains the information that will vary in a form letter.

Data type Specification that tells Access what kind of information can be stored in a field.

Decrypting Removing the encryption. The decryption process unscrambles the encryption code so that a database file displays meaningful information.

Default Setting used unless another option is chosen.

Descending sort Sort that arranges records from Z to A or largest to smallest.

Defragmenting Compacting a database by removing unused space within the database file.

Delete query Query that deletes records within a table.

Design view Where you design and modify objects.

Desktop Space where you access and work with programs and files.

Detail Section in a form or report that displays the records.

Dialog box A message box asking for further instructions before a command can be performed.

E

Entry The actual data entered into a field.

Encrypting Scrambling the code that makes a database file readable. When you encrypt a database, Access compacts the database file and then makes it indecipherable.

Event properties Similar to macro actions. It is the event or activity that takes place to trigger the conditional macro to execute.

Exporting Placing data from one program into another program.

Expression Typically a calculation in an unbound control or query.

Expression Builder The Access feature that helps you create calculations when you are not sure how to enter the expression.

F

Field Unit of information that contains one type of data. In a table, fields are displayed in columns. In a form, fields are represented by rectangles containing the information.

Field names The name that represents a specific category of information in a record within a database.

Field properties Specifications that allow you to customize a field beyond choosing a data type.

Field selectors Located at the top of a table, they contain the field name.

Filter A method of screening out all records except those that match your selection criteria.

Folder A place where other files and folders are stored on a disk.

Form footer Section that displays information that remains the same for every record. Appears once at the end of the form.

Form header Section that displays information that remains the same for every record. Appears once at beginning of form.

Form Wizard A step-by-step process of creating forms.

Fragmentation Process in which parts of the database file become scattered over an area of the disk where the application is stored. This can cause the database to run slower and less efficiently.

Function A software routine that performs a task.

G

Grouping Organizing records into parts or groups based on the contents of a field.

H

Home page First page that appears when you start your browser.

Hyperlink An address embedded in a file that links the file with an object stored elsewhere in the computer or on the Internet.

Hypertext Markup Language (HTML) The standard document format used on the World Wide Web.

I

Icon Small pictures that represent an item or object, that also remind you of each button's function.

Importing Bringing information from one program into another.

Indexing Feature of databases that allows a field to be more quickly searched.

Input mask Predetermined format for data entry.

Integrated software package Computer program that combines common tools into one program.

Internet Vast network of computers linked to one another.

Internet Explorer Browser for navigating the Web.

Intranet A company's private Web.

L

Link Colored, underlined text that "jumps" to a document containing additional information when clicked.

Lookup field Field that pulls data from a field in another table or query in the database.

M

Macro Commands and instructions grouped together as a single command to complete a task automatically.

Main document The information that stays the same in a form letter.

Make-table query Query that creates a new table using the records found from one or more tables.

Maximize button Button at the right side of the title bar that enlarges a window to its maximum size.

Menu List of options from which to choose.

Menu bar A row of titles located at the top of the screen, each of which represents a separate pull-down menu.

Merge fields Fields in a main document where you want to print the information from a data source.

Minimize button Button at the right side of the title bar that reduces a window to a button on the taskbar.

Mnemonic Underlined letter that is pressed in combination with the Alt key to access items in the menu bar, pull-down menus, and dialog boxes.

Multitable query Query that searches related tables.

My Computer Program to help you organize and manage your files.

N

Navigation buttons Buttons that allow you to move to different records in your table or form.

Network Neighborhood Shows all the folders and printers that are available to you through the network connection, if you have one.

New Record button A button located with the navigation buttons that allows you to enter a new record.

O

One-to-many relationship A relationship in which a table whose common field is a primary

key field is linked to a table that does not have the common field as a primary key field.

One-to-one relationship A relationship in which each record in Table A can have only one matching record in Table B and each record in Table B can have only one matching record in Table A.

Open Process of loading a file from a disk onto the screen.

P

Page (see also Data access page) An Access object that lets you create and display information for the Web.

Parameter query Query in which you are prompted to enter the criteria each time you run the query.

Primary key A field designated by the user that uniquely identifies a record. Prevents duplicate information from being entered into a field.

Primary table A table with a primary key field that contains the same data as that stored in the common field of another table.

Pull-down menu A list of commands that appears below each title in the menu bar.

Q

Query An object used to find and display records that meet the criteria you specify.

Quick Launch toolbar Contains icons so you can display the desktop or quickly start frequently used programs.

R

Read-only file File that can be viewed but not changed.

Record Complete set of database fields.

Record pointer The pointer that Access uses internally to keep track of the current record.

Record selector The symbol that Access uses to identify the record your mouse pointer is currently in. This symbol is a triangle.

Records Collections of information about particular people or items. A database is divided into records.

Recycle Bin Place to get rid of files or folders that are no longer needed.

Referential integrity Having Access check new data as it is entered into related fields.

Related table A table joined to another through a related field containing the same data type.

Relationship Link between tables that have a common field, allowing you to create forms, queries and reports using fields from all tables in the relationship.

Relational database A database that can read information from other tables with a common field.

Report A database object that is designed specifically for printing.

Report Wizard A step-by-step process of creating reports.

Restore button Button at the right side of the title bar that returns a maximized window to its previous size.

S

Save Process of storing a file on disk.

Scroll arrows Moves the window in that direction over the contents of the window when clicked.

Scroll bars Located at the bottom and right sides of the window, they allow you to move quickly to other areas of the document.

Scroll box Small box in the scroll bar that indicates your position within the contents of the window.

Search criteria In a query, it's the information for which you are searching.

Search operators Mathematical symbols used in queries. Examples of operators are <, >, <=, >=, <>, and =.

Start Button on the taskbar that brings up menus with a variety of options.

Subdatasheet In tables that are related, you can show records from one table in the related record in the primary table.

Subform A form that is placed within another form. Usually these forms contain related information.

T

Taskbar A bar located at the bottom of the Windows 98 screens that shows the Start button, the Quick Launch toolbar and all open programs.

Title bar Bar at the top of every window that contains the name of the open program, window, document, or folder.

U

Unbound control An unbound control does not get its information from a field in a table or query. An unbound control gets its information from other sources, such as Microsoft ClipArt.

Uniform Resource Locator (URL) A unique address for each Internet page that defines the route to that page.

Update query Query that changes the values of a specified field in a specified group of records.

W

Web browser Software used to display Web pages on your computer monitor.

Wildcard A symbol that stands for any character or a series of characters.

World Wide Web System of computers that share information by means of hypertext links.

INDEX

A

Access
add-in applications, AA-130, AA-134 to AA-136
command summary, IA-119 to IA-121, AA-140
exiting, IA-18
functions, IA-2
integration with Excel, IA-92, IA-105 to IA-106, AA-92 to AA-93
integration with Word, IA-105
screen, IA-4, IA-5
starting, IA-3
startup options, AA-133 to AA-134
See also databases
Access startup dialog box, IA-3
Action list, IA-97 to IA-99
action queries, AA-59
append, AA-59
delete, AA-59, AA-60 to AA-61
make-table, AA-59, AA-63 to AA-65
update, AA-59, AA-61 to AA-63
add-in applications, AA-130, AA-134 to AA-136
adding. *See* creating; inserting
Advanced Filter/Sort, IA-66, IA-67 to IA-68, IA-70 to IA-71
And operator, IA-64
And queries, AA-49 to AA-50
Answer Wizard, IN-8 to IN-9
applications
add-in, AA-130, AA-134 to AA-136
exiting, IN-11
in Office 2000, IN-2
starting, IN-3 to IN-4
See also integration
arguments, in macros, IA-98

ascending sort, IA-69
autoexec macros, AA-103
AutoPage, AA-118

B

backing up databases, IA-106
bound controls, IA-49, AA-69
buttons
macro, AA-100 to AA-101
See also toolbars

C

calculated controls, IA-53 to IA-55, AA-69, AA-71
calculations
Expression Builder, AA-42 to AA-45
in queries, AA-42, AA-46 to AA-47
in reports, IA-89, AA-69 to AA-71
summary queries, AA-46 to AA-47
captions, field, IA-35
Category Footer, IA-94
Category Header, IA-94
cells, IA-15
editing, IA-26
undoing changes, IA-26
changing
column widths, IA-31 to IA-32
data access page designs, AA-123 to AA-124
Datasheet layout, IA-30 to IA-33
field properties, IA-34 to IA-35
form designs, IA-49 to IA-53
query designs, IA-64, AA-55 to AA-56
report designs, AA-69 to AA-74
subform properties, AA-36

table designs, IA-14

See also editing

Chart Wizard, AA-74 to AA-78

charts

    in forms, IA-91

    in reports, IA-91

        creating, AA-74 to AA-78

        modifying, AA-76

clip art

    inserting in forms, AA-38

    inserting in reports, AA-79 to AA-80

    See also pictures

closing

    documents, IN-7

    See also exiting

Column Width dialog box, IA-31 to IA-32

columns, in datasheets

    changing widths, IA-31 to IA-32

    freezing, IA-33

    rearranging, IA-32

    See also fields

commands

    Access, IA-119 to IA-121, AA-140

    on menus, IN-7

compacting databases, IA-29, IA-55, AA-130 to AA-131

concatenation, AA-48

conditional macros, AA-104

    attaching to field, AA-104

    creating, AA-104

    multiple actions, AA-107 to AA-109

controls

    bound, IA-49, AA-69

    calculated, IA-53 to IA-55, AA-69, AA-71

    in forms, IA-49

    image, IA-92

    moving, AA-71

    in reports, IA-94, AA-69 to AA-72

    unbound, IA-49, AA-69, AA-70 to AA-71

converting databases to previous versions of Access, AA-130

copying

    data between applications, AA-92 to AA-93

    database entries, IA-29 to IA-30

    database objects, IA-29

    databases

        by compacting, AA-130 to AA-131

        replicating, AA-133

    records, IA-29

correcting errors. *See* errors, correcting

Create Labels dialog box, IA-114

creating

    action queries, AA-59 to AA-65

    blank documents, IN-3

    charts, AA-74 to AA-78

    conditional macros, AA-104

    data access pages, AA-118 to AA-122

    databases, IA-7 to IA-8

    filters, IA-66 to IA-69

    form letters, IA-108 to IA-111

    forms

        in Design view, AA-37 to AA-38

        with Form Wizard, IA-42 to IA-47

    input masks, AA-2 to AA-7

    macros, IA-97 to IA-99, AA-96 to AA-99

        with Macro Builder, AA-109 to AA-110

    mailing labels, IA-113

    queries, IA-62 to IA-65

    relationships, IA-72 to IA-73, AA-17 to AA-19

    reports

        in Design view, AA-79 to AA-80

        with Report Wizard, IA-85 to IA-92

    subforms, AA-31 to AA-35

    subreports, AA-80

    switchboards, AA-101 to AA-102

    tables, IA-9 to IA-13, AA-63 to AA-65

    See also inserting

Currency data type, IA-10, IA-11

    decimal places, IA-35

    entering data, IA-35

cutting and pasting database entries, IA-29

D

data access pages, AA-118
  creating, AA-118 to AA-122
  grouping, AA-120
  modifying, AA-123 to AA-124
  previewing, AA-118, AA-124
  purpose, IA-5
  sorting, AA-120
  viewing records, AA-122
data source for mail merge, tables as, IA-108
data types
  default, IA-10
  fields, IA-10, IA-11
  validation of, IA-15
data validation. *See* validation rules
database management systems (DBMS), IA-2
database objects, IA-4
  copying, IA-29
  in Database window, IA-4 to IA-5
  deleting, IA-29
  hyperlinks in, AA-115 to AA-117
  purposes, IA-5
  saving as Web pages, IA-65
  viewing, IA-6
Database Splitter, AA-135
Database window, IA-4
  Objects bar, IA-4 to IA-5
databases
  backing up, IA-106
  compacting, IA-29, IA-55, AA-130 to AA-131
  converting to previous versions of Access, AA-130
  creating, IA-7 to IA-8
  decrypting, AA-131
  encrypting, AA-131
  fragmentation, AA-130
  opening, IA-3 to IA-4
  passwords, AA-131 to AA-132
  repairing, IA-55
  replication, AA-133
  searching, IA-60 to IA-61
  splitting into two files, AA-135

See also tables
Datasheet view, IA-15
  changing layout, IA-30 to IA-33
  entering data, IA-15 to IA-16
  navigating in tables, IA-15
  printing, IA-17
DBMS. *See* database management systems
decimal places, in fields, IA-35
decrypting databases, AA-131
default settings, IN-10
default values, IA-10, IA-35
defragmenting databases, AA-130 to AA-131
delete queries, AA-59, AA-60 to AA-61
deleting
  database objects, IA-29
  fields, IA-14
  records, IA-28
    with delete queries, AA-59, AA-60 to AA-61
    referential integrity, AA-19
  relationships, AA-22, AA-23
  tables, IA-14
  text boxes in reports, IA-95
descending sort, IA-69
Design view
  changing field properties, IA-34 to IA-35
  creating macros with Macro Builder, AA-109 to AA-110
  creating queries in, IA-62 to IA-65
  creating tables in, IA-9 to IA-13
  modifying forms, IA-49 to IA-53
  modifying reports, IA-93 to IA-95
  modifying tables, IA-14
  switching to, IA-15
  Toolbox, IA-49, IA-50
designing tables, IA-10 to IA-12
dial-up connections, IN-12
direct access to Internet, IN-12
displaying
  Office Assistant, IN-10
  Web toolbar, IN-12
documents
  closing, IN-7

creating blank, IN-3

filenames, IN-6

locating, IN-5

opening, IN-4 to IN-5

opening recently used, IN-8

read-only, IN-5

saving, IN-6 to IN-7

documents, Word, copying data to and from databases, IA-105

dragging and dropping data between applications, AA-92 to AA-93

E

Edit Relationships dialog box, IA-74, AA-18 to AA-19

editing

database entries, IA-26

hyperlinks, AA-117

macros, AA-99

queries, IA-64, AA-55 to AA-56

records

in Datasheet view, IA-26

in forms, IA-47

relationships, AA-22

reports, IA-93 to IA-95

See also changing

encrypting databases, AA-131

Enter Parameter Value dialog box, AA-58

entering

data in tables

Datasheet view, IA-15 to IA-16

input masks, AA-8

in subforms, AA-35

validation rules, AA-8 to AA-9

field names, IA-10

entries, database, IA-6

concatenation, AA-48

copying, IA-29 to IA-30

data type validation, IA-15

editing

in Datasheet view, IA-26

in forms, IA-47

importing from worksheets, AA-86 to AA-90

moving, IA-29

searching for, IA-61

Text Box controls in forms, IA-49

undoing changes, IA-26

errors, correcting

in database entries, IA-26

in Design view, IA-14

event properties, of fields, AA-104 to AA-105

Excel, integration with Access, IA-92, IA-105 to IA-106, AA-92 to AA-93

exiting

Access, IA-18

applications, IN-11

exporting data, AA-85, AA-91

Expression Builder, AA-42 to AA-45

Expression Builder dialog box, AA-43 to AA-44

external data. *See* importing data

F

Favorites, IN-12

field names, IA-6

entering, IA-10

Label Controls in forms, IA-49

Field Properties dialog box, AA-46

field selectors, IA-27

fields, IA-6

adding to forms, IA-44

adding to queries, AA-55

adding to tables, IA-14

calculated controls, IA-53

captions, IA-35

changing properties, IA-34 to IA-35

column width in datasheet, IA-31 to IA-32

concatenation, AA-48

in data access pages, AA-120, AA-123 to AA-124

data types. *See* data types

decimal places, IA-35

default values, IA-10, IA-35

defining relationships on, IA-72 to IA-73

deleting, IA-14

deleting from queries, AA-55

descriptions, IA-10

designing, IA-10

event properties, AA-104 to AA-105

in Expression Builder, AA-44 to AA-45

formats, IA-35

in forms, IA-44

 conditional macros, AA-104 to AA-109

indexing, IA-71, AA-59

input masks, IA-35

lookup, AA-10 to AA-11

primary keys, IA-12 to IA-13, IA-14, IA-72

in queries, IA-64, AA-55

 properties, AA-46

rearranging in datasheets, IA-32

in reports, IA-86

required, IA-35, AA-9 to AA-10

search criteria in queries, IA-64

searching for data in, IA-61

selecting, IA-27

sizes, IA-34

validation rules, AA-8 to AA-9

See also input masks; merge fields

File New Database dialog box, IA-7

files

 importing into tables, AA-85 to AA-86

 names, IN-6

 See also documents

filters, IA-66

 advanced, IA-66, IA-67 to IA-68, IA-70 to IA-71

 applying in queries, AA-51

 by form, IA-66, IA-67, AA-51

 by selection, IA-66, IA-67, AA-51

 creating, IA-66 to IA-69

 excluding selection, IA-66

 removing, IA-68, AA-51

 sorting with, IA-70 to IA-71

 types, IA-66

Find and Replace dialog box, IA-60 to IA-61

finding. *See* searching

folders, finding files in, IN-5

fonts

 in forms, IA-50

in reports, IA-94

footers

 in forms, IA-49, IA-52

 in reports, IA-94

foreign keys, IA-72, AA-16

form letters

 creating, IA-108 to IA-111

 printing, IA-111 to IA-112

 using queries to select for printing, IA-111 to IA-112

Form Wizard, IA-42 to IA-47

Form Wizard dialog box, IA-44

Form/Report Formatting toolbar, AA-70

formats

 charts, AA-76

 field, IA-35

 forms, IA-50

 reports, IA-94

forms

 calculated controls, IA-53 to IA-55

 charts in, IA-91

 columnar layout, IA-45

 conditional macros, AA-104 to AA-109

 creating

  in Design view, AA-37 to AA-38

  with Form Wizard, IA-42 to IA-47

 creating macros with Macro Builder, AA-109 to AA-110

 Design view, IA-49

 detail section, IA-49

 entering data, IA-47

 filter by, IA-66, IA-67

 form footer section, IA-49, IA-52

 form header section, IA-49, IA-51

 graphics in, AA-38

 hyperlinks in, AA-115 to AA-117

 layouts, IA-45

 macro buttons, AA-100 to AA-101

 modifying, IA-49 to IA-53

 names, IA-46

 navigating, IA-47 to IA-48

 printing, IA-48

 purpose, IA-5

saving as Web pages, IA-65

styles, IA-46

subforms, AA-30 to AA-35

switchboards, AA-101 to AA-103

tabular layout, IA-45

formulas, Expression Builder, AA-42 to AA-45

fragmentation, of databases, AA-130

freezing columns, IA-33

functions, AA-46 to AA-47

in Expression Builder, AA-42 to AA-43

summaries, AA-46 to AA-47

G

graphics. *See* clip art; pictures

graphs. *See* charts

grouping

in data access pages, AA-120

in reports, IA-87 to IA-88

H

headers

in forms, IA-49, IA-51

in reports, IA-94

Help, IN-8

Answer Wizard, IN-8 to IN-9

contents, IN-8

index, IN-9 to IN-10

links between topics, IN-8

searching for topics, IN-8 to IN-11

See also Office Assistant

Help dialog box, IN-8

home pages, IN-12

HTML files. *See* Web pages

hyperlinks

in database objects, AA-115 to AA-117

editing, AA-117

on Web pages, AA-115

I

image controls, IA-92

Import dialog box, IA-106, IA-107

Import Spreadsheet Wizard, IA-106, AA-87 to AA-90

importing data, AA-85

types of files, AA-86

from Word tables, IA-105

from worksheets, IA-106, AA-86 to AA-90

index, Help, IN-9 to IN-10

indexing database fields, IA-71, AA-59

Input Mask Wizard, AA-3 to AA-7

input masks, IA-35, AA-2

applying to fields with existing data, AA-4

creating, AA-2 to AA-7

entering data, AA-8

formats, AA-3

Phone Number, AA-2

placeholders, AA-4

Insert Hyperlink dialog box, AA-116

Insert Subdatasheets dialog box, IA-76

inserting

clip art

in forms, AA-38

in reports, AA-79 to AA-80

fields, IA-14

hyperlinks, in database objects, AA-115 to AA-117

See also creating

insertion point, moving in Datasheet view, IA-15

integrated software packages, IN-2

integration

copying data between applications, AA-92 to AA-93

Excel and Access, IA-92, IA-105 to IA-106

exporting data from Access tables, AA-48

form letters, IA-108 to IA-112

linked objects, AA-92

mailing labels, IA-113

moving data between applications, AA-92 to AA-93

Word and Access, IA-105

See also importing data

Internet, IN-11

    connecting to, IN-12

    dial-up connections, IN-12

    direct access, IN-12

    See also Web

Internet Explorer, IN-12

Intranets, IN-12

J

joining tables in queries, AA-23 to AA-24

K

keyboard shortcuts

    navigating forms, IA-48

    navigating in tables, IA-15

keys. *See* foreign keys; primary keys

L

Label controls, IA-49

Label Options dialog box, IA-114

labels

    in reports, AA-71 to AA-72

    See also mailing labels

layouts, of reports, IA-90 to IA-91

letters. *See* form letters

Link Spreadsheet Wizard, AA-92

linked objects, worksheets, AA-92

links

    between Help topics, IN-8

    See also hyperlinks

lookup fields, AA-10 to AA-11

Lookup Wizard, AA-10

M

Macro Builder, AA-109 to AA-110

Macro Design window, AA-96 to AA-97

    Condition column, AA-104

Macro message box, IA-100

Macro window, IA-97

macros, IA-97

    action arguments, IA-98, AA-96

    Action list, IA-97 to IA-99

    actions, AA-96

    autoexec, AA-103

    buttons in forms, AA-100 to AA-101

    conditional, AA-104 to AA-109

    creating, IA-97 to IA-99, AA-96 to AA-99

        with Macro Builder, AA-109 to AA-110

    editing, AA-99

    purpose, IA-5

    running, IA-99 to IA-100, AA-97

    saving, IA-99

    switchboards, AA-101 to AA-103

mail merge

    data source, IA-108

    form letters, IA-108 to IA-111

    mailing labels, IA-113

    main document, IA-108

    merge fields, IA-108, IA-109

Mail Merge Helper dialog box, IA-108, IA-109, IA-113

Mail Merge toolbar, IA-109

mailing labels, IA-113

main document, mail merge, IA-108

Make Table dialog box, AA-63 to AA-64

make-table queries, AA-59, AA-63 to AA-65

many-to-many relationships, AA-25 to AA-27

menus, commands on, IN-7

Merge dialog box, IA-112

merge fields, IA-108, IA-109

merging. *See* mail merge

Microsoft Access. *See* Access

Microsoft Excel. *See* Excel

Microsoft Office 2000. *See* Office 2000

Microsoft Web site, IN-2

Microsoft Word. *See* Word

modules, IA-5

mouse

    dragging and dropping, AA-92 to AA-93

    navigating in tables, IA-15, IA-26

moving

    controls, AA-71

    data between applications, AA-92 to AA-93

    database entries, IA-29

    Text Box controls, IA-95

multitable queries, IA-77 to IA-78

N

names

    file, IN-6

    form, IA-46

    query, IA-64

    report, IA-92

    table, IA-12

    See also field names

navigating

    forms, IA-47 to IA-48

    tables

        buttons, IA-25 to IA-26

        in Datasheet view, IA-15

    Web pages, IN-12, IN-13

New Data Access Page dialog box, AA-119

New dialog box, IA-7

New Form dialog box, IA-43

New Office Document dialog box, General tab, IN-3

New Query dialog box, IA-62

New Record button, IA-25

New Report dialog box, IA-85

New Table dialog box, IA-9

normalizing tables, AA-135 to AA-136

Number data type, IA-10, IA-11

    decimal places, IA-35

    internal type, IA-34

O

objects. *See* database objects; linked objects

Office 2000 applications, IN-2

    See also integration

Office Assistant, IN-10

    displaying, IN-10, IA-4

    options, IN-10

    searching for topics with, IN-10 to IN-11

    turning off, IN-8

one-to-many relationships, IA-73, AA-16 to AA-17

    symbols in Relationships window, AA-20

one-to-one relationships, AA-25

Open Data Source dialog box, IA-108

Open dialog box, IN-4 to IN-5

Open Office Document dialog box, IN-4 to IN-5

opening

    databases, IA-3 to IA-4

    documents, IN-4 to IN-5

    switchboards, AA-103

    tables, IA-6

operators

    in Expression Builder, AA-42 to AA-43

    in queries, IA-64

Or operator, IA-64

Or queries, AA-50 to AA-51

orientation, of reports, IA-90

P

Page Design view, AA-123

Page Footers, IA-94

    changing properties, AA-73 to AA-74

Page Header, IA-94

Page Setup dialog box, IA-17

Page Wizard, AA-118, AA-120 to AA-122

pages, data access. *See* data access pages

parameter queries, AA-57 to AA-58

Password dialog box, AA-132

passwords, for databases, AA-131 to AA-132

Paste Append command, IA-29

pasting database entries, IA-29 to IA-30

Phone Number input mask, AA-2

pictures

    in reports, IA-92

    See also clip art

placeholders, for input masks, AA-4

previewing data access pages, AA-118, AA-124

primary keys, IA-12 to IA-13, IA-14

    designating, IA-72

    in relationships, IA-72, AA-16 to AA-17

Print dialog box, IA-17, IA-48

printing

    form letters, IA-111 to IA-112

    forms, IA-48

    query results, IA-65

    relationships, IA-75

    reports, IA-95

    tables, IA-17 to IA-18

Programs menu, IN-3

Publish to the Web Wizard, IA-65

names, IA-64

operators, IA-64

option with form letters, IA-111 to IA-112

parameter, AA-57 to AA-58

printing results, IA-65

purpose, IA-5

running, IA-64

saving, IA-64

    as Web pages, IA-65

search criteria, IA-64

    multiple (AND), AA-49 to AA-50

    multiple (OR), AA-50 to AA-51

    parameters, AA-57 to AA-58

sorting results, IA-64

speeding up, AA-59

summary, AA-46 to AA-47

using in reports, IA-85

Query Options dialog box, IA-111 to IA-112

Query window, IA-63 to IA-64, IA-77

quitting. *See* exiting

Q

queries, IA-62

    action, AA-59

        append, AA-59

        delete, AA-59, AA-60 to AA-61

        make-table, AA-59, AA-63 to AA-65

        update, AA-59, AA-61 to AA-63

    calculating with, AA-42

    concatenating fields, AA-48

    copying data to worksheets, AA-92 to AA-93

    creating, IA-62 to IA-65

    defining relationships in, AA-23 to AA-24

    Expression Builder, AA-42 to AA-45

    field properties, AA-46

    fields in, IA-64

    filters in, AA-51

    joining tables in, AA-23 to AA-24

    modifying, IA-64, AA-55 to AA-56

    multitable, IA-77 to IA-78

R

read-only files, IN-5

Record number box, IA-25

record pointers, IA-26

record selectors, IA-27

records, IA-6

    adding in subforms, AA-35

    copying, IA-29

    deleting, IA-28

        with delete queries, AA-59, AA-60 to AA-61

        referential integrity, AA-19

    displaying in data access pages, AA-122

    editing

        in Datasheet view, IA-26

        in forms, IA-47

    entering

        in Datasheet view, IA-15 to IA-16

        in forms, IA-47

        New Record button, IA-25

filters, IA-66 to IA-69

heights of rows in datasheets, IA-30 to IA-31

navigating, IA-25 to IA-26

printing, IA-48

saving, IA-15

selecting, IA-27

sorting, IA-69 to IA-70

updating

referential integrity, AA-19

with update queries, AA-59, AA-61 to AA-63

viewing related on subdatasheets, IA-76

referential integrity, IA-73, AA-17, AA-19

relationships, AA-16

adding tables to, AA-22

creating, IA-72 to IA-73, AA-17 to AA-19

defining in queries, AA-23 to AA-24

deleting, AA-22, AA-23

editing, AA-22

many-to-many, AA-25 to AA-27

one-to-many, IA-73, AA-16 to AA-17, AA-20

one-to-one, AA-25

printing, IA-75

queries using, IA-77 to IA-78

referential integrity rules, IA-73, AA-17, AA-19

symbols in Relationships window, AA-20

viewing related records, IA-76

See also subforms

Relationships window, IA-74, AA-20

repairing databases, IA-55

replication, database, AA-133

Report Footer, IA-94

Report Header, IA-94

formatting, AA-79

hiding page footer, AA-73 to AA-74

as title page, AA-72 to AA-73

Report Wizard, IA-85 to IA-92

reports, IA-84

charts in, IA-91, AA-74 to AA-78

controls, IA-94, AA-69 to AA-72

creating

in Design view, AA-79 to AA-80

with Report Wizard, IA-85 to IA-92

fields in, IA-86

graphics in, IA-92, AA-79 to AA-80

grouping, IA-87 to IA-88

labels, AA-71 to AA-72

layouts, IA-90 to IA-91

macro buttons, AA-100 to AA-101

modifying, IA-93 to IA-95, AA-69 to AA-74

names, IA-92

orientation, IA-90

printing, IA-95

purpose, IA-5

sections, IA-93 to IA-94

sorting, IA-88

styles, IA-90 to IA-91

subreports, AA-79

summary options, IA-89

title pages, AA-72 to AA-73

required fields, IA-35, AA-9 to AA-10

resizing Text Box controls, IA-95

rows

in datasheets

heights, IA-30 to IA-31

See also records

in tables, Design View. *See* fields

running

macros, IA-99 to IA-100, AA-97

queries, IA-64

S

Save As dialog box, IA-12 to IA-13

saving

database objects as Web pages, IA-65

documents, IN-6 to IN-7

macros, IA-99

queries, IA-64

records, IA-15

search criteria

in filters, IA-66

parameter queries, AA-57 to AA-58

in queries, IA-64

AND, AA-49 to AA-50

OR, AA-50 to AA-51

searching
> databases, IA-60 to IA-61
>> *See also* filters; queries
> for help topics, IN-8 to IN-11
> Web, IN-14

security
> encrypting databases, AA-131
> passwords, AA-131 to AA-132

selecting
> all records, IA-27
> fields, IA-27
> records, IA-27

shortcut keys. *See* keyboard shortcuts

Show Table dialog box, IA-63, IA-74, AA-17 to AA-18

sorting
> data access pages, AA-120
> with filters, IA-70 to IA-71
> query results, IA-64
> records, IA-69 to IA-70
> reports, IA-88

splitting databases into two files, AA-135

spreadsheets. *See* worksheets

Start menu, IN-3

starting
> Access, IA-3
> applications, IN-3 to IN-4

Startup dialog box, AA-133 to AA-134

startup options, AA-133 to AA-134

styles
> form, IA-46
> report, IA-90 to IA-91

subdatasheets, IA-76

Subform/Subreport Wizard, AA-31 to AA-35, AA-80

subforms, AA-30 to AA-31
> adding records, AA-35
> creating, AA-31 to AA-35
> modifying, AA-36

subreports, AA-79
> creating, AA-80
> synchronizing, AA-80

SUM function, AA-46 to AA-47

summaries, in reports, IA-89

Summary Options dialog box, IA-89 to IA-90

summary queries, AA-46 to AA-47

switchboards, AA-101
> creating, AA-101 to AA-102
> opening automatically, AA-103

T

Table Analyzer, AA-135 to AA-136

Table Wizard, IA-9

tables
> copying data to and from Word documents, IA-105
> copying data to and from worksheets, IA-105 to IA-106
> creating, IA-9 to IA-13
>> with make-table queries, AA-63 to AA-65
> as data source for mail merge, IA-108
> deleting, IA-14
> designing, IA-10 to IA-12
> exporting to other applications, AA-91
> filters, IA-66 to IA-69
> finding duplicate data, AA-135 to AA-136
> importing data, IA-106, AA-85, AA-86 to AA-90
> indexing, IA-71
> linking to worksheets, AA-92
> modifying designs, IA-14
> names, IA-12
> normalizing, AA-135 to AA-136
> opening, IA-6
> primary keys, IA-12 to IA-13, IA-14, IA-72
> printing, IA-17 to IA-18
> purpose, IA-5
> queries on, IA-63
> saving as Web pages, IA-65
> *See also* records; relationships

tables, Word, copying data to and from databases, IA-105

Text Box controls
> deleting, IA-95
> in forms, IA-49
> moving, IA-95

in reports, IA-94 to IA-95

resizing, IA-95

title pages, of reports, AA-72 to AA-73

toolbars

Form/Report Formatting, AA-70

Mail Merge, IA-109

More Buttons list, IN-13

Web, IN-12, AA-117

Toolbox, AA-69, AA-70

Design view, IA-49, IA-50, IA-94

U

unbound controls, IA-49, AA-69, AA-70 to AA-71

labels, AA-71 to AA-72

unfreezing columns, IA-33

Uniform Resource Locators. *See* URLs

update queries, AA-59, AA-61 to AA-63

URLs (Uniform Resource Locators), IN-12

See also hyperlinks

V

validation rules

for fields, AA-8 to AA-9

referential integrity, AA-17, AA-19

views. *See* Datasheet view; Design view

W

Web, IN-12

searching, IN-14

Web browsers, IN-12

Web pages

Favorites, IN-12

home, IN-12

hyperlinks, AA-115

navigating with toolbar, IN-12, IN-13

saving database objects as, IA-65

searching for, IN-14

See also data access pages

Web sites, Microsoft, IN-2

Web toolbar, IN-12, AA-117

displaying, IN-12

Word

form letters, IA-108 to IA-112

integration with Access, IA-105

mailing labels, IA-113

worksheets

copying data from tables to, AA-92 to AA-93

copying data to and from databases, IA-105 to IA-106

exporting data to, AA-91

importing data from, IA-106, AA-86 to AA-90

linking to tables, AA-92

World Wide Web. *See* Web

Z

Zoom dialog box, AA-48, AA-49